NEWSPAPER CIRCULATION:

Marketing the News

THORN, William J. Newspaper circulation: marketing the news, by William J. Thorn with Mary Pat Pfeil. Longman, 1987. 333p index 86-27577. 34.95 ISBN 0-582-28637-9. PN 4784. CIP
This book deals comprehensively with two aspects of newspaper circulation: (1) a general consideration of the role of newspaper circulation from an industrial and historical point of view, and (2) a specific consideration of the problems to be solved in the day-to-day management of circulation departments. In its general section, the book deals with current essential elements in the overall subject of circulation: its uses as a measure of audience and as an index of commercial value; the history of circulation; circulation and the marketing concept; newspaper promotion and circulation; and laws involving circulation. In its management section, it deals with the physical problems of newspaper delivery and with computerization. It also offers 11 case studies of individual newspaper circulation departments. It fills a gap in the literature of newspaper management in that no other source so thoroughly describes the function and management of circulation departments. The authors are well qualified. The book is documented with mostly industry sources, and the index is useful. Printing is attractive and clear, but illustrations contribute little. The content is valuable to newspaper circulation managers and other professionals, but is much more detailed than what the casual student of media economics would require.—*R. Halverson, University of Oregon*

NEWSPAPER CIRCULATION:

Marketing the News

William J. Thorn
with
Mary Pat Pfeil

College of Journalism
Marquette University

Longman
New York & London

Executive Editor: Gordon T. R. Anderson
Production Editor: Pamela Nelson/Helen B. Ambrosio
Text Design: Steven August Krastin
Cover Design: Steven August Krastin
Cover Illustration/Photo: Steven August Krastin
Production Supervisor: Eduardo Castillo
Compositor: Graphicraft Typesetters Ltd.
Printer and Binder: The Alpine Press, Inc.

Newspaper Circulation

Copyright © 1987 by Longman Inc.

Longman Inc.
95 Church Street
White Plains, N.Y. 10601

Associated companies:
Longman Group Ltd., London
Longman Cheshire Pty., Melbourne
Longman Paul Pty., Auckland
Copp Clark Pitman, Toronto
Pitman Publishing Inc., New York

Library of Congress Cataloging-in-Publication Data

Thorn, William J.
  Newspaper circulation.

  Includes index.
  1. Newspapers—Circulation.   2. American newspapers—
Circulation.   I. Pfeil, Mary Pat. II. Title.
PN4784.C6T47   1987   070'.0688   86-27577
ISBN 0-582-28637-9

87 88 89 90 9 8 7 6 5 4 3 2 1

Dedicated to Harold Schwartz

A circulation manager's circulation manager
and one of the industry's finest gentlemen

CONTENTS

FOREWORD I

This book is a response to the request of journalism educators for authoritative material on newspaper circulation to be used in connection with media study programs in American and Canadian colleges. In 1980, at a meeting in Madison, Wisconsin, attended by James M. Hoyt, acting director of the Department of Journalism at the University of Wisconsin; James M. Scotton, then Dean of the College of Journalism of Marquette University; Joseph Forsee, General Manager of the International Circulation Managers Association; and William J. Thorn, Ph.D., of Marquette University, educators asked for the industry's assistance in producing material on the principles and practices of newspaper circulation.

Dr. Thorn agreed to prepare a book and spent several years studying American and Canadian newspapers, visiting newspaper operations in all sections of the United States and Canada, interviewing publishers and circulation directors of many newspapers, and researching the history of newspaper circulation. Dr. Gail Barwis reviewed early drafts, and Mary Pat Pfeil of Marquette University edited and reworked the manuscript, adding new material in Part II as well.

Newpaper circulation is the very foundation of the newspaper industry. It is the only business in the United States that provides door-to-door service every day of the year. It depends on an army of a million carriers, both youths and adults, and generates more than $12 million a day in the United States alone. Much of this is collected in nickels and dimes totaling annual newspaper revenue in excess of $4 billion—approximately 25 percent of total newspaper revenue.

Circulation operating methods, service standards, and distribution techniques vary considerably in different areas of North America. Newspapers in the North and East rely on their youth carrier program as the mainstay of circulation, while some newspapers in the South and West turn to adult distribution. Single copy sales is becoming more important. In the Snowbelt areas of our continent, carriers "porch" the papers; while in the South and West, carriers throw the papers on the lawn or driveway as standard operating procedure.

This book tells the history of North American newspaper distribution, analyzes operating procedures in various sections of the continent, and discusses trends in promotion and circulation development.

We extend our thanks to the many individuals who cooperated in this endeavor and to the newspaper companies that made it possible. With the increase in competition for readers' time, newspaper management is devoting greater resources to the circulation operation. Circulation today is an essential part of the overall marketing structure of the daily newspaper.

HAROLD A. SCHWARTZ

Past President
International Circulation
Managers Association

FOREWORD II

The term newspaper circulation conjures up obvious images—faded pictures of nineteenth-century newsboys hawking their wares or modern delivery trucks inching their way through urban traffic. But there is more, much more. While there is rarely much visible public or industry discussion of newspaper circulation, this important activity is the final and most vital link in the survival and success of the modern newspaper. Without vigorous circulation departments and imaginative plans for the sale and distribution of the newspaper, now frequently called "the product," there would be no point in discussing freedom of the press, patterns of news coverage, or the power of the editorial voice. Whatever newspapers are and have become in American life, they owe to the "little merchants" of earlier days and to the modern circulation manager.

Until recently, neither leaders of the newspaper industry nor scholarly commentators gave much attention to newspaper circulation. It got backseat (if any) treatment at the annual meetings of newspaper publishers and only the most cursory mention in histories of the press. Perhaps that was because newspaper circulation was growing rapidly, and delivering the paper was simply something that was done routinely. With the decline of newspaper circulation figures and the much reported "death in the afternoon" of many American dailies, greater attention has come to the topic of circulation.

This topic is now front and center on the programs of industry and professional associations; even editors who once expressed little interest now recognize the important relationship between their editorial product and what people will buy, use, and regard as indispensable. Newspapers and those concerned about them are now self-conscious about circulation. People speak of the death of the mass media and of the mass audience as we enter an era of market segmentation and demographic development. Newspapers are challenged as advertising vehicles by the electronic media, magazines, free circulation shoppers, and other media, some of them emerging only today

Journalism schools have begun adding media management to the traditional menu of reporting and editing courses considered invaluable to tomorrow's editors and publishers. Here, too, circulation is emerging as a vital component of any effort to understand how newspapers can be managed for success.

There could be no more appropriate time for the appearance of *Newspaper Circulation*, which is by far the most thoughtful and most comprehensive treatment ever written on this subject. Dr. William Thorn, a professor of journalism at Marquette University, brings the tools of a former editor and reporter, a trained observer, and a journalism historian to the problem of newspaper circulation. He defines it, treats its history, and then takes the reader into the main problems of circulation both in a broad, analytical sense and then on the scene at several newspapers. Indeed, this makes the book unique, because it is a national portrait with many fresh examples gathered by Dr. Thorn's visits to a large number of newspapers. The yield of his extensive interviews with publishers, business managers, advertising and circulation personnel is evident in this splendid book. The author identifies exemplars among the nation's circulation departments and presents both a practical and scholarly report that will, no doubt, become essential reading in the newspaper industry and a text for prospective circulation managers and publishers.

Blessedly, this book brings into full view for the newspaper specialist and the public what has heretofore been a behind-the-scenes function in modern communication. Understanding circulation is akin to understanding the audience, its tastes, and its preferences. In such understanding there is intelligence for the field of advertising and for writers and editors whose work must ultimately resonate to and with the people for whom it is produced. In this thorough analysis, text, and handbook, Dr. Thorn shows us why circulation is so vital—and, assuredly, it is.

EVERETTE E. DENNIS
Executive Director
Gannett Center for Media Studies
Columbia University

PREFACE

This book began amidst a major circulation crisis at the *Milwaukee Journal*. While I was discussing a university program in media management with one of the vice-presidents of the company, we learned that the Pope had been shot. It was about 10 a.m. on a Wednesday, and the vice-president was Harold Schwartz, head of circulation. Immediately, the problem popped out: a major surge of single copy sales but a limited number of preprinted food sections. Circulation executives were in and out of the office for the next half hour relaying figures, newsroom deadlines, special coverage. By 10:40, the circulation decision had been made.

From that moment, I've never been able to view circulation as I once did from my perspectives as a youth carrier and then as a reporter and editor. I subsequently spent summers in the circulation department and weeks on the road going from newspaper to newspaper, coast to coast. During a sabbatical in Rome, I even spent time studying Italian circulation practices. In short, I was hooked by a world that I had generally ignored. I met hundreds of dedicated newspaper professionals, and I learned that unlike newsrooms, circulation departments are highly individual operations. No two circulation systems are identical, and only those in a common newspaper group are even highly similar. This, I came to understand, is as it should be, for circulation is the most localized aspect of newspaper work: finding and servicing every single person who wants to buy the newspaper.

I also came to understand newspaper circulation as the most complex part of the newspaper industry. The complexity of circulation arises in part from its multiple tasks—sales, delivery, and collection—and in a larger part from the very nature of moving such a highly perishable product from presses to porches within two to four hours every day, every week, every month, every year. No other business would attempt it at so little cost, let alone tie it to sales and collection.

The complexity also arises from the amount of information handled by circulation departments: stops and starts, vacation holds, complaints, address changes, and carrier phone numbers. Nothing, it seems, is simple about circulation except the basic adage: Circulation increases come one at a time, but circulation drops come in droves.

As a former reporter and editor, I was astonished to discover that circulation workers knew both their newspaper and its readers far better than I had ever imagined. Indeed, they demonstrated time and again that they often understood the reader's perception of the newspaper better than most reporters and editors. And, they are readers, too—readers who go door to door trying to sell what the reporters and editors produce. In his textbook on reporting, Everette E. Dennis notes that reporters today suffer from isolation: They are middle-class people with college degrees who cover the major figures and institutions around them. In that isolation, he argues, they lose touch with the readers and their concerns. Circulation workers never lose touch with the readers because their working life is spent in direct contact with them.

The final, inescapable fact is that this book contains only the major themes and issues in newspaper circulation. Not only are there a hundred variations for every example I used, but the changes sweeping through newspapers and society are keeping circulation practices in constant flux. But then, the story of circulation is one of constant adaptation to local conditions.

Several people played a major role in this book. Harold Schwartz, to whom the book is dedicated, inspired the original research and writing. With boundless enthusiasm he supported the project through several drafts and revisions. Mary Pat Pfeil edited and revised gummy and obtuse prose, and she added her own material to the latter chapters. Without these two people, this might still be a 600-page manuscript in search of a publisher. Richard Robinson provided the basic material and concepts for the chapter on marketing. Gail Barwis provided perceptive criticisms, particularly to the early drafts. James Scotton, Dean of the College of Journalism at Marquette, lent his own unique support.

The book would not exist if the International Circulation Managers had not provided a study grant for gathering the basic material, and that grant would have been wasted if the circulation managers and staffs of more than 40 newspapers had not opened their doors to an inquiring author. I am most conscious of the frank, honest, and sometimes highly confidential material these professionals entrusted to me, seeking always to explain their systems and sometimes sound out their problems. In several years of meeting with circulation managers and trying to fathom the underlying issues and problems they face, I came to know them as people of complex minds, individuals able to manage operations that of necessity have numerous exceptions, variations, and special approaches.

William J. Thorn

INTRODUCTION

The Newspaper in America

Newspaper circulation being the topic of this book, our initial task must be a quick survey of the basic structure of American newspapers. The first question is, "What is a newspaper?" For a seemingly simple question, there is no simple answer, only a few more questions. For example, is every periodical regularly published on newsprint a newspaper? The frequency of publication is not entirely helpful, for newspapers can be monthly, bimonthly, weekly, biweekly, triweekly, and daily. In this book a newspaper means a mechanically produced publication appearing regularly at least biweekly, covering current events and issues, and being available to anyone of ordinary financial and literary means. Two other newspaper hallmarks are timeliness and stability. This definition includes mass circulation newspapers aimed at a broad public, special interest newspapers for narrow publics such as businesspeople, and institutional newspapers aimed at members of religions and associations.

American press history demonstrates the power of three fundamental concepts that underlie its 250 years of development: The press is a social/political institution, the press is a business, and the press is a link between an organization and its members. These three concepts often lead to conflicting demands, for example, the needs both to turn a profit and to expose corrupt advertisers or sponsors. Nonetheless, American newspapers spring from these roots, and publishers work out the conflicts time and time again, some opting for profitable silence or sensationalism, others sacrificing profit for service, and still others striving for a careful balance. Circulation can be properly understood within the unique character of American journalism.

THE NEWSPAPER AS A SOCIAL INSTITUTION

As a social institution newspapers and the press generally play a formal role, particularly in politics, economics, the exchange of ideas, and entertainment. The press has been called the Fourth Estate, indicating its power in political life rivaling that of the nobility, Church, and business class. The press has also been called the democratizing force that expands the rights of common people and allows for a democratic society.[1]

Today, two basic press-government relationships seem to have evolved in the world: a press controlled or manipulated by the government to serve its leaders and a politically independent press that serves the citizens. A government-controlled or manipulated press restricts what the public can learn about society and the world at large, coloring and shaping the news for propaganda purposes. In this capacity, newspapers proclaim the views of their nation's leaders. An autonomous press, while allied to the interests of the nation, is free to monitor government performance and to evaluate the behavior of leaders on behalf of the citizens. In this capacity, the press is a voice of the people.

In formulating his theory of democratic government, John Locke posited the people as the source of power and the government as the servant of the people.[2] In this system a free press is an essential element because it can inform the electorate and hold government accountable for its actions, providing there is widespread literacy and an available press. Thomas Jefferson wrote clearly about the role of the press in a democracy:

> The people are the only censors of their governors: and even their errors will tend to keep these to the true principles of their institution. To punish these errors too severely would be to suppress the only safeguard of the public liberty. The way to prevent these irregular interpositions of the people, is to give them full information of their affairs through the channel of public papers, and to contrive that those papers should penetrate the whole mass of the people. The basis of our government being the opinion of the people, the very first object should be to keep that right; and were it left to me to decide whether we should have a government with newspapers, or newspapers without government, I should not hesitate a moment to prefer the latter. But I should mean that every man should receive those papers, and be capable of reading them.[3]

Once elected president, Jefferson became the target of brutal criticism from the opposition press, and he noted the darker side of the "opinion of the public": "Indeed, the abuses of the freedom of the press here have been carried to a length never before known or borne by civilized man."[4] Inherent in an autonomous press is its ability to abuse its power.

The social institutional role of newspapers extends beyond politics into almost every facet of social life, from monitoring crime and business to explaining new trends and scientific developments. In a complex society, the press becomes the institution that tells a society about itself; as such, it has power to shape the way people see and think about their society. Newspapers serve society by reflecting its diversity and similarity, sometimes through cartoons and editorials as well as through news and feature articles. The extent to which a newspaper fulfills its social institutional role—that is, how well it meets the needs of the society it serves—can have a positive or negative impact on its circulation.

THE NEWSPAPER AS A BUSINESS

As a business newspapers survive by earning a profit, unless they are subsidized by an institution such as a church, business, or labor union. In a democratic society, therefore, commercial newspapers have two powerful and potentially conflicting obligations: to play a decisive informational role in their community's life and to attract enough readers and advertisers to achieve financial stability. These two activities lead to a split personality when the newspaper succeeds admirably in one role but fails in the other. While Jefferson tolerated inaccuracy and outright hostility in the press, he deplored the tendency of editors to compromise their calling by appealing to baser tastes in their readers in order to maintain profits:

> Defamation is becoming a necessary of life; insomuch, that a dish of tea in the morning or evening cannot be digested without this stimulant. Even those who do not believe these abominations still read them with complaisance to their auditors, and instead of the abhorrence and indignation which should fill a voracious mind, betray a secret pleasure in the possibility that some may believe them, though they do not themselves. It seems to escape them, that it is not he who prints, but he who pays for printing a slander, who is the real author.[5]

The search for financial success in the newspaper business has produced the kind of content that falls far short of Jefferson's ideal. American press history runs full with news accounts of scandal, horror, fraud, and sensationalism because people will pay for this news.

Each publisher chooses a balance between the business and social institutional roles of the newspaper by establishing a series of policies. In so doing, the publisher defines circulation, as well as editorial and advertising success. The dual nature of a commercial newspaper in a democratic society often forces uncomfortable compromises based on what the readers want, what the revenues will allow, and what the publisher expects. Nonetheless, profitability, as Joseph Pulitzer pointed out, is the only sure means to editorial autonomy and full independence for a commercial newspaper in a democratic system.

As businesses, newspapers have two potential sources of major revenue: selling the newspaper to readers and selling space to advertisers. Commercial newspapers can be grouped by their revenue sources into three types: purchase newspapers, free newspapers (shoppers), and voluntary pay newspapers.

Purchase Newspapers

The dominant style among dailies and weeklies, the purchase newspaper receives a stated price for each copy or subscription, perhaps adjusted in special sales campaigns. Most newspapers derive 20 to 30 percent of their income from circulation sales and the balance from the sale of advertising space.[6] Thus, purchase newspapers have two distinct sets of customers: those who buy the newspaper and those who buy advertising space in the newspaper. While they are sometimes the same people, advertisers being also readers, these two groups have different needs, which the newspaper must satisfy in order to achieve commercial success. Moreover, as the number of paying readers increases, the desirability and price of the advertising space also increase. This text concentrates on purchase newspapers because they form the largest segment of weekly and daily press, and because the twin demands from advertisers and readers has produced the widest range of management problems and solutions.

Free Distribution Newspapers

Free distribution newspapers, also called "shoppers," are delivered at no cost to every household within a defined geographic area or are offered at no charge to everyone passing a newspaper rack. Publishers of shoppers offset this lack of circulation revenue by setting their advertising rates high enough to guarantee profitability. Compared with competing purchase newspapers, shoppers are usually smaller and contain a higher proportion of advertising content.

Like purchase newspapers, shoppers deliver their readers to their advertisers. However, shoppers provide saturation coverage of a defined circulation zone. This makes them desirable for merchants who wish to reach specific populations; thus they become direct competitors for newspaper advertising. Over the past decade, shoppers have become successful by insuring that every home in a target circulation zone receives the newspaper, particularly in areas where purchase newspapers reach only

30 to 50 percent of the population. In some parts of the country, particularly the South and Southwest, legal government notices have moved from purchase newspapers to shoppers in recognition of this higher coverage. Because legal notices provide substantial regular revenue, this has been a serious issue for small dailies, particularly those based in the county seat.

At the core, shoppers are less news vehicles than advertising vehicles, but they remain newspapers as long as they contain some editorial content. Whatever their content, they face significant circulation problems.

Voluntary Pay Newspapers

Voluntary pay newspapers are delivered to each household in a defined area, then payment is requested. However, delivery will not stop if the customer refuses to pay. Some offer a Sunday magazine supplement or inexpensive premium to those who pay, but mostly they rely on the customers' sense of justice. Economically, voluntary pay newspapers operate like shoppers: They charge advertisers a premium rate and guarantee saturation coverage of a target area. The difference is that they rely on voluntary payment to support the carriers and perhaps offset a small portion of the operating costs.

As a hybrid system, the voluntary pay method in a competitive market survives only when the newspaper offers something superior to that provided by either purchase newspapers or shoppers. The voluntary pay system proved successful for the *Contra Costa Times* in San Francisco's East Bay area, where approximately 45 percent of the customers paid. This income allowed the *Times* to increase its local news coverage and to expand daily porch delivery. Rising newsprint costs forced conversion to a purchase newspaper, but only after competing dailies had abandoned the area to the *Times*. Other voluntary pay newspapers trimmed editorial costs and increased the proportion of advertising space to remain profitable. The voluntary pay newspapers were a phenomenon of the 1970s, particularly on the West Coast. Today, however, rising production costs have forced most voluntary pay newspapers to a subscription status or else out of business.

Competition from shoppers and voluntary pay newspapers have forced purchase newspapers to create their own versions of free distribution products in order to satisfy advertisers who want the heavy saturation of shoppers. In the 1980s purchase newspapers of all sizes began delivering a free copy to all nonsubscribers in target zones in order to provide total market coverage (TMC) for advertisers.

Each type of newspaper shapes its business dimension by imposing its own profitability pressures, which in turn affect the definition of success-ful circulation. A purchase newspaper, because of the revenue generated by circulation, will have a more complex circulation system in order to both collect the purchase price and sell the newspaper to new customers. Its circulation system will include provisions not only for home delivery but for the sale of single copies as well. A free distribution newspaper will have a simple circulation system but will pay close attention to verifica-tion of delivery because nonpaying readers are less likely to complain about missed delivery or damaged copies. A voluntary pay newspaper will have the collection concerns of a purchase newspaper and the deliv-ery verification problems of a shopper. In response to these and other circulation demands, each newspaper will develop a circulation system and a definition of circulation that best meets its needs and maintains the character of the newspaper as defined by the publisher.

THE NEWSPAPER AS AN ORGANIZATIONAL LINK

The American press contains a large number of institutional newspapers produced by churches, unions, professional associations, and other mem-bership groups, such as the American Automobile Association. These newspapers have two basic roles. First, they fulfill the need for news and information among the members and they offer a forum for discussion of internal issues. Second, they are the public voice of the organization, commenting on politics, court decisions, and current events. In this latter role, the institutional press provides the general community with alter-nate voices whose political and social views are part of the tradition of a free press long defended by the Supreme Court.

Some institutional newspapers operate like purchase newspapers: they sell subscriptions and advertising space, and they are expected at least to break even. Others include the subscription cost in the mem-bership fee. Still others do not sell advertising space or subscriptions but ask for contributions, much like voluntary pay newspapers.

Whatever their revenue system, institutional newspapers face sub-stantial pressures to compromise. However fair, balanced, and accurate, a story about an institutional scandal or problem can create ferocious reac-tion from the institution's leaders. Unpopular stands taken by leaders can antagonize rank and filers. A newspaper's credibility among members and the general public can be diminished if it attempts to hide problems or to misrepresent the facts. In addition, a guaranteed subsidy can blind the editor and staff to disaffection among their readers, whose lack of interest in the content or style is not translated into declining circulation and therefore goes unnoted. No less than their commercial counterparts, institutional newspapers need strong marketing programs to keep the paper adjusted to their audiences and not simply to the organizations' leaders.

The roles of institutional papers include binding together their associations or denominations and presenting the views of special groups to the public. Yet, institutional newspapers cannot ignore or resist the circulation problems faced by their commercial cousins, whether in the form of postal rates, sales campaigns, computerization, or declining readership. Not only do these newspapers form an important part of the mosaic of the American press system, but they also compete for readers with each other and with commercial weeklies and dailies. In that competition the American press finds the mainspring for its adjustment to the needs of its readers. Those that do not adjust eventually fade away. That, too, is part of the American press tradition.

NOTES

1. John Jessup, *The Third Estate* (New York: Time, Inc., 1980), 17. Former *Life* magazine editorial editor Jessup argued that journalists have no reason to separate themselves from the Third Estate—the common people—from whom the rights to freedom of the press and democracy spring.
2. John Locke, *Social Contract*. Modern research by Garry Wills suggests that the inspiration for democratic theory as understood by Thomas Jefferson came not from *Social Contract* but from earlier tracts Locke wrote about Scottish communities. Nonetheless, John Locke's conception is basic to democracy.
3. Jefferson to Carrington, 1787, *Writings of Thomas Jefferson*, ed. Andrew A. Lipscomb (Washington, D.C.: The Thomas Jefferson Association, 1903), vol. VI, pp. 57–58.
4. Jefferson to Mr. Pictet, 1801. Lipscomb, vol. X, pp. 355–356.
5. Jefferson to J. Norvell, 1807. Lipscomb, vol. XI, pp. 222–226.
6. Benjamin Compaine, *The Newspaper Industry in the 1980s* (White Plains, N.Y.: Knowledge Industry Publications, 1980), 15; see also Ben Bagdickian, "The Bu$ine$$ of Newspapers," *Mass Media Issues*, eds., Leonard Sellers and William L. Rivers (Englewood Cliffs, N.J.: Prentice-Hall, Inc., 1977), 233–240.

The Forces That Shape a
Circulation System

Today's newspaper circulation system involves far more than the way newspapers move from the printing press to the reader, although that remains the crucial task. Circulation includes the sales efforts that attract new subscribers and single copy buyers, and the collection of money. Newspaper sales and promotion have become so important in the past decade, that marketing has moved to the foreground in administrative planning and operations. Collection has adapted to the computer and credit card age. But circulation is more than these elements.

Even within newspaper circles, the term "circulation" has several different implications. Circulation can refer to measure of audience, a financial yardstick of the newspaper's market value, a guide to the newspaper's impact on the community, and a structural unit within the newspaper. Chapter 1 explores these aspects of newspaper circulation.

The major tasks of circulation—delivery, sales, and collection—have a long and fascinating history that begins with the first newspaper and the very first American newspaper carrier, Ben Franklin. The current circulation issues and problems are extensions of historical trends whose roots are traced back through World War II to the turn of the century. As Chapter 2 demonstrates, success has come to those who adapted to the underlying changes in the newspaper business.

Marketing, which has become an integral part of contemporary business, has but a short history in the newspaper industry. Almost every daily newspaper has looked to the marketing concept as a means to survival or improved profits. In either instance, the route to success leads right through circulation. Almost every circulation executive has been affected by marketing, and all recognize the increasing importance of the link between marketing and circulation.

Marketing inevitably leads to promotion and sales, major circulation tasks that existed long before the marketing was even a concept. Chapter 4 begins with the assumption that one major task of circulation is to replace ex-readers with new readers, to encourage irregular readers to read daily, and to transform single copy buyers into subscribers. The methods reviewed in this chapter range from traditional sales efforts to special gimmicks and offers. Contemporary life-styles raise special problems that require special sales efforts.

Every circulation department bears the stamp of the publisher and top executives. As part of the company, the circulation department presents part of the newspaper's image to the community. At the same time, the circulation department can carry customers' concerns back to the corporation. This unique role, formed by sales effort and by daily contacts with both readers and newspaper staff, forces its own adaptations on circulation units. Specific market factors like climate and competition also create pressure and offer opportunities that encourage uniquely local answers to basic circulation challenges.

Circulation, while sometimes wild, cannot be lawless. Chapter 6 reviews the major legal concerns that daily face circulation executives. These laws, particularly those governing unions, child labor, monopolistic practices, liability, workmen's compensation, and rack ordinances, play an important part in the design of every circulation system. In circulation, ignorance of the laws produces an inadequate understanding of why circulation systems develop as they do.

Part I outlines some of the basic forces that play upon every circulation system and describes some of the basic building blocks that comprise the foundation. Part II will examine each structural component of circulation in all its variety and assess its role in the overall system.

CHAPTER
1

The Scope of Newspaper Circulation

In the contemporary newspaper, circulation activity ranges from market planning among top executives through distribution and collection to collaboration with advertising on targeted delivery of special sections. Circulation business is conducted simultaneously in executive offices, in mailrooms and on loading docks, on street corners and front porches, and in newspaper counting rooms. The scope of circulation work changes from newspaper to newspaper, reflecting differences in circulation, frequency of publication, labor conditions, and management philosophies. It goes beyond the actual distribution of the newspaper, because in the American press system, circulation is the basis for almost all revenue.

More specifically, questions of readership, audience, local influence, corporate structure, customer service, promotion, and sales all fit into the scope of circulation. Authors and circulation managers have periodically tried to sort out and separate the various elements covered by the term *circulation* in order to lay the foundation for better understanding. Overall, circulation embraces the following six distinct components:

1. A system for selling and delivering newspapers and collecting the purchase price
2. A measure of sales, readership, and audience
3. An index of commercial value
4. An index of community value and responsibility
5. A department within a newspaper
6. A profession requiring special skills and training

A SALES, DELIVERY, AND COLLECTION SYSTEM

When most people hear the word circulation, they think of the system that delivers the newspaper. This system, including sales and collection as well as distribution, has evolved over 200 years into a complex operation. Traditionally known as the 3-legged stool supporting the newspaper, sales, distribution, and collection are the major tasks of circulation.

FIGURE 1.1 Newsboys remain important to single-copy sales wherever people gather in large cities daily and during special events. Courtesy *Newsday*, Long Island, NY.

FIGURE 1.2   The importance of information and opinions in competing news-papers can be seen in major metropolitan airports and here, in Washington, D.C., where sales justify single-copy boxes from 23 different newspapers at one location. Courtesty *Washington Post*, Washington, D.C.

Selling the newspaper to subscribers or to single copy customers is only the first step, one not required for free distribution shoppers or institutional newspapers. Accurate, prompt, and efficient service are re-quired to retain customers. Home delivery, in particular, requires stren-uous efforts to overcome the problems of traffic and mobility plaguing larger cities. Distribution includes a record-keeping system that swiftly and accurately begins service to new customers, resolves problems of established customers, and provides special services like vacation holds. Collecting poses its own problems, including deciding when and how to drop those who fail to pay. Buried between the lines are a dozen other tasks, ranging from deciding how much to charge for the newspaper to increasing driver safety and retaining youth carriers.

A MEASURE OF SALES, READERSHIP, AND AUDIENCE

The concept of circulation reflects the commercial nature of newspapers and the contribution circulation makes to a newspaper's profitability. Circulation provides direct income through newspaper sales and indirect income through advertising revenue. Thus, the newspaper's circulation is the basis for calculating the net worth of a newspaper property.

In all of these measures, circulation is a number—either of those who pay for the newspaper or of those who read it. Despite the seeming simplicity of the terms sales, readership, and audience, the calculation of these figures remains a source of constant debate. Nonetheless, each has a precise technical definition that rests on such basic questions as: "Who is a newspaper reader?" "What must one do to be considered a reader —read a headline? a cartoon?" The terms represent totally different methods of determining the number of people reached by a newspaper.

Measure of Sales

Circulation is the number of newspapers, whether purchase, free distribution, or voluntary pay, commercial or organizational. For purchase newspapers, circulation is the number of copies sold on a particular day or over a defined period (weekly or monthly average, for example). For free distribution and voluntary pay newspapers, circulation is the number of newspapers delivered to homes in a defined area or the number of newspapers given away at newsstands, racks, and other sites. For organizational newspapers, circulation is the number of members or member households if everyone automatically receives the publication; or it may be only the number of dues-paying members. Some organizational newspapers operate like purchase newspapers, charging a subscription fee even if the organization subsidizes part of the cost, which means they use a purchase newspaper definition.

In all cases, circulation differs from the pressrun, or the total number of newspapers printed. The pressrun may exceed circulation by as much as 20 percent because the newspaper must provide enough copies to supply newsstands, vending boxes, and other single copy outlets where sales are unpredictable. Additional copies are printed to replace wet, stolen, or damaged copies; to make up for missed deliveries; to be used by employees or departments; for back copy files; for advertising tear sheets; and for other internal needs.

Establishing an accurate circulation figure has not always been possible for those outside the publisher's office. In the 1800s, no standard definition of newspaper sales existed among publishers or advertisers; but even if it had, the figures would have been greeted with justifiable suspicion. Publishers inflated circulation to appear more successful, to attract attention, or to appeal to advertisers. Independent newspaper space sales agents, who sold advertising space on behalf of many newspapers, inflated circulation figures to justify higher space rates (and their commissions). Inadequate accounting procedures prevented accurate and comparable circulation figures, even when publishers strove to be scrupulously honest. Circulation wars encouraged publishers to grossly overestimate circulation for competitive reasons. The New York circulation war in the 1890s between Joseph Pulitzer and William Randolph Hearst was the most notorious battle of inflated figures, but far from the first or last.

To standardize circulation figures and make them reliable and comparable, advertisers and publishers established the Audit Bureau of Circulations (ABC) in 1913 as a voluntary organization of newspaper publishers. Today ABC sets the standards for newspaper sales and audits 95 percent of all daily newspaper circulation in the United States.[1] ABC established strict criteria defining a newspaper sale as the basis for calculating circulation, and it established a standardized system for auditing the calculation of total sales by member newspapers. ABC thereby established net paid circulation as a standard figure, comparable among all member newspapers. Net paid circulation is calculated on a daily basis (net paid daily) and averaged over a five-day period (average weekly net paid) according to uniform practices. For most purposes the average weekly net paid provides a more reliable figure because it accommodates the natural fluctuation in sales from one day to the next caused by predictable elements such as special food section and workdays or by unpredictable elements such as news stories, weather, and reader life-style, which vary from day to day and season to season. The daily net paid figure is most useful for Sunday sales, which normally differ greatly from weekday sales.

Free distribution newspapers can be audited by Verified Audit of Circulation, Marina del Rey, California, or Certified Audit of Circulation, Inc., of Fairfield, New Jersey; but many newspapers hire their own verification service or have employees spot-check distribution to monitor the percentage of accurate deliveries. Verification techniques include door-to-door surveys, telephone surveys, and observation of carriers. Such systems are essential, for carriers have been known to dump bundles of undelivered newspapers in the trash or sell them for scrap. The circulation manager of a daily shopper in California discovered his adult carriers delivered only half of the papers each day and sold the other half to scrap dealers. Nonpaying customers are much less likely to complain about nondelivery, making verification crucial to reliable circulation figures.

For some purposes, the net paid circulation figure offers insufficiently precise data about the nature of circulation within the newspaper's circulation territory, which may include the surrounding county or a large portion of the state. Larger newspapers divide their delivery area into a newspaper designated market area (NDMA) and all other zones (AOZ) to provide a more refined picture of circulation levels. The NDMA is the commercial and residential zone closest to the newspaper's central city, and the AOZ is the territory beyond that core. Definition of the NDMA and AOZ follows ABC guidelines, as does the calculation of net paid circulation within the zones, ensuring accurate depiction of sales patterns. Included in the NDMA description are state and federal population and commercial figures; thus, the NDMA is often nearly identical to the standard metropolitan statistical area (SMSA) used in federal census studies, although it need not be if ABC and the newspaper agree on another geographical boundary.

For their own purposes, some newspapers use a variation of the NDMA/AOZ division by subdividing their territory into a city zone (CZ) and a retail trading zone (RTZ), and perhaps an AOZ. The CZ includes the core city and surrounding suburban developments; the RTZ includes the area beyond the CZ that is a commercial extension of the central city; and the AOZ is the territory beyond that. An ABC member newspaper cannot arbitrarily shift zones but coordinates the definitions with ABC guidelines, because the zones are important to advertisers and advertising agencies for whom the whole ABC system was established. For a newspaper, the zone definition may reflect separate editions of the newspaper or organizational structure of the delivery system as well as the character of its territory. Whatever description of the zones a newspaper chooses, it will likely differ from the audience zones used by competing broadcasters.

Newspapers report net paid figures by circulation zone. Each quarter the ABC produces a printed list, entitled *Fas Fax*, of the net paid circulation by zone for each member newspaper. Compared over time, these quarterly figures describe the stability of a newspaper's audience within zones. Comparisons across newspapers provide regional and national circulation patterns with standardized, uniform figures. Thus, *Fas Fax* provides both advertisers and newspaper executives with valuable circulation data.

An even more defined and descriptive gauge of net paid circulation is the household penetration figure, but it is also potentially more misleading. Household penetration is the percentage of occupied dwelling units in a circulation zone that probably receive the newspaper. The figure is obtained by dividing the number of occupied housing units by the net paid weekly or daily figure. This figure establishes a comparison of circulation to the number of residences and thus measures the appeal of the newspaper in a very general way.

For example, the *Milwaukee Journal* has a net paid weekly average of 258,284 and a Sunday net paid circulation of 390,242 in the NDMA. The Milwaukee NDMA comprises 523,100 occupied dwelling units, so the daily household penetration is 52 percent and the Sunday penetration is

72 percent in the NDMA. Household penetration is seldom calculated for the AOZ because it is insignificant for advertisers who already understand that penetration drops off rapidly beyond the NDMA or RTZ. Free distribution and voluntary pay newspapers should have a household penetration close to 100 percent, and certainly above 95 percent. The mobility of Americans plus a normal margin of error in apartment complexes, new housing developments, and inner city reconstruction precludes 100 percent circulation beyond a very limited geographic area. Homeowners who adamantly refuse delivery also prevent perfect saturation.

Household penetration figures, while valuable as a gross measure of a newspaper's attraction and impact, can be misleading because the number of occupied dwelling units has become increasingly hard to calculate. High turnover in apartment complexes, the rising number of single people working on the road and returning home for only the weekend, and abandoned homes and apartments distort the very basis for calculation. Further, many people own multiple homes, either for vacations or for retirement, living in each for only part of the year. Their homes may be counted as occupied dwelling units in two different states. As the poor, the functionally illiterate, and the non-English-speaking immigrants have moved into the central city areas, the value of household penetration figures has declined proportionately. Contemporary metropolitan life makes household penetration figures more difficult to interpret accurately, but the figure remains valuable as a rough guide to a newspaper's reach into the community.

Both net paid circulation and household penetration figures have been complicated as comparative tools by newspapers like the *Boston Globe* and *Detroit News*, which offer editions throughout the day as all-day newspapers. In contrast, the overwhelming majority of newspapers offer either a morning or afternoon newspaper, even if it has multiple editions. All-day newspapers are a response to changing readership patterns, typically with home delivery in the morning and single copy sales in the afternoon. In general, each edition is a part of the day's production, so each sale is part of the day's net paid circulation, even if individual customers purchase both morning and afternoon editions. Advertisers buying space in such newspapers face a unique problem that net paid and household penetration figures do not fully resolve because they do not indicate the number of different households or paying customers.

As a basic standard, the net paid circulation figure provides a solid and useful measure, but one lacking the refinement necessary to gauge a newspaper's precise readership. Household penetration moves one step closer, but it remains a gross measure of raw totals: newspapers sold and housing units. Lacking in these measures are the nature of the newspaper's readers, the movement of the newspaper among readers, and the variation among readers from day to day. Moreover, circulation and penetration figures are not comparable with audience measures used by radio and television stations.

Measure of Readership

Circulation as a measure of readership and audience moves beyond the gross figures to a more refined analysis of a newspaper's readers, both as individuals and in groups. Readership is almost always larger than circulation sales. Together, the figures provide a more accurate and sophisticated profile of a newspaper's reach into its market and the character of its audience.

Readership is the number of people who actually read a particular headline, caption, article, or advertisement. Because very few people read every item in the newspaper, readership is measured for particular content. It excludes those who merely glance at the newspaper or add it to their stack of unfinished reading. Readership research includes a wide range of studies on a reader's ability to comprehend and remember the content, type legibility, layout effectiveness, the ease with which a story can be read, and even attitudes toward reading the newspaper.[2]

Research results can pinpoint items and writers that bore, excite, enrage, please, and alienate readers. By covering readers in demographic or psychological groups characterized by age, income, education, occupational status, sex, geography, or attitudes, readership studies further refine a newspaper's understanding of how a particular segment of the audience uses the newspaper. Properly used, readership research enables editors and publishers to develop content that best serves the patterns and needs of specific groups within the audience. Attention to readership preferences can increase circulation.

Another, less scientific method of assessing readership preference is by listening to the reports of circulation employees who sell subscriptions door to door and newsstand dealers. They learn by conversation with their prospective customers which parts of the newspaper irritate or attract particular groups of readers. In the early 1970s, publisher Katherine Graham learned of the deficiencies of the *Washington Post* sports section from a newsstand dealer. Subscription salespeople refine their sales approaches to emphasize the attractive and minimize the irritating facets of their newspaper.

Although readership is a precise technical term describing the number of people who read a particular item, newspaper people often use it synonymously with audience, or the total number of people who look at any part of the newspaper. In circulation studies, it is essential to clarify whether the author means readership or total audience.

Duplicate readership, or the number of people who read multiple newspapers in a market, contributes to the confusion. Duplicate readership sometimes means duplicate subscribership, or the number of people subscribing to more than one newspaper. Don't forget, though, that subscribing is not necessarily a measure of reading. For advertisers, duplicate readership is important in calculating the impact of advertisements because it clarifies the number of different readers. Duplicate circulation was once a major source of subscription sales, and newspapers mounted special campaigns to develop subscribers among those who also purchased a competing newspaper. The increased price of newspapers, though, has steadily diminished duplicate readership over the past two decades.

Measure of Audience

Audience is a general term for two types of circulation measures: the number of people who look at a copy of the newspaper and the percentage of possible newspaper readers who receive a copy. As the number of people who look at the newspaper, the audience is always larger than both net paid circulation and readership because it includes everyone who sees even a small part of the newspaper. It is expressed in one of two figures, readers per copy and turnover rate. As the percentage of possible readers, audience is normally higher than household penetration because it is calculated for specific groups in the market and may exclude the functionally illiterate and non-English-speaking population.

Readers per copy (RPC) is the number of people beyond the purchaser who read any part of the newspaper, and it is sometimes called the "pass along rate." Calculated by reliable scientific survey techniques, the readers per copy figure is a multiplier of net paid circulation and a powerfully reliable estimate of total audience. The Three Sigma Study of 124 daily and 89 Sunday newspapers set the national RPC rate at 2.6, a rise from the previous 2.17.[3] This means that a newspaper with a net paid circulation of 100,000 has an audience of 260,000. The RPC measures the movement of newspapers in families, in apartment buildings and group homes, and in the workplace. Scientifically derived, the readers per copy figure is as reliable and more accurate than the net paid figure.

Turnover rate is a recently developed measure of audience that counts the number of different readers reached by the newspaper over several days. It is based on research that found that sequential issues of the newspaper reach different readers, even though their net paid circulation figures may be almost identical. The turnover rate is the percentage of readers who differ from one day to the next. Three Sigma found the national turnover rate to be 28.5 percent, with substantial variation from city to city.[4] High turnover can be caused by tourists, traveling professional sales and management people, irregular readers, and regular but nondaily readers. Whatever the precise cause, the signficance of the turnover rate is clear: Of every 10,000 readers, 2850 change each day. In Dallas, the 39 percent turnover rate means the *Dallas Morning News* reaches 111,912 different readers from one day to the next with its net paid average circulation of 286,955. When the turnover rate is based on the readers per copy rate of 2.6, the net paid average becomes an audience of 746,083 (286,955 × 2.6) with a total audience turnover of 290,972 (746,083 × .39) each day. The total audience turnover exceeds the net paid average by 4000!

The combined readers per copy and turnover rates describe an audience with a much more dynamic and irregular relationship to the newspaper than the net paid circulation figure describes. Over a 20-day period the *Dallas Morning News* may reach 1,037,055 different people, even though its net paid average remains steady at 286,955. Obviously, a booming metropolitan area like Dallas has a far different turnover rate than a smaller, quieter area like Des Moines has; but the audience magnitude represented by these two figures underscores the difficulties a circulation manager and staff face in a fluid and changing marketplace. For advertisers, the turnover rate may ultimately prove far more important than either net paid or readers per copy rates because it affects the scheduling of advertisements.[5]

Audience as a percentage of possible readers can be calculated like household penetration, with the occupied dwelling units decreased by the functional illiteracy rate and the number of non-English-speaking households (functional illiterates and non-English-speakers are quite different). Essentially, this is no more unreasonable than subtracting the percentage of vacant, abandoned, and second homes or adjusting for the percentage of residents dwelling out of town part of the year. More valuable is the percentage of audience calculated for specific demographic groups, for example, college graduates, 18- to 24-year-old males, and the like. For this calculation, the circulation is studied in a way different from net paid circulation, normally with a survey of subscribers and single copy purchasers. These figures may vary substantially from the household penetration figures in either direction, depending on the newspaper and the market.

The differences among these figures can be seen in Table 1.1 based on figures for the *Milwaukee Journal*.

TABLE 1.1
Circulation Data Comparison[6]

Type of Circulation Data	Daily	Sunday
Net paid average	323,932	515,108
Household penetration (NDMA)	57.26%	74.69%
Readers per copy	2.3	2.2
Total audience	745,043	1,133,238
Percentage readership:		
among adults 18 years of age and older	54%	70%
among males 18–24	60%	68%
among females 18–24	44%	75%
among college graduates, postgraduates	55%	79%
among managers/officials/proprietors	59%	81%
among those earning $25,000 to $34,000 per year	59%	76%

Circulation as a measure of sales, audience, and readership is its most important task for a newspaper because it links the number of newspapers sold to the dynamics of the local marketplace and captures changes in subscription and reading habits. The ABC net paid circulation figure is extremely vital for many purposes, including cross-newspaper comparisons. It is least susceptible to rapid changes in the marketplace and statistical error or flawed research design; however, it is also least reflective of the actual relationship between a newspaper and its readers and least comparable with measures of broadcast audience. This need to measure the total audience is filled by reader per copy and turnover figures, just as the need to understand circulation within specific groups is satisfied by studying readership by demographic groups.

COMPARISONS TO BROADCAST AUDIENCE FIGURES

Comparing circulation with broadcast audience figures causes constant debate and not a little confusion among media salespeople, advertisers, and employees in newspapers and broadcast stations. Most audience figures are noncomparable simply because they use different concepts and different numerical bases in their calculations. Broadcasters not only use different terminology, but they also have different territorial boundaries and a different audience-measuring system. The result is that newspaper net paid figures and household penetration figures do not express the same facts as broadcast audience measures and look small in comparison, even though a newspaper may reach more people or a higher percentage of the audience.

Broadcasters use the area of dominant influence (ADI) as their basic measure of territory. The ADI comprises whole counties where more than half of all viewing households are tuned to stations in a particular market. Created by the American Research Bureau, which conducts the Arbitron surveys, the ADI almost never coincides with the newspaper's NDMA or RTZ and automatically excludes counties where the broadcasters do not attract a large audience.

There are two technical definitions for broadcast audience. The first is the number of people tuned to the station at a particular time, as determined by surveys. As the number of listeners or viewers, audience is closest to the total audience figure of newspapers (net paid circulation times readers per copy). Like newspaper audience figures, these broadcast audience figures can be broken down by demographic groups and adjusted for those incapable of being in the audience.

The second definition is the share of audience, or simply the *share*. This is the percentage of listeners or viewers tuned to a specific station at a particular time. It is, then, a percentage of a percentage, although it is commonly stated as a whole number, e.g., 40 share. If 50 percent of adults watch television at 10 p.m., a 40 share means that 40 percent of the 50 percent are watching one particular station, for a total of 20 percent of adults. Share of audience is comparable to readership of a particular item, but because it is seldom expressed as a percentage and because there is little reason to do so, the two figures are seldom compared.

A group of major metropolitan newspapers, among them the *Los Angeles Times*, the *New York Times*, and the *Toronto Globe and Mail*, have challenged the Audit Bureau of Circulations to change its reliance solely on the net paid figure and develop audience measures comparable to those used in broadcasting. Their request is due to their loss of advertising revenue to broadcasters and the new categories of newspaper readers. Advertisers are resisting these changes, however, because they have come to implicitly trust net paid figures and view audience measures as susceptible to manipulation. Major advertisers, educated for 70 years to depend on the solid and reliable character of net paid figures, question the need for change to another system. Small-town publishers resist spending money on a new circulation measurement system solely to satisfy a few large-city publishers. Some publishers in cities with competing dailies fear the temptation to manipulate audience figures will prove irresistible, particularly for the second newspaper.

Properly conducted by qualified professionals, newspaper audience research could produce figures as reliable as net paid circulation. For some purposes, the figures would be more accurate and precise because they would describe the way the newspaper fits into its market and the lives of its readers. The refined figures would help editors and advertising and circulation managers better understand their own newspaper and its audience. These figures would be more directly comparable to broadcast audience measures and thus could increase advertising sales.

CIRCULATION AS AN INDEX OF COMMERCIAL VALUE

One of the definitions of a newspaper cited earlier in this chapter stressed the profit-making role of the newspaper as a business. In this sense, circulation figures, along with advertising revenues, capital goods, property, and other economic factors, are a measure of a newspaper's commercial value. Circulation figures are used to determine the newspaper's market position, its revenues, and its net worth.

Index of Market Position

Circulation as an index of market position describes the groups of readers within the market to whom the newspaper appeals or seeks to appeal. As such, its primary value lies within larger metropolitan areas, where multiple newspapers are readily available and advertisers want a precise profile of the newspaper's audience.

Market positioning has determined the success and failure of newspapers. In Boston, in the 1960s, three daily newspapers appealed to three different parts of the overall population; that is, they had different market positions. The *Herald* appealed to upscale, well-educated people; the *Globe* appealed to midddle-class citizens; and the *American* appealed to blue-collar workers and the lower class. When the *Herald* and *American* merged, its new market position created a serious problem for editors and advertising and circulation managers because they had a newspaper whose market position included the top and bottom in education, income, and social status. Against that diversity in taste and reading interest, the *Globe* had a single market whose proximity to the upper-class *Herald* readers permitted expansion with little conflict. Straddling the market position of the *Globe*, the *Herald-American* had an untenable position and gradually ceded its upper-class readers to the *Globe* and tried to expand its market position into the blue-collar segment of the *Globe* readership. The circulation of these two newspapers, expressed in terms of demographic groups and social class, points out a fundamental problem for newspaper managers: Where does a particular newspaper fit in the market? The answer to that question guides decisions on content, advertising, and circulation sales efforts.

Another aspect of market position is the appeal of a particular type of circulation for major advertisers. The *Los Angeles Times* has a circulation of over 900,000 daily with a household penetration of less than 23 percent. On Sundays its penetration rises to 28 percent with a circulation of nearly 1,200,000. Despite the low penetration figure, the *Times* has maintained the highest advertising linage each year for over a decade. Its market position, as the newspaper of the upper middle and upper classes, makes it essential for major advertisers in southern California. In other words, although the *Times* reaches only 23 percent of Los Angeles's households, it has the right 23 percent for advertisers; the net paid circulation and penetration are less important figures than market position. At the root, market position is simply a demographic refinement of circulation as a measure of audience, based on socioeconomic status. Its value lies in its description of the newspaper's competitive posture against other newspapers and advertising media.

Revenue Base

Circulation as a basis for all revenues defines the financial relationship between the audience figures and revenues from both circulation sales and advertising. For all newspapers the audience determines the income, both directly and indirectly. Direct income is derived from the sale of the newspaper through subscriptions and single copies or from membership fees, whereas indirect income is derived from the sale of advertising space, whose value is directly proportional to the circulation. Both the desirability and cost of advertising space depend on the size and demographics of the newspaper audience, that is, the circulation.

Prior to 1833, subscribers paid the full cost of producing the newspaper, often as much as 6 cents per copy, a working man's wage for half a day. The cost limited newspaper sales to the affluent and meant advertising was carried more as a service to readers than as a source of revenue. Benjamin Day revolutionized this system in 1833 by pricing his *New York Sun* newspaper at a penny and charging advertisers a rate that guaranteed profitability and rose with circulation. Day's financial system carries through to this day. A 92-page copy of the *Toronto Star* selling for 25 cents contains 31 cents in raw materials alone (newsprint and ink). The price differential for a five-pound Sunday newspaper is even greater.

Advertisers buy space to reach potential customers, which means the newspaper sells its audience to advertisers. Today, an increasing number of advertisers reach these customers with preprinted inserts rather than advertisements appearing on the newspaper pages (called run-of-paper [ROP] ads), but the newspaper is the vehicle for delivering advertisements. Some newspapers even insert free samples and small catalogs in the newspaper in order to increase advertising revenue. If a newspaper's household penetration or net paid circulation falls below a certain level, some major advertisers shift their preprints to direct mail or free distribution newspapers. In an effort to retain preprint advertisers like Sears and K-Mart, some newspapers augment their net paid circulation with free distribution newspapers and total market coverage products for nonsubscribers in crucial parts of the market.

Measure of Net Worth

A newspaper's market value as a commercial property at the time of sale is determined, in part, by its circulation. Paid circulation is used in two different ways in appraising a newspaper's value. The first method divides total circulation revenue by the individual subscription price to produce a per paper revenue figure. When compared with the cost per paper and the advertising revenue per paper, this figure yields a quick analysis of profitability. The second method places a specific value on circulation, either a dollar figure per subscriber or as a multiplier of earnings. The Tribune Company of Chicago paid $200 million for the Newport News Daily News Company in 1986. This translates to about $1200 per subscriber or four times the annual revenue. The per-subscriber rate is typical for monopoly markets; the typical multiplier is 2.9 times revenue. The dollar figure, based on revenue, yields a total circulation value. The percentage figure reduces total circulation revenue to a profitability gauge. All such figures amount to approximate values, and they vary by the size of the newspaper and the nature of the local market. In appraisal, circulation is but one of several figures, such as advertising revenue, value of mechanical equipment, and net assets; but it is nonetheless important.

CIRCULATION AS AN INDEX OF VALUE AND RESPONSIBILITY

Definitions of circulation in this group focus on the value of the newspaper in society beyond its commercial nature or its audience or revenue. While important to the commercial success of the newspaper, the measures discussed offer little to those who ponder a newspaper's contribution to the public good as a participant in the democratic system. The founding fathers established the first amendment to protect the press in its public service as a government watchdog and a forum for public opinion.

In all, the press fulfills four different roles in American society: informing readers about community and world events, commenting on the news to provide focus and understanding, entertaining readers, and offering merchants a means to advertise their goods and services. In as much as it measures reach into the community, circulation measures a newspaper's service to the community, creates an index of its influence, and becomes the product of editorial responsibility and advertising value.

Service to the Community

Newspapers foster the process of public discussion, which marks a healthy democracy. In a letter to one of his editors, Joseph Pulitzer described the service a newspaper should provide for its community:[7]

> Every issue of the paper presents an opportunity and a duty to say something courageous and true; to rise above the mediocre and conventional; to say something that will command the respect of the intelligent, the educated, the independent part of the community; to rise above the fear of partisanship and fear of popular prejudice. I would rather have one article a day of this sort; and these ten or twenty lines might readily represent a whole day's hard work in the way of concentrated, intense thinking and revision, polish of style, weighing.

Each day the *Chicago Tribune* publishes a statement of its creed:

> The newspaper is an institution developed by modern civilization to present the news of the day, to foster commerce and industry, to inform and lead public opinion, and to furnish that check upon government which no constitution has ever been able to provide.

Similar creeds mark the origins and philosophy of most newspapers because publishers, editors, and readers recognize the role of the press in public life. Each newspaper, rooted in a unique community, differs from others because of its location and its publisher's philosophy. As a local voice with overriding concerns in its own community, the newspaper shares responsibility in the community for the common good.

In this context, circulation assures that a newspaper is widely available and that all who can read have access to it. Thus, circulation fulfills the democratic ideal of a free press in a free society. Beyond that, circulation measures the extent to which the newspaper serves the community and meets the needs of the citizens. At times, circulation may decline because the newspaper exposes the dark side of life: corruption, scandal, political malfeasance, religious chicanery, and threats to public health and safety.

Newspapers celebrating community life may find their sales increasing, but the number of readers willing to pay for the newspaper provides a measure of how well the newspaper fits the needs of its readers more than the amount of press freedom.

Another group of newspapers addresses communities significantly different from the towns and cities served by dailies. These national newspapers—the *Wall Street Journal*, the *Christian Science Monitor*, the *New York Times*, and *USA Today*—serve the needs of demographic and special interest audiences and have few geographic boundaries. As the voice of the business community, the *Wall Street Journal* provides essential, credible information in a narrow area, and it offers a national editorial voice that speaks to the nation on behalf of business. The *Christian Science Monitor* offers the news of the day in perspective to those who have no use for the violent, sensational, or titillating. Known for its careful and reliable editing, the *Monitor* provides opinions rooted in its religious understanding on the editorial page; and it derives substantial support from the national religious body. As the newspaper of record, the *New York Times* has more readership outside the city of New York than inside the boroughs. Its circulation in Washington, D.C., and among the opinion leaders and influential in virtually every state capitol and major university gives it powerful national influence and service. It also serves as the most respected newspaper among journalists. *USA Today*, the newcomer among these papers, appeals to a national audience interested in a brief summary of news, extensive coverage of sports and entertainment, business news, and snappy graphics in attractive colors. Its community remains somewhat amorphous and changing, but *USA Today* appeals to those without a strong commitment to the local community or its newspapers: travelers, newly arrived singles and young marrieds, young professionals, and other occasional readers. For each of these newspapers, circulation measures service of a different sort—a national perspective, a particular perspective, an outside voice, a fulfilling alternative to locally available newspapers.

Index of Influence

Newspapers help to shape public discussion, formulate public policy, and develop public opinion. Influence in this context means the ability to affect readers' lives, community operation, legislation movement, and law enforcement. The community may be local, regional, or national because citizens play a part in multiple levels of authority. The key questions related to influence are: Is the newspaper read by leaders? Is it frequently cited by the influential or the citizens? Is it considered a voice of the people? Does it faithfully monitor government? Is its support crucial to the success of a community project? The ultimate question is: Does the newspaper, by its coverage and editorials, force consideration of changes and change itself?

If a newspaper is so important in its community that it must be read by those who wish to stay informed, it is a newspaper of influence. Just as the *New York Times* exerts influence because it is read by politicians, editors of other newspapers, and other leaders, a newspaper like the *Dubuque Telegraph Herald* or the *Salt Lake City Desert News* exerts influence because it affects the way people in a portion of Iowa or Utah perceive their community. In that role, these newspapers exert an influence measurable only at the local level, directly by those who read the paper and indirectly by those who learn of its stories and opinions from others. Although editorial support of political candidates seems the obvious and prominent influence, it is probably less important than the subtle and pervasive ways in which a newspaper influences community life. A newspaper provides the community with a self-image, a reflection of life and the times. When a newspaper has a monopoly on readers in its market, circulation figures may be less a measure of influence than simple necessity, but even a politically weak newspaper provides a particular community image and may serve it well in nonpolitical ways.

Product of Editorial Desirability and Advertising Value

Circulation depends on the appeal of the newspaper. Net paid circulation is an accumulation of individual purchase decisions, each based on the newspaper's value and its role in the buyer's life. Significant changes in the customer's life, the newspaper, or the informational marketplace can alter these purchase decisions and increase or decrease circulation. To compete with other sources of information, opinion, and entertainment, the newspaper must keep pace with its present readers and find ways to attract nonreaders.

Desirable editorial content comprises news accounts, editorials, letters to the editor, columns, comics, sports stories, crossword puzzles, stock market figures, chess and bridge columns, radio and TV listings, and special sections. Each element in the newspaper draws a particular type of reader, eventually through habit. Content alteration can produce fierce protests and threats of cancellation. Judiciously allocating space among the various content possibilities requires a keen sense of reader interest and the overall audience if circulation is to be maximized.

Advertising value goes beyond the savings that a newspaper's coupons offer to news about new products and prices, jobs, cars, homes and apartments, pets, and personals. For some readers the importance of advertising content outweighs editorial material on a given day because the readers are looking for a job, home, or car. They may need an appliance, furniture, or clothes; or they may simply enjoy monitoring the prices of goods listed in the classified advertisements. The success of small newspapers filled with only classified advertisements demonstrates the appeal of this content for a group of readers. A decline in advertising value can trigger a decline in circulation, just as a decline in circulation can cause a decrease in advertising linage. In a competitive market serious decline can prove fatal. As soon as the circulation of the *Philadelphia Bulletin* fell below that of the competing *Inquirer*, advertisers deserted the *Bulletin*, which soon went out of business. The relationship between advertising and circulation lies at the heart of a newspaper's financial success.

In the mid-1970s the *Minneapolis Star* radically altered its image by emphasizing lengthy news analysis. The front page often contained only three or four stories and at times contained but one. The paper aimed at young, active readers and shifted from its market position among families and married homeowners. Almost immediately the newspaper lost 2000 subscribers per month, and within four years the flaccid *Star* merged with the morning *Tribune*. It lost its editorial and advertising desirability for too many readers. On the other hand, the *Sacramento Bee*, which had lost significant AOZ circulation, converted from evening to morning publication and increased its circulation 17 percent within a year. Like many other Sunbelt newspapers, it found its content substantially more desirable in the morning.

The rise of cable television systems with classified and retail advertising and the proliferation of small shoppers have alarmed newspaper publishers because both threaten advertising revenue and the advertising value of the newspaper. Not only do newspapers receive a smaller portion of advertising expenditures, but other media meet consumers' advertising needs. Specialized classified advertising publications for cars, homes, appliances, recreational vehicles, and the like cost newspapers advertising and circulation revenue and reduce the possibility that a nonreader interested in advertising will become interested in some other feature of the newspaper on a regular basis.

CIRCULATION AS A NEWSPAPER DEPARTMENT

Circulation, advertising, and editorial are the three major newspaper departments because they provide the income and define the product. The other departments—production, accounting, maintenance, personnel, promotion, data processing—play an important but supporting role. Department interaction is inherent in some of the definitions of circulation already discussed. Circulation partly depends on editorial and advertising content. Advertising rates depend on circulation totals. Circulation employees depend on the production department to meet printing deadlines, on the accounting department to maintain billing records, and, on many newspapers, on the data processing department to maintain updated subscriber lists.

The number of employees performing circulation work varies with the newspaper's size and its circulation philosophy, but circulation emerges as a separate department for newspapers with circulation above 5000. This number of subscribers justifies a separate person responsible for sales, service, and collections, and supervision of the carriers, drivers, and dealers. On a small newspaper like the *Goldsboro News-Argus* in North Carolina, one person is both business manager and circulation manager, has an assistant circulation manager, and supervises a number of full- and part-time employees. On a metropolitan daily, a vice-president may supervise a circulation unit with hundreds of employees and thousands of carriers and agents. In some newspapers, circulation is part of a marketing division or department; in others, marketing is part of the circulation unit. These variations in size and structure reaffirm the point that newspapers are local businesses guided by very different people and are highly local in nature.

As discussed in Chapter 7, some circulation departments take charge of the newspaper as soon as it leaves the presses, in the mailroom where papers are bundled for shipping; others only take charge after the newspaper leaves the delivery truck. The truck fleet and drivers may be under the circulation department or supervised by another department head. Even the garage and vehicle maintenance employees can be found in some circulation departments. If the newspaper produces its own total market coverage product, the circulation department may employ writers, advertising salespeople, and a layout staff; or it may simply deliver the finished product. Also, maintenance of subscriber and nonsubscriber files (see Chapter 10) in a computer system may fall to circulation employees. Some circulation departments increase profits by delivering magazines and free samples.

Whatever the mix of these extended tasks, most circulation departments share responsibility for three traditional functions: sales, service, and collections. Sales involves selling subscriptions and single copies. Service includes two distinct activities: delivery of the newspaper to single copy outlets and subscriber homes and service for customers forgotten by their carriers or cursed with damaged newspapers. Collection involves taking in circulation revenue from subscribers and single copy outlets. Each of these functions, discussed in greater detail in Chapters 8 and 9, includes an array of tasks and responsibilities that are easy to define but difficult to accomplish across the department.

As one department, circulation also has corporate connections and responsibilities; but as a functional unit, circulation works in the world of subscribers and readers rather than in the corporate world. Circulation workers drive the streets, walk the sidelines, meet readers while delivering and collecting, and try to persuade nonsubscribers to give the newspaper a chance for only a few weeks. Observing community life as they go about their tasks, circulation workers are the scouts of community change, the eyes and ears of the newspaper across the circulation territory. Their familiarity with their readers and their community provides a unique and invaluable set of reports for circulation management. As a department, circulation connects the newspaper to the readers.

CIRCULATION AS A PROFESSION

Circulation is sometimes defined in terms of its job responsibilities. Circulation management has been called a profession involving a wide variety of skills, including salesmanship, organizational ability, public speaking, literary competence, imagination, and mathematical aptitude.[8] Whether circulation management or any other occupation is a true profession raises a substantial debate among sociologists and those in the three classical professions: law, medicine, and education. The true professions meet the following three criteria:

1. They are based on theoretical knowledge.
2. Their members command special skills and competence.
3. Professional conduct is guided by a code of ethics, the focus of which is service to the client.[9]

Rather than debating the extent to which circulation management is a profession, the discussion should concentrate on circulation managers as professionals. Professionals are those who earn their living at a particular activity and who do something with great skill, as well as being those who work in the defined professions. A professional demonstrates high competence in an occupation and establishes a high standard of performance. In this sense, circulation work challenges many to professional performance across sales, service, and collections, each of which requires a full set of distinctive skills and specialized knowledge.

As Leo Bogart of the Newspaper Advertising Bureau concluded from his study of newspaper circulation, circulation managers have several standing assignments.

To sell subscriptions in the areas the paper regards as its market
To retain those subscriptions with minimum loss and turnover by providing timely and satisfactory service
To facilitate complete and prompt collection of the payments required from subscribers
To sell as many single copies as possible to people who have not been persuaded to subscribe on a regular basis or for whom no delivery service can be economically arranged
To strive for cost efficiency by reducing the waste that is involved in turnover at all levels: among subscribers, carriers, and carrier supervisors or district managers.[10]

Circulation has its own professional association, the International Circulation Managers Association (ICMA), which has provided a full range of services since its founding in 1893. ICMA informs its members of changes in the newspaper industry, impending government regulations and legislation, court decisions, postal rates, and labor legislation. It has been the national voice of newspaper circulation and a driving force for educational programs in circulation management.

NOTES

1. Chuck Bennett, Audit Bureau of Circulations, interview with author, 3 June 1986.
2. George Gallup, "A Scientific Method for Determining Reader Interest," *Journalism Quarterly* 7, 1 (March 1930): 1–13. Gallup began an approach to the assessment that expanded rapidly from study of particular articles to photographs, headlines, advertising, and then readability of type. Rudolph Flesch developed a formula for measuring readability, and contemporary audience research studies the image of the newspaper among its readers and nonreaders. See, for example, Malcom MacLean Jr., "Mass Media Audiences: City, Small City, Village and Farm," *Journalism Quarterly* 29 (Summer 1952): 271–282, for early studies
3. This 1980 study, conducted at the Three Sigma Research Center, Larchmont, New York, was the first syndicated newspaper study of the 31 largest metropolitan areas. It was privately released to newspapers in 1981.
4. Ibid.
5. Mark Mattison, "What's Happening to Newspaper Readers," *Marketing & Media Decisions* 17 (February 1982): 140–141. Mattison is marketing manager for Knight-Ridder newspapers.

6. *Milwaukee Journal* figures were obtained from ABC Publisher's Statement and Three Sigma Study for the same time period.
7. Don Seitz, *Joseph Pulitzer: His Life and Letters* (New York: Simon and Schuster, Inc., 1924), 286.
8. ICMA President Harold Schwartz to Joseph Forsee, 10 January 1980.
9. Amitai Etzioni, *The Semi-Professions and Their Organization* (New York: Free Press, 1969), 142.
10. Leo Bogart, "Circulation: The Key to Successful Newspaper Marketing," address to the International Circulation Managers Association convention, New York City, 21 June 1982.

CHAPTER
2

The History of
Newspaper Circulation

The history of newspapers is the history not only of content but of how people got their news. News in the sense of knowing what's going on in the world around us originated in the oral histories passed on from generation to generation. As early as 449 B.C. news reports on the actions of the Roman Senate and gossip from Rome circulated throughout the Roman Empire.[1] Athenian dramatists recorded the history of Greece.

In approximately 1 A.D., written news reports were introduced with *Acta Diurna*. The daily, handwritten accounts were delivered to the homes of subscribers, posted on the walls of Rome, and stored in a government archives where citizens could review back copies.[2] One subscriber, the Roman senator Cicero, cancelled his subscription to protest content editing.

In 1566 the Venetian government initiated a daily newspaper to report its war with Dalmatia, posting copies on the city walls and selling single copies for a *gazetta* (a small coin). In Germany, regular daily newspapers began appearing in 1609. Government regulations prevented independent newspapers in London until 1702, but the Dutch printed English language newspapers and smuggled them into London long before that. These early newspapers were generally delivered to the homes of a few subscribers, inns, and coffee houses, and were sold on street corners; delivering an illegal newspaper could lead to arrest and imprisonment on the grounds of treason and sedition. The "legal" newspapers in England were only those that were licensed and government-controlled.

COLONIAL NEWSPAPER DISTRIBUTION

Colonists brought British press tradition with them to the New World, so the first colonial newspapers were government newspapers, licensed by the authorities and controlled by the postmaster, who served as editor, publisher, and circulation manager. These postmaster newspapers were additional sources of income, which the postmaster sent through the mail at no charge.[3] Sitting at the hub of colonial communication, postmasters had access to all the news from government, from foreign and domestic newspapers, and from letters patrons shared with the community. They quickly realized they might be able to sell the information passing through their offices and invoke government support by publishing official announcements. Through them, weekly publication became the norm; and from them, weekly newspapers developed into the dominant form for nearly 300 years.

John Campbell, whose *Boston News-Letter* was the first successful newspaper, charged 2 pence (4¢) per copy; but he seldom made a profit. Several times during his 19 years as postmaster he received government subsidies to avoid closing the newspaper. After falling from political favor and losing his postal position, Campbell continued publishing the *News-Letter* until competition from the new postmaster's newspaper, the *Gazette*, drove him out of business. Without the postal frank, Campbell could not deliver the newspaper inexpensively, partly because the new postmaster set the newspaper postal rate.

As official government newspapers delivered by the government postal system, the *News-Letter* and *Gazette* contained only politically safe material. Ben Franklin's older brother James established the *New England Courant* as a voice of opposition to the severe Puritan rule in Boston; the *Courant* did not have an official license. As long as the paper criticized Puritan leaders Cotton Mather and Increase Mather, the colonial government allowed it to circulate freely; but when it criticized the British defenses in the harbor, James was jailed for seditious libel and ultimately lost his right to print the *Courant*. The *Courant* relied heavily on home delivery; and Ben Franklin, as the printer's apprentice, became America's first newspaper carrier, carrying the still warm news sheets around Boston.[4] The *Courant*'s subscribers included local taverns, reading rooms, inns, and homes of upper-class merchants. The legal controls on the press in Boston caused Ben to sell the *Courant* once he controlled it and move to Philadelphia, where the press operated in freedom.

Delinquent subscribers posed the greatest financial threat to Campbell, Franklin, and subsequent publishers for over 100 years. In the colonial period and the first decades of the new republic, a subscriber signed up for a quarterly or annual period and was not billed until the end of the subscription period. Known as billing in arrears (because the customer owed for issues already delivered), this system offered the publisher two unattractive choices if the subscriber did not pay. He could cancel the subscription and assure the temporary loss of a customer with small chance of repayment if the subscriber was embarrassed or angered, or he could continue delivery and plead for repayment. Publisher Hugh Gaine continued to serve one wealthy subscriber for 10 years without payment. Royalist editor James Rivington pleaded with British officers and loyalists during the Revolutionary War to pay their newspaper bills before fleeing Boston.[5] Because advance payment was unacceptable at the time, colonial publishers had little choice but to extend credit and beg for payment. Newspapers from the first years until well after the Revolution commonly carried advertisements begging subscribers for partial repayment of their bill with goods, if not with cash. One such ad, appearing in the final issue of the *New York Weekly Journal*, read: "My every day Cloaths are almost worne out, send the poor printer a few Gammons, or some Meal, some Butter, Cheese, Poultry, &c."[6]

The postal system, which favored postmaster publishers, proved an inadequate and unsatisfactory delivery system for publishers as the newspaper industry grew in the 1700s, particularly in the decade preceding the Revolution. At first, publishers relied on apprentices like Ben Franklin to serve local customers and used the postal system only for rural landholders and middle-class burghers in outlying villages; but growth and competition led to a complex system involving youth carriers, newsboys, and post riders.

Delivery by Youth Carriers

Youth carriers were hired specifically to replace apprentices for newspaper delivery as early as the 1760s, when New York publisher Hugh Gaine advertised for a "nice boy" to deliver the *Mercury*. Expanding cities and enlarged subscription lists created a home delivery network too large and far flung for the apprentice, who had obligations in the print shop as well. Youth carriers worked for a pittance, but they were allowed to solicit subscribers for gifts each New Year's Day to supplement their wages. Going door to door, they joined watchmen, lamplighters, and other public servants in town.

The carriers soon learned that a bit of verse spoken at a subscriber's door would open a purse, so they began creating carriers' addresses, a

New Year's tradition lasting into the 1880s. The typical carriers' address began cheerfully.

> Since 'tis the Custom ev'ry Year
> When it begins, for to appear
> In an emphatic Rhimish Mode
> To greet you at your own Abode,
> Relating to you Things again
> Which now are past; in humble Strain
> Wishing you all a happy Year
> With Peace, and plenty of good Cheer

The carrier would then recount a few major news events of the year in rhyme and conclude with a plea for a cash gift.

> Hoping you will not think it strange
> That Something's wanting in Exchange
> Kind Sirs:—I do not name the Sum;
> But what you please; and I'll be gone.[7]

For over 150 years youth carriers annually repeated the rite at Christmastime, updating the carrier address in anticipation of a seasonal gift of cash. Economic necessity maintained the tradition: In the midst of the Civil War, *New York Herald* managing editor Frederic Hudson estimated that poorly paid carriers received about $5000 in New Year's tips.[8] The *Herald* soon thereafter ended the tradition for its own carriers by raising their income. The *Kansas City Star* forbade the carrier address after 1880 on the grounds that it was a form of begging. To aid carriers in their annual appeal, the *Philadelphia Ledger* gave its carriers almanacs as gifts for subscribers; by 1885, almanacs and calendars replaced the carrier address as an inducement for seasonal generosity. They are still used by youth carriers in many cities.

Delivery by Newsboys

Newsboys first appeared in London in the form of buxom "Mercurie Girls," who stood on the street corners and hawked copies of the *London Mercurie* in 1638. Puritan morals quickly outlawed the Mercurie girls, who were replaced by young boys.[9] The French were not so sensitive, for women sold newspapers on street corners unimpeded for several centuries. Americans copied the British, with young men shouting the headlines to sell single copies on colonial streets by 1765, when Samuel Sweeney was the foremost newsboy for the *Constitutional Courant*.

Newsboys aided colonial newspapers in two ways: They increased circulation by attracting customers who would not subscribe regularly, and they brought in cash for each issue. The improved cashflow broke reliance on quarterly and annual subscription bills and moderated the effect of delinquent subscribers; it did not fully resolve the problem, however, because single copy sales were erratic. Furthermore, single copy sales appealed less to upper-class customers than to those who could not afford regular home delivery.

Delivery by Post Riders

Post riders delivered newspapers to outlying post offices since the appearance of the first issues of the *Boston News-Letter*, and for a fee they dropped off copies at homes along the post roads. Post riders were the long-distance mail carriers of the colonial period, carrying gossip and tales of city life along with the mail. Moving on horseback along trails and rutted roads through snow and rain, ice and mud, heat and dust, post riders connected isolated villages with the outside world. Like the Wells Fargo drivers and Mississippi riverboat captains of a later era, the post rider knew the value of a grand entrance to each hamlet along the post road. Not that the post rider could move the newspapers swiftly. Under ideal conditions it took one week for the mail to move between New York and Boston; in winter, it required two weeks. A two-day ride separated New York and Philadelphia; but two-day-old news was better than none, so the post rider played a major role in newspaper distribution.

In their 1758 revision of the Royal Postal System, publishers Ben Franklin and William Hunter also revamped the newspaper collection system by empowering post riders to sell subscriptions and collect the subscription fee, from which they kept 20 percent as a collection fee. The revision established an annual newspaper delivery fee for post riders, and it continued the practice of free delivery of newspapers to editor/publishers throughout the colonies. These exchange newspapers, from which editors clipped stories about foreign and domestic events, were the primary source of news of the hinterlands for city newspapers and the sole source of news for rural newspapers. Post riders were integral to the news flow; and they served publishers as a delivery, sales, and collection force outside the local area.

Lawrence Sweeney, who delivered the *New York Mercury* in rural areas, was but one of a number of private post riders specializing in newspaper delivery, particularly to customers not living along post roads. Peter Robinson carved out a substantial career as a delivery agent for all the Boston newspapers, delivering them to every subscriber in Amherst and to those living along the road. The private post rider system ensured that royal censors would not confiscate newspapers that seemed too critical of the government. As the Revolution neared, ship captains aided newspaper delivery by carrying newspapers, along with bundles of mail, to coffee houses in ports of call.

After the Revolution, post riders became official collection and delivery agents, paying publishers for the newspapers they delivered and keeping half of their collections as a fee. While this improved the financial condition of publishers, it guaranteed post riders an impoverished existence. A post rider for the *Farmer's Weekly Museum* reminded delinquent subscribers of the hardship they caused him with the following verse:

> You think that I can ride, I say
> Two full years without a farthing's pay;
> So full of dark ingratitude,
> Pray don't complain if you are sued.
> A Sheriff soon I mean to send,
> And on my word you may depend,
> And if you wish to know my name,
> I will make known to you the same;
> 'Tis Abner Felt, your poor post rider
> So poor he can't buy wine, nor cider.[10]

CHANGES IN NEWSPAPERS AFTER THE REVOLUTION

Although the multiple distribution systems introduced in colonial America provided effective delivery of newspapers and citizens clamored for news during the American Revolution, newspapers remained a luxury item, affordable only to the affluent. Circulation growth was slight; for instance, a Boston newspaper had a circulation of 600 in 1765 and reached only 700 subscribers in 1800. Costs of presses and type and production time limited circulation growth.

Readers could choose between two widely different types of newspapers. The mercantile press contained vital information about shipping, prices, clients, and competitors; because of its content, it was essential to merchants. The partisan political newspapers, specializing in government affairs, required frequent infusions of cash to remain afloat, because they attracted few advertisers and small circulations, yet they formed an important link among the growing communities of the new nation.

Newspapers began to grow with the industrialization of the Northeast. In the late 1700s and early 1800s the newspaper industry made three significant strides toward an important, independent, ongoing role in the nation's affairs. The first was advance payment, which provided greater economic security. The second was a mutually beneficial partnership with the postal service, which encouraged mutual development. The third was the emergence of daily newspapers.

Advance Payment

The first effort to resolve the arrears billing system, which plagued post riders and publishers, was the mandatory advance payment system established in Salem, Massachusetts, in 1786. The publisher of the *Salem Gazette* required all subscribers to pay cash in advance at the newspaper office. Youth carriers and post riders were then paid a delivery fee. This proved a cost-efficient system, known as the office control method, and quickly spread to other newspapers because it ended the bad debt burden.[11] Even though it limited circulation growth, advance payment assured a regular income to carriers and post riders and allowed publishers to devote more time to soliciting advertising. Because it limited circulation, it was a system more suited to smaller newspapers than to the competitive newspapers in Boston, New York, and Philadelphia. While the office control method did not guarantee profitability, it removed a major economic threat to newspapers.

Postal Service and Newspaper Expansion

The pre-Revolutionary relationship between publishers and postmasters took on new importance as debates over the government and organization of the new nation fostered heavy use of exchange newspapers. Newspapers carried the *Federalist Papers* and other articles on the proposed constitution and bill of rights, and editors pleaded for expansion of the postal system to speed delivery of exchanges. Congressmen, responding to their local editors, authorized major improvements. The 75 post offices of 1790 increased to 4500 by 1820; and the 1875 miles of post roads grew to 73,492 in the same 30 years.[12] Newspapers moved swiftly in stagecoaches along the great post road from Maine to Savannah and by horseback along other post roads into the West and Southwest over the Alleghenies. The trip from New York to Philadelphia took only 22 hours, but it took more than three weeks for a newspaper to travel from Philadelphia to the western frontier at Lexington, Kentucky.[13]

The development of a better system was not smooth and uneventful, however. Editors and postal system proponents had to learn to work together in the new political system. The 1792 Post Office Act fixed the newspaper delivery rate at 1¢ for the first 100 miles and 1.5¢ beyond 100 miles and continued the free delivery of exchange newspapers among all post offices from the coast to the frontier territories of Ohio, Pennsylvania, Kentucky, and Tennessee. George Washington took special note of the value of this system in 1793 and pleaded for expansion of the Post Office Act through repeal of any delivery tariff on newspapers because of their essential role in the relation between the government and the governed. He told Congress the relation was critical, because no other resource was

> so firm for the Government of the United States as the affections of the people, guided by an enlightened policy; and to this primary good nothing can conduce more than a faithful representation of public proceedings, diffused without restraint throughout the United States.[14]

Americans were proving, as Washington knew, to be heavy newspaper consumers. Noah Webster wrote in his newspaper, *American Minerva*, that most citizens were able to read English and had the income and inclination to buy and read newspapers to such an extent that newspapers circulated more generally in America than in any other country, including Great Britain.[15] But despite Washington's pleas, Congress curtailed funds for the postal system after its initial expansion in the 1790s. As secondary post roads deteriorated, post riders abandoned newspaper bundles in the mountains in order to finish their ride. Angered by the loss of their primary source of news, editors demanded improved postal service and stagecoach roads to the West. By 1806 stagecoaches carried newspapers and mail to the western frontier. The lesson was not lost on editors: Inattention to postal regulations could prove disastrous for news flow and newspaper delivery. Concern about free exchange newspapers diminished with the development of wire service news reports after the Civil War, but postal routes and tariffs still concern publishers, ad managers, and circulation directors.

Daily Newspapers

The limited capacity for news gathering, printing, and circulation produced only weekly newspapers in the colonies prior to the American Revolution. In the boom following the truce, increased mercantile news and advertising, coupled with cheaper American-made presses and types, allowed publishers to move to twice-weekly, then thrice-weekly publication. Youth carriers, newsboys, and post riders proved more than adequate as delivery agents for frequent publication. In 1783 Benjamin Towne converted his *Pennsylvania Evening Post* to the *Pennsylvania Evening Post and Daily Advertiser*, primarily to serve customers in Philadelphia's mercantile exchanges. With revenue from advertisements, which took up 80 percent of the page space, Towne printed all the mercantile news he could obtain from the coffee houses, inns, docks, and exchanges. Ultimately the newspaper, deriving its information from coffee house conversations of the merchants, drove the coffee houses out of business by replacing them as information centers.

Towne set out to attract the ordinary workers as well as the merchants by creating a newspaper that would appeal to all classes in content and price. At that time, annual weekly subscriptions cost anywhere from $1.50 to $5.00; Towne's thrice-weekly *Evening Post* cost 4¢ per issue, which was simply too high for the common laborer earning 80¢ per week. Towne decided to offer his daily at half price and emphasize single copy street sales to pick up additional customers. To boost sales, Towne himself strode the streets of Philadelphia, newspapers under his arm, shouting, "All the news for two coppers."[16] He also established a monthly subscription rate in addition to the traditional quarterly and annual payment schedules. For a year, Towne's approach proved successful; but the appearance of a competitor, the *Pennsylvania Packet and Daily Advertiser*, dashed his hopes of a mass circulation newspaper. The *Packet* appealed to strictly upper-class readers (ridiculing Towne's lower-class appeal), charged 4¢ per copy, and sold exclusively through home delivery. Snob appeal worked; the *Evening Post* died within two years as upper-class readers abandoned it.

In emphasizing street sales, Towne deviated from the norm in the major cities. Upper-class readers insisted on home delivery and generous interpretation of advance payment. To survive, publishers complied, even though the bad debt amounted to 25 percent of the subscription rate. The *New York Evening Post* made readers wishing to purchase a single copy go to the office and pay double the subscription price, 12.5¢. It sold no copies on the street, lest it be thought of as less than genteel. The *Philadelphia Daily Chronicle* announced that it took care to "procure diligent and trustworthy carriers—but as mistakes may happen in the commencement, subscribers, who find themselves neglected, are requested to give notice at the publication office."[17] Competition in the big cities demonstrated that the newspaper business could be profitable: By 1800 Philadelphia had six dailies; New York, five; Baltimore, three; and Charleston, two. Boston, which steadily declined as a commercial port and business center, could not support a daily newspaper until after 1800.

In rural areas, newspapers changed less rapidly and had smaller circulation. Publishers were more flexible about payment, often bartering like the publisher of the *Kentucky Gazette*, who offered to take corn, wheat, linen, linseed, sugar, whiskey, or a few well-cured bacon hams as payment for subscription fees. Newspapers moved from press to reader by post rider or delivery agent; but at least one publisher, Charles Freer, delivered his own *Ulster County Gazette* and its competitor, the *Plebeian*, in order to make a little more money.[18] Only gradually did the changes sweeping major cities influence newspapers in the rural areas.

DAILY NEWSPAPERS FOR THE MASSES CHANGE CIRCULATION

Benjamin Towne was simply 50 years ahead of his time. The first successful newspaper written for common people appeared in 1833 as the culmination of massive changes in the social, political, and technological aspects of American life. The mass newspaper, sold for a penny, revolutionized the economic structure and newspaper content to such an extent that it redefined news and circulation. Increasing immigration, westward migration, and a rapidly expanding factory manufacturing system brought the rise of the commoner and the decline of the American aristocrats as political forces.

Waves of literate immigrants from soot-blackened London and impoverished Ireland flooded American cities with a lower-class population looking for newspapers like those they left behind. They were joined in every large city by young men and women who were abandoning the long hours of drudgery on the farm for wage labor in the humming factories and mills, in dry goods stores and inns, on the docks, and in the homes of the newly affluent. This large, new class had literacy, cash, and curiosity about their world; yet they were uninterested in the political and business newspapers or unwilling to pay for them.

Politically, this class came into power with universal male suffrage—the right to vote, which put Andrew Jackson in the White House in 1828 and elected many other politicians who represented the landless laboring class. This "bloodless revolution" brought politics to the common people and created interest in politicians who represented them. Small newspapers linking politics and the laboring class arose in New York to argue the cause of organized labor, decent wages and hours, better working conditions, and the right to organize.

Technological development hit the newspaper industry in 1814 with the introduction of power presses that could print 800 copies per hour. By 1832 American manufacturer R. Hoe and Company offered a press that could print 4000 copies per hour. A newly invented paper manufacturing machine could produce an endless "web" of paper 100 inches wide at the rate of 500 feet per minute, replacing the hand manufacturing system in which people beat, ground, soaked, strained, and squeezed rags into sheets of paper. Webs allowed higher speed printing than did stacks of single sheets. Rags remained the primary raw ingredient for newsprint; experiments with straw and wood pulp failed to produce the tensile strength necessary for a high-speed web press, although small amounts of these pulps were added to rags to reduce costs. Typesetting alone remained an unchanged hand operation amidst the mechanical improvements.

An enterprising young compositor, 24-year-old Benjamin H. Day, took advantage of these changes and offered New Yorkers a one-cent daily newspaper aimed specifically at lower-class readers. The *New York Sun* ("It Shines For All") started a new era in American newspapers when it hit the streets September 3, 1833. In competition with the six-penny papers written for the political and mercantile elite, the *Sun* imitated successful London mass newspapers that emphasized local events, news from police courts, and whatever the readers were likely to discuss. Day's newspaper specialized in covering sensational trials, favoring upper-class paternity suits and any court cases pitting the common people against the upper class. Crime reports and gory murders received constant, intense attention. Nor was the *Sun* bound by truth. It freely embellished scandalous events, and it fabricated a seven-part series about life on the moon, ostensibly written by a South African astronomer who described what he saw through his telescope, including the life and habits of moon folk. Such coverage quickly swelled the *Sun*'s daily circulation to 19,000, at least 2000 more than London's largest newspaper. Underpinning the sensational success of the *Sun* were two major innovations in the newspaper business, a revision of advertising's role and the London Plan of Circulation. These, in turn, spawned other changes in newspaper delivery, such as the Philadelphia Plan and the introduction of wholesale distributors.

Changes in Advertising Revenue

The *Sun* took full advantage of technological innovations, but it could not produce a newspaper for substantially less than the six-penny publishers. To generate a profit with a one-cent purchase price, Day increased the advertising space rate. Unlike his fellow publishers who viewed advertising as a service for readers, Day viewed the newspaper as a means for delivering customers to advertisers. *Sun* advertising rates also rose with circulation on the grounds that advertisements received more exposure. Advertising revenue thus became the dominant source of income, made the newspaper affordable to all working people, and increased financial stability by reducing the impact of delinquent subscribers.

This reliance on advertising, rather than circulation, revenues continues in the twentieth century. Newspapers receive approximately 80 percent of their revenues from advertising, compared with 20 percent from circulation.

The London Plan of Circulation

To free the newspaper of delinquent subscribers and allow maximum circulation growth with minimal business risk, Day instituted the London Plan of Circulation, a newspaper sales and circulation system borrowed from that city's lower-class newspapers. The London Plan established a mercantile relationship between the newspaper and the carrier by making carriers and newsboys middlemen, selling them the newspaper at a wholesale rate, payable in advance. Carriers then sold the newspaper to customers and profited on the difference between wholesale and retail rates. No subscriber dealt directly with the *Sun*, but rather with the local carrier or news agent. The London Plan put all the commercial advantages on the side of the *Sun*. By demanding advance payment from middlemen, Day solved the delinquent subscriber problem and assured regular cashflow. Moreover, all bookkeeping related to subscriber accounts moved out of the publisher's offices into the middleman's office or back pocket. The newspaper was able to keep books for a large number of wholesalers without substantially increasing office costs as circulation rose.

The London Plan also motivated carriers and newsboys, whose profits rose in proportion to sales. Not surprisingly, competition among newsboys led to fistfights over the rights to sell on a high-volume street corner. The increased emphasis on single copy street sales attracted laborers who might only have an occasional penny for a newspaper. The net effect of the London Plan was a system that assured high daily cashflow, low office overhead, and high competition for circulation sales.

To quickly build street sales and establish the *Sun* in New York, Day established circulation districts, gathered a group of young men, gave each one 125 newspapers, and paid them $2 per week plus 9¢ for each 12 newspapers sold. The youths could sell on street corners or build subscriber routes and provide home delivery; they had full control over their territory. These newsboys soon sold enough newspapers to earn $5 per week at a time when journeymen printers earned $10 per week. The profits quickly attracted adults, who created additional circulation zones and hired their own newsboys. Within one year, a *Sun* route paid $30 to $60 per week. Adult middlemen steadily gained control of the distribution system, creating large territories that yielded $600 to $700 per week by 1836.

The *Sun* spawned a number of competitors in New York and every other large city in the country, including papers written especially for women; but few matched the style and success of the *Sun*, and most died within a few months, unable to find a large audience. The *New York Herald*, which featured the finest Wall Street reporting of the day and the most aggressive news coverage, found new ways to outrage readers regularly; but it also found a substantial market of businessmen and lower-class readers. When the *New York Tribune* tried to wedge into the penny-paper market, the other publishers threatened to boycott any carrier, newsboy, or dealer who handled it. Horace Greeley, *Tribune* editor and publisher, created his own circulation system, as Day had. Circulation wars among the penny papers were frequent; but within a decade the *Sun*, the *Herald*, and the *Tribune* dominated New York. Each sold more than 15,000 copies per day, with circulation zones extending into adjoining cities and states and even to Albany, Hartford, Troy, Philadelphia, and Washington, D.C. When Day sold the *Sun* to his brother-in-law for $40,000 in 1839, he had irrevocably changed the content, financial structure, and circulation system of American newspapers.

The Philadelphia Plan of Circulation

What worked for Ben Day in New York did not appeal to advertisers in Philadelphia, because penny papers had notoriously unpredictable circulation from day to day and largely unknown customers. Advertisers thus encouraged the local penny paper, the *Philadelphia Public Ledger*, to justify its high advertising rates. The *Ledger*'s publisher decided to maintain the financial structure of the London Plan but to emphasize home delivery and establish a direct relation between subscribers and the newspaper.

Philadelphia was divided into circulation districts; employees canvassed door to door for subscriptions; and the *Ledger* maintained a file of all subscribers in the office, where advertisers could review it. To further emphasize subscriptions and home delivery, youth carriers received their newspapers first; copies were sold to dealers and newsboys an hour after the last carrier left on his route to deliver his papers. By 1870 80 percent of the *Public Ledger*'s 70,000 circulation was home delivered by youth carriers. Newsboys sold a mere 3700 copies of this penny paper. The remaining newspapers were sold through cigar stores, newsstands, and other dealers. With the same financial structure and definition of news content as the *New York Sun*, the *Public Ledger* created a significantly different circulation system, the Philadelphia Plan.

At the root, the London and Philadelphia Plans represent the two major philosophies of circulation management, which grew out of mass circulation newspapers. Mass circulation required the solution of a new problem: Economic success depended on high volume, low-cost circulation, and high advertising rates keyed to circulation; but advertisers were unable to verify circulation and grew skeptical of circulation figures built dominantly on single copy street sales. The publishers had to choose between the roles of retailer and wholesaler. As a retailer, the publisher retained control of subscribers and delivery at high office costs in order to maintain accountability for advertisers; as a wholesaler, the publisher turned control of delivery and subscribers over to middlemen in order to generate maximum sales at low office cost. As the retailer, the publisher maintained a direct relationship with subscribers; as a wholesaler, the publisher dealt only with the middlemen, whose customers were the readers and subscribers.

The London Plan represented the least complicated system, but the one least responsive to advertiser and subscriber complaints. Advertisers had to accept the *Sun*'s circulation figures on trust, and subscribers had to deal with someone other than a *Sun* employee. The Philadelphia Plan was far more responsive to advertisers and subscribers, but it created a large employee force and costly recordkeeping. The simplicity of the London Plan swiftly and efficiently accommodated major changes in circulation by putting the burden on middlemen. The office paperwork of the Philadelphia Plan made such changes more costly and slower. Both systems were profitable; but one gave priority to the manufacture and sale of newspapers, while the other gave priority to control of the entire delivery system. The chosen plan reflected the publisher's philosophy and the local market. Local advertisers played a major role in determining which system developed: New York advertisers supported the London Plan; Philadelphia advertisers preferred the Philadelphia Plan.

As six-penny papers died away, one-penny papers began looking outside the metropolitan area for new readers. Horace Greeley began a weekly edition of the *Tribune* that carried news of interest to people in the West, making it a national newspaper. James Gordon Bennett, publisher and editor, developed three separate editions of the morning *New York Herald* in an effort to reach more rural readers and suburban commuters. The first edition went to post offices for delivery to rural customers, the second went by horse and wagon to outlying areas, and the final edition went to city newsboys and carriers. After unsuccessful experiments, Bennett finally found a combination of one early morning edition delivered before breakfast and two afternoon editions at 1 p.m. and 3 p.m., which suited both commuters and rural postal route subscribers. Afternoon newspapers in communities distant from New York suddenly found themselves competing with the major New York penny papers delivered by mail and brought home by commuters. The competition was the forerunner of problems facing newspapers in metropolitan areas to this day.

Wholesale Companies for Newspaper Circulation

The proliferation of penny newspapers in urban areas created problems for the dealers, who began working as middlemen for several publishers, and for the carriers, who likewise delivered several newspapers and had to pick up their papers from several locations before beginning delivery. A few distributors realized they could build a profitable business as brokers among all the publishers and dealers. Publishers welcomed the new wholesale brokers because they simplified billing for reducing the number of accounts to a handful and daily paid cash on delivery. Distributors didn't mind the small wholesale charge because the wholesalers picked up all the newspapers and delivered them to carriers, newsboys, newsstands, cigar stores, and other retail outlets.

Street violence erupted in the fierce competition among wholesalers for control of territory, leading to monopolies and cartels. Philadelphia wholesalers, tired of violence, merged into the Central New Company and pioneered the central station system in which horse-drawn wagons hauled newspapers to a single building where all dealers and carriers came to collect their papers. In 1874 the morning newspaper publishers formed a cooperative delivery system, which endured until the 1920s. United by their supply system, the carriers formed the Morning Newspaper Carriers' Beneficial and Protective Association to advance their labor interests. The largest wholesaler was A. S. Tuttle, who moved New York newspapers on his own railroad cars to dealers outside the city by 1854. When this company expanded into the American News Company, it owned or controlled over 20,000 newspaper agencies across the United States.

Inevitably, the wholesalers' ability to strangle circulation with a strike or boycott empowered them to advance their own financial interests at the expense of publishers and retailers. When James Gordon Bennett cut the newspaper's price and the dealer margin to meet the competition, wholesalers boycotted the *Herald* or ignored the new prices. Bennett established his own circulation system of boys dressed in red caps for street sales and home delivery. The Manhattan News Company, which controlled all sales on commuter and long-distance railroads and trolleys, continued to charge the old price. After 20 months, Bennett caved in and raised the price to the old level; but he immediately began trying to persuade other publishers to form their own cooperative distribution system to end the tyranny of wholesalers. However, friction and competition among publishers prevented success.

After World War I, newspapers challenged wholesalers for control of the distribution system and its profits. Wholesalers controlled geographic distribution zones and funneled newspapers from all local publishers to their own carriers and dealers, enabling them to force unsatisfactory prices and customer service on newspapers facing rising costs and sharper competition. Powerful publishers used the wholesale system to handicap newcomers, but shrinking profits caused publishers to seek control of their own circulation system. After the federal courts upheld the *Chicago Tribune's* right to order its dealers not to carry competing newspapers in 1922, newspapers across the country broke away from wholesalers and established their own circulation systems. By 1930, over 90 percent of the newspapers dealt directly with their carriers and subscribers.

DEALING WITH CIRCULATION GROWTH

The mass newspaper system spread across the country, permanently changing the newspaper industry. In bringing profitability and new readers to newspapers, the system required enormous production capacity, a constant search for advertising, and a large corps of youth carriers. Steady technological improvement increased press capacity, which allowed newspapers to take full advantage of major news events like the Civil War. Publishers like William Randolph Hearst and Joseph Pulitzer recognized the circulation sales value of news content and built mammoth circulations by providing extensive coverage of news events. They, and others, began promoting circulation with a wide variety of stunts and games, having little connection with the news. Circulation figures, always unreliable with heavy street sales in the penny press, reached new heights of exaggeration and fraud in the highly competitive atmosphere. To attract readers and advertisers, publishers desperately needed other advertisers; to increase business, advertisers needed newspapers. Although advertising agents brought advertisers and newspapers together, they had little impact on unreliable circulation figures or deceptive and tasteless advertising. Newsboys, streetwise and tough, became the target of social reformers, particularly as big-city circulation wars turned violent. From the Civil War through World War I, newspapers faced the problems created by rapid growth and unscrupulous publishers.

Technological Developments

Even before the Civil War began, successive waves of immigrants and steady urban growth took newspaper circulations ever higher, as wage laborers looked for entertainment, information, and advertising. When the *Sun* first appeared in 1833, circulations had not reached 5000; yet in 1860 the *Herald* sold 70,000 copies per day, a world record and one of the wonders of the age. The *New York Weekly Ledger* claimed 400,000 weekly sales, and Greeley's *Weekly Tribune* was sold wherever railroad tracks were laid. The mass circulation newspaper had not only arrived, within a generation it had fundamentally altered newspapers.

The Civil War drove circulation to new peaks by providing rapid telegraph accounts from the fronts and lists of the dead and wounded in each battle. When Fort Sumter was shelled, the *Herald* sold 107,000 copies of its first edition, then another 136,600 in subsequent editions. By 1862 its daily sales hit 100,000. Both the *Boston Herald* and the *Philadelphia Inquirer* sold over 90,000 copies daily during the war. Readers were served late-breaking dispatches, as publishers mastered the techniques of multiple daily editions and reporters telegraphed correspondence from the battlefields. News moved so swiftly from the front to the front pages that Union generals read news accounts of their strategies before the battles were concluded. Working multiple shifts and long hours, pressmen, distributors, carriers, and newsboys adapted to the new demands from readers.

Peace brought circulation back to prewar levels for most publishers, except for the occasional major story that sent circulation above 100,000 for a single day. The majority of newspapers sold 20,000 or fewer copies each day, but 4295 dailies served American communities in each state and territory by 1870. Printers went West with the railroads, and newspapers from the West were circulated among prospective migrants as proof that the frontier was civilized. Newspapers circulated heavily in newly established commercial centers like St. Louis, Chicago, St. Paul, and Denver.

Technology, which allowed newspapers to produce 20,000 copies per hour by the start of the Civil War, created further efficiencies. A new press, which used a solid slab of lead in place of individual types on each printing cylinder, doubled, then tripled, press speeds. By 1890 the fastest press could produce 48,000 12-page newspapers in an hour. Newsprint prices skyrocketed to $440 per ton during the Civil War in response to scarcity of rags, and experiments with alternate materials remained unsatisfactory. However, following the war, a new process mixed as much as 25 percent woodpulp with rags without significant loss in tensile strength. By 1900 the process yielded 100 percent woodpulp newsprint, which held up under the stress of high press speeds. Newsprint prices tumbled to $36 per ton and the cost of materials was no longer a problem with massive circulation and its thousands of unsold copies. Rolls or webs of newsprint reduced press loading time, and automatic folding devices replaced the hand labor of youth carriers and newsboys while permitting maximum press speed.

The invention of the Linotype™ machine, which set whole lines of type in solid lead, tripled the output of typesetters, moved deadlines closer to press time, and permitted more editions of each newspaper. Constant improvements of printing equipment and lowered costs of production allowed newspapers to produce inexpensive copies for growing audiences and created stiffer competition.

Newsboys and Child Labor Reform

From 1850 to World War II, social reformers periodically focused their attention on ridding the streets and newspapers of newsboys and at times threatened the whole youth carrier system. The Penny Press system created the newsboy, a ragged, filthy, foul-mouthed youth who earned money the hard way—by being tough and streetwise. Far from the middle-class ideal, newsboys mixed with streetwise adults; and more than a few became gamblers and criminals. Others, however, were the sole support of widowed mothers or one of several breadwinners for a poor family.

Reformers of the 1850–1880 period demanded that newspapers provide decent earnings and cold-weather clothes for newsboys, encourage education, and discourage streetlife. In 1850 New York established a home for newsboys, caring for over 10,000 before it closed in 1865. The *Philadelphia Star* gave winter coats and clothes to its 500 youths, a practice which became common. The *New York Times* sought charitable donations for its annual newsboy picnic. As mandatory school attendance laws moved through the country, newspapers began working out relations with the local schools to ensure that carriers complied with the law. Some even provided tutorial sessions for carriers who missed part of the school day.

Aggressive circulation practices demanded aggressive street sales, and newsboys literally fought with their fists for a good street corner. The toughest newsboy got the best corner, where he might double his income as long as he could beat all challengers. The level of violence escalated sharply in Chicago, where the Annenberg brothers, Max and Moses, created street gangs to boost circulation by intimidating newsboys, newsstand dealers, and anyone else working for the opposing paper. Newspaper sluggers and gunmen burned newsstands, stole trucks, and kidnapped newsboys. Reformers quickly noted the risks to youths.

Chicago's circulation war seemed unbelievable in almost every other American city, but the connection between crime and newspaper work was regularly raised. In his 1921 book, *The Newsboy at Night in Philadelphia*, Scott Nearing wrote that the professional newsboy is the embryo criminal. The wave of child labor reform set off investigations in city after city. Coupled with the national movement to eliminate child labor in sweat shops, mines, and mills, this effort led Congress to propose a constitutional amendment prohibiting and regulating labor by those under 18 years of age. The ensuing 16-year debate was ended by World War II, and the postwar changes made the issue all but irrelevant.

Throughout this period the International Circulation Managers Association insisted that most youth were "little merchants" who were learning the American commercial system, future leaders and self-starters. In fact, many youths put bread on the family table during the Depression by working for newspapers. Labor reformers argued that youths worked too long for too little, were under too much pressure, and were forced to absorb the newspaper's bad debt. The reform effort had two effects. Some newspapers followed the lead of St. Louis, Kansas City, and Baltimore and moved to adult carriers. Many states established a minimum age for newspaper work, generally 10 or 12.

The reform movement that focused on big-city problems made far less sense in the small towns, where most youths delivered newspapers door to door, collected from subscribers, and suffered most from unleashed dogs and bicycle accidents. Nonetheless, the reform movement encouraged newspapers to evaluate their labor practices. As they defended youth carriers and newsboys, circulation managers and publishers also studied the benefits of adult carriers and improved supervision of the Little Merchants.

First Circulation Managers

Rapid circulation growth threatened to crush the traditional circulation system despite the continuing capacity for large-scale distribution. Profitability began to depend on the planning and organization of circulation sales to avoid unprofitable press overruns. Publishers, particularly those outside the highly competitive big-city markets, preferred the controlled circulation growth of the Philadelphia Plan rather than the unpredictable cycle of sellouts and major overruns typical of the London Plan. Postal regulations, competition, expanded carrier forces, complex distribution routes, and increased raw material costs required specialized knowledge.

FIGURE 2.1   Soda shops, cigar stores, and other businesses became newspaper substations during the mass newspaper era of the nineteenth century. These newsboys and carriers were photographed in the 1890s outside of their substation. Courtesy The Journal Company, Milwaukee, WI.

Publishers created the position of circulation manager, removing responsibility for circulation from the advertising manager or business manager. In 1874 the *Detroit Evening Sun* hired M. A. McRae as circulation manager. McRae, along with Alex Thompson of the *New York Evening Post*, was an early leader in circulation management.

For these new managers, training carriers posed a major task, particularly after compulsory school attendance laws were enacted from state to state, limiting the hours youth carriers could work. After moving to the *Cincinnati Post*, McRae began educating his carriers in business methods by treating them as "little merchants," who had to understand the profit system, sales, efficiency, and the newspaper system. Each night after school McRae provided sales training for newsboys and carriers alike; however, attracting youths became a problem. Newsboys' bands, gymnasiums, and special school sessions were tried. With a brass band, gym hours, and Sunday socials, the *Grand Rapids Gazette* increased its youth force from 17 to 1200. *Editor and Publisher*, the new voice of the newspaper industry, urged publishers to see these benefits as essential tools for attracting the little merchants upon whom circulation depended. The fortunes of a multimillion-dollar industry rested on newsboys and independent carriers; circulation managers now added youth carriers to their growing list of responsibilities.

Circulation Wars

In 1883 Joseph Pulitzer defined journalism as a major business enterprise of massive circulation, massive budgets, and massive promotion. After purchasing the moribund *New York World*, he drove its circulation from 10,000 to 100,000 in less than a year, to 374,000 in less than a decade, and to 1,000,000 by 1900. Like Benjamin Day, Pulitzer reached out for a new class of readers, the laborers and immigrants who could afford his one-cent paper and enjoyed his editorial attacks on their enemies. In addition to ceaselessly attacking fraud, corruption, big business, and big businessmen, the *World* demanded solutions for the poor, homeless, and hungry of New York. Hotly sensational headlines and front page cartoons attracted lower-class readers and guaranteed that the *World* would be a conversation piece.

Pulitzer also introduced large-scale promotion as a means to increase circulation sales. When circulation hit 100,000, the cannon in New York's City Hall Park boomed 100 times. A commemorative coin celebrated 250,000 circulation. The *World* provided the poor with coal in winter, ice in summer, free medical care, Christmas dinners, and unending excitement. Reporter Nellie Bly went around the world for the *World* in less than 80 days. Front page headlines boasted of each new circulation milestone. A new Sunday issue brought in more readers with major topical sections, illustrations, the use of color for comics, special features, and constant entertainment. Amidst the promotions were Pulitzer's commitment to accuracy and a newspaper that championed the causes of the underprivileged. For 12 unrivaled years, the *World* had its own way: high circulation, incomparable accuracy, beautifully thoughtful editorials, serious investigative reporting, and entertainment.

When William Randolph Hearst bought the dying *Journal* in 1895, the modern circulation war began. Hearst brought millions of dollars from his family's silver mines and a keen understanding of sensationalism with him. After studying the *Boston Globe* and the *World* as a Harvard student, Hearst took over his father's newspaper, the *San Francisco Examiner*, and experimented successfully with the techniques he learned back East. The circulation war began when Hearst, from his office in the *World* building, hired away most of the Sunday *World* staff by doubling or tripling their salaries. Encouraged to forego restraint and produce the most exciting newspaper, the *Journal* staff drove circulation to 380,000 on Sunday by 1896. The next year it matched the *World*'s 600,000, by 1900 it averaged 1,250,000. The day after the presidential election in 1896, the *World* and *Journal* each claimed sales over 1,500,000.

Hearst boosted sales with screaming headlines, partially factual articles, and outright hoaxes. To ensure success, Hearst poured more than $7.5 million into the *Journal*. He bought the most advanced printing equipment available. His eight Hoe presses could produce eight pages with color, and the *Journal* announced the new product as "eight pages of irridescent polychromous effulgence that makes the rainbow look like a lead pipe."[19] When Hearst bought the cartoonist who created the Yellow Kid comic strip but lost the copyright fight over the name Yellow Kid, the journalism of the circulation war, with its sensationalism and disregard for accuracy, became known as *yellow journalism*.

The Spanish-American War seemed an ideal opportunity to send circulation to new heights; it was the last major battle in the circulation war. Hearst sent a boatload of reporters and photographers to Cuba, and Pulitzer had little choice but to send his own corps. Unlimited by costs or facts, the *Journal* put out 40 separate war editions in a single day with little news to justify them. Pulitzer, embarrassed by the excessive sensationalism and declining credibility of yellow journalism, ordered his editor to reverse course and stress responsible coverage. Hearst won, and the *Journal*'s circulation roared ahead of the *World*'s by 250,000. Both newspapers were multimillion-dollar businesses by the turn of the century.

Circulation Sales Promotion

Pulitzer's genius, in part, lay in his recognition of constant self-promotion as a circulation tool of broad reach.

> Circulation promotion, viewed fully, includes the whole public relations program of a daily newspaper, the contacts of all newspaper workers with actual or potential readers. From the circulation manager's standpoint, it has included the exploitation of news coverage, actual news hoaxes, crusades, fiction, and articles signed by "big names"; the organization of parades, pageants, and welfare work; and the development of campaigns, contests, and enticing "house" advertisements.[20]

After the Spanish-American War, science became a prime promotional topic. The *New York Times* paid $4000 for exclusive rights to Perry's story of his Antarctic expedition, and the *Washington Star* funded two unsuccessful expeditions to the North Pole. In the hands of a Hearst editor, science coverage took a unique form.

> Suppose it's Haley's comet. Well, first you have a half-page of decoration showing the comet, with historical pictures of previous appearances thrown in. If you can work a pretty girl into the decoration, so much the better. If not, get some good nightmare idea like the inhabitants of Mars watching it pass. Then you want a quarter of a page of big-type heads snappy. Then four inches of story, written right off the bat. Then a picture of Professor Haley down here and another of Professor Lowell up there, and a two-column boxed freak containing a scientific opinion, which nobody will understand, just to give it class.[21]

Not all publishers followed Hearst's example, but sensationalism was hardly limited to New York and the big cities. In small towns, however, consistent inaccuracy and sensationalism simply reduced the reputation and business of the newspaper. In small communities delicacy and accuracy weighed more than fabrication as promotional tools because the publisher was part of the community leadership.

Rewards, prizes, and cash giveaways were promotional tools available without prejudice to all publishers. Free turkeys, gifts from local merchants, small cash awards from lotteries, or names and numbers hidden in the newspaper content boosted sales. The *New York Recorder* favored a lottery involving numbered tintographs (cheaply printed color images) inserted in each paper. Advertisers would exchange winning tintographs for diamonds, clothes, jewelry, real estate, insurance, cigars, or furniture. The publisher of the *Denver Post* had a siren on the roof, setting it off on whim to call attention to the newspaper; and each afternoon at 4 p.m., he threw a bagful of coins into the street to draw people to the newspaper. James Gordon Bennett offered free trips around the world. In competitive situations, the premiums could exceed the subscription price.

Many publishers rejected such promotions because they detracted from their basic business: providing news and opinion. They promoted service and reliability. The *Philadelphia Bulletin* proudly advertised that its 1899 Daimler electric wagons, the first automobiles used in the newspaper business, improved delivery. The *Kansas City Star* promised enlightening editorials and consistent accuracy in reporting. Others encouraged subscriber complaints and promised to reduce delivery errors.

Pulitzer had taught other publishers that civic service could be a promotional device. Milk and food for the hungry, clothing and shelter for the homeless, parades, athletic events, and free public entertainment were several methods used to demonstrate civic responsibility. The

Chicago Tribune declared that the newspaper had taken on an additional role, that of "parish priest, guide, counsellor, and friend."[22] To outsiders, the newspaper became a town booster, promoting its civic virtues and congeniality as a place to live and work.

THE DEMAND FOR CIRCULATION ACCOUNTABILITY

The mammoth circulations and rapid expansion of newspapers using the penny-press financial system rested on advertisers, a point not lost on those who paid the higher linage rates. The relationship between publisher and advertiser changed with the increased size and complexity of the newspaper business, moving from one of fellow small businessmen in the early 1800s to one of suspicion and even hostility after the Civil War. Advertising rates rose with circulation, yet an increasing number of newspapers competed for the advertiser's dollar; the system seemed to defy the law of supply and demand. Even more disturbing to advertisers was the unreliability of circulation figures, business secrets known only to publishers. Advertisers trained salesmen to listen at printing plant walls and count press vibrations as a gauge of circulation. Others bribed pressmen to obtain press run figures, but publishers retaliated by installing lock boxes around the counters.

Resistance to the publishing of circulation figures was almost universal. Some publishers lied shamelessly about their circulation; others considered the question an infringement of their right to business secrets; still others felt pressured by competitors to inflate the figures; and almost all of them were simply unable to provide an accurate figure for paid circulation. Neither a standard definition of paid circulation nor a standard circulation accounting system existed during the nineteenth century. Most publishers inflated or discounted the total pressrun by an arbitrary amount. Ben Day, for example, refused to accept unsold copies of the *Sun*, called *returns*, for credit or cash because he discovered carriers collected discarded copies from subscribers and taverns and then turned them in as unsold copies. Without a firm figure for unsold copies, publishers could only guess at circulation.

The proliferation of newspapers, even in suburbs outside the major cities, meant each advertiser had to know how to buy space in several newspapers, judge the value of each, and provide material to those chosen without necessarily ever meeting the publishers. Advertisers found themselves the supporters and potential victims of newspaper growth.

Publishers, too, found the new relationship troubling, for the system pressured them to accept any advertiser, local or distant, who could pay for the space. So desperate were publishers to fill advertising space that they had few scruples about the products advertised to their readers. Penny publishers even warned readers they would not be responsible for the content of any ads. The *Philadelphia Ledger* excluded only what was illegal or offensive to the decency and morals of everyone. Income drove publishers to disregard content: The *Sun* had four pages of ads for every page of news. The *Pittsburgh Gazette* devoted 83 to 85 percent of its space to ads. Despite the outrage of critics and readers, fraudulent ads continued to appear as long as the advertisers paid their rates. Horace Greeley accused the *Sun* and *Herald* of running indecent and thieving ads; but he continued to accept bawdy theater ads in the *Tribune*, even though he thought them injurious to the community. Freedom of the press, rather than economic necessity, was the most frequent defense proclaimed by publishers when challenged.

Publishers and advertisers found themselves in a new and uncomfortable relationship. Publishers had to sell large amounts of advertising space to stay in business, and advertisers had to purchase ads in several newspapers to maintain or increase sales. Out of this new relationship grew advertising agencies, newspaper circulation directories, and more insistent cries for reliable circulation figures.

Advertising Agencies

Into the complex relationship between publisher and advertiser moved a plump and pompous man who learned the newspaper business from his father, the publisher of the *Mt. Holly Mirror* in New Jersey. Volney Palmer opened his first advertising office in Philadelphia to solicit ads for a small Pennsylvania paper and soon learned he could build a profitable business as a middleman between newspapers and advertisers. For 25 percent of the linage charge, Palmer found advertisers, obtained the copy, forwarded it to the newspaper, and collected the bill. Palmer legally operated as a solicitor for publishers, empowered by them to contract for advertising space. Palmer soon had branch offices in New York, Boston, and Baltimore as he began representing a far-flung group of newspapers and advertisers. Imitators followed the scent of success so that by the Civil War 20 newspaper advertising agencies operated in New York and at least 10 had offices in several cities.

In the heat of competition, agents began inflating circulation figures to whatever level seemed necessary to close a sale. They had little fear of correction because publishers jealously guarded pressrun and net paid figures. Publishers publicly challenged each other's circulation figures, perhaps because they knew how inaccurate their own were. Competition also encouraged advertisers to seek the lowest bids by submitting copy to several agencies. Because publishers granted no exclusive solicitation rights, agents competed to sell the same newspaper space. Publishers suffered financially from the bidding war because agents cut the linage rate rather than their own 25 percent fee. Trapped by the option of a discounted linage rate or no advertising, publishers accepted the discount rate to the benefit of advertisers and agents. Newspaper advertising was worth $7,584,000 by 1865; it broke $39 million in 1880; and it approached $96 million by 1900.

Newspaper Circulation Directories

Each advertising agency kept its own secret list of newspapers across the United States and the approximate circulation of each one because no public list existed. George Rowell, owner of a Boston agency, revised the agency system by buying advertising space in bulk quantities at wholesale prices in anticipation of advertising. More importantly, he drafted a catalog of American newspapers and his estimate of their actual circulations. His *American Newspaper Directory* appeared in 1869 as the first effort to organize and publish newspaper circulation figures. Rowell's directory spawned competitors, including the *N. W. Ayer Directory*, which eventually purchased his and exists to this day.

Rowell obtained signed circulation statements from cooperative publishers, taking them at their word as gentlemen. Others he marked as "claimed" or "estimated." To improve the directory, he introduced a typographical bull's eye for the newspapers with the following traits:[23]

Circulation among a prosperous class of readers.

Circulation almost exclusively among people who buy and pay for the publication because they have learned to know and appreciate its special appeal.

Circulation among a regular list of yearly subscribers.

When the character of the circulation is to be considered, papers marked with the centered circle are to be counted as the very best.

Newspapers especially valuable to advertisers in exerting a special influence, having a long-established hold upon the community, which causes them to be more thoroughly read and more highly esteemed than others.

Only four newspapers earned Rowell's mark of distinction the first year. Rowell's directory and the American Newspaper Annual of N. W. Ayer and Son helped deflate newspaper circulation figures in their own competition for accuracy. Along the way Rowell grew skeptical of publishers' signed statements; they were simply not to be believed. Advertisers, supported by Rowell's experience, pressed harder for a reliable, uniform circulation reporting system; but as local merchants and manufacturers, they had little effect on the national newspaper industry.

The International Circulation Managers Association

Advertisers' concerns over reliable circulation figures and the prizes, contests, and promotional stunts of forced circulation techniques became regular convention issues for the National Association of Newspaper Circulation Managers (NANCM), which began in 1898 as a group of 35 publishers, advertisers, and circulation managers. Bringing reliability to circulation figures by standardizing circulation accounting was the topic of the first national meeting. At the first national convention, the publisher of the *Montgomery* (Alabama) *Advertiser* called circulation management a specialty within newspapers so demanding that no one should be responsible for managing both advertising and circulation.

NANCM grew slowly until 1910, when Canadian newspapers joined the association and conventioneers adopted the name International Circulation Managers Association. Rapid growth followed, and ICMA developed a strong regional structure, which addressed local problems and mounted conventions where circulation issues drew local experts' attention. The regional structure allowed ICMA to emerge as a powerful, thoughtful advocate at state and national levels.

As ICMA aggressively addressed circulation management problems, it provided a forum for debate, information about court decisions, and impending legislation. It became the voice of the circulation manager within the newspaper industry. But unlike associations that were thinly veiled labor unions concerned only with wages and working conditions, ICMA developed as an association dedicated to circulation management and circulation problems of editors, publishers, and advertisers. The American Newspaper Publishers Association and the National Editors and Publishers Association turned to ICMA for recommendations on employee relations with carriers and newsboys. Forced circulation turned up annually as a convention topic, both as a review of techniques and a philosophical debate of its value.

Audit Bureau of Circulations

The appearance of nationally marketed brands of soap and baking powder in the 1890s, followed by 150 other companies and 2500 products within a decade, created national advertising budgets that finally drew publishers' attention. These manufacturers bypassed the established advertising agencies and hired their own advertising representatives to buy newspaper space as part of national promotions. In short order, the agents learned the complexities and inconsistencies of newspaper circulation. Among the 2179 dailies, 15,660 weeklies, and 567 less frequently published newspapers, agents found considerable variation in publisher attitude and circulation size. The average circulation among dailies was 6784; but New York had 29 newspapers whose average circulation reached 92,000, including the mammoth 1,250,000 circulation *Journal* and the 1,000,000 circulation *World*. Further compounding the problem, both the *World* and *Journal*, like their counterparts in Philadelphia, Boston, and other major cities, offered morning and evening editions plus varying numbers of extra editions throughout the day. Very few publishers encouraged the drive for credible circulation figures, and more than a few continued to produce fraudulent figures.

The Association of American Advertisers was formed in 1899 to sort out newspaper circulation and establish a system for obtaining true statements. The first task was defining a common circulation base. Rowell advised reliance on press run totals because fewer than 10 percent of publishers could accurately calculate paid circulation. However, AAA defined net paid circulation as the total circulation minus returned, unsold, and waste copies and established it as the national standard for comparison. As a definition it had one flaw: It allowed publishers to include sales obtained with large discounts and valuable premiums (sometimes equal to the value of the newspaper) or subscriptions bartered for goods and services.

The AAA then devised an audit procedure whereby auditors entered newspaper offices if the publisher agreed to cooperate. The audit began with a form requesting sworn circulation figures and permission to visit the plant for an audit. During the audit the publisher provided full access to all records on the previous month's circulation and sufficient circulation history for an accurate appraisal. For his cooperation, the publisher received a net paid circulation certificate and a favorable reputation among national advertisers. Within three years 400 newspapers in 57 cities were audited, but the system began to flounder. Fewer than one in four publishers cooperated, and many demanded an active role in the AAA audit policy decisions. The audits became too expensive for the 50 advertisers who actively supported them.

In 1913 publishers became active members of the audit board, and the AAA system became known as the Audit Bureau of Circulations. Advertisers and advertising agencies retained majority control of the Audit Bureau, and publishers agreed to underwrite most audit costs. The representatives worked out a standard definition of net paid circulation and devised a simple, standard formula for calculating it.

The U.S. Postal Act of 1912 provided compelling reasons for publishers to cooperate in circulation audits. Congress, frightened that foreign countries, socialists, or labor leaders might secretly own newspapers, required every daily newspaper to publish and file a sworn statement of ownership, management, and circulation twice each year. The U.S. Supreme Court upheld the law, and publishers had little choice. They declared full support for strict enforcement of the law, as did the International Circulation Managers Association. ABC rules quickly became the standard guide for circulation managers and publishers filing their federal statements, and ABC audited figures provided advertisers their long-sought goal. Simplified forms for small dailies and weeklies appeared in 1935. From auditing newspapers, the ABC moved to auditing circulations of consumer magazines, farm publications, and business publications.

MODERNIZATION OF NEWSPAPER CIRCULATION

Following World War I, basic social and economic changes introduced a period of consolidation and change within the newspaper industry that continues through the present time. By 1920 the United States was an urban, industrial society served by new highways and an efficient mass transit system. Cities expanded into nearby counties, absorbing once independent communities. The promise of high wages and good times lured increasing numbers of rural youth into the cities, where they joined recent waves of immigrants and native city dwellers.

Radio, which crackled and sputtered for two decades, took on new significance during the Depression and World War II, eventually falling behind television as the dominant form of family entertainment. Following World War II, an unprecedented period of prosperity and university education accelerated the changes begun in the 1920s and stalled by the Depression. Americans became increasingly mobile, increasingly affluent, and increasingly urban. As readers changed their life-style and the economics of publishing changed the way newspapers were run, well-known newspapers died, new papers flourished, and circulation managers began devising new methods for reaching readers in suburbs and high-rise apartments.

Newspaper Consolidation, 1914–1945

As the industrial age altered established cities and as westward movement produced large cities in the Midwest and West, newspapers entered

FIGURE 2.2   Gas-powered trucks quickly became an integral part of newspaper circulation, often advertised as a mark of progressive spirit. This newspaper truck fleet was photographed during World War I. Courtesy The Journal Company, Milwaukee, WI.

a period of major change. Despite the emergence of several thousand newspapers, the number of newspapers began declining in 1914, setting off a series of suspensions and mergers, which halted for the prosperous decade following World War II. The number of English-language dailies peaked in 1914 at over 2200, slid to 1942 by 1930, to 1772 in 1950, and to 1763 in 1980. The trend was far more complex than a simple decline; even as established newspapers suspended publication or merged, new newspapers arose. For example, between 1914 and 1930, 1495 new newspapers appeared on the market and 1753 dailies merged, died, or shifted to weekly publication. Weeklies faced a similar decline as the newspaper market adapted to changing conditions. In town after town, competing newspapers disappeared, leaving about one in four with competing dailies and one in five with competing weeklies by 1930. Long before broadcasting became a major competitor, most communities had but one local source of news opinion and advertising.

Despite the best efforts of editors and circulation managers, a major shakeout moved relentlessly through the newspaper industry, the changes resulting from seven fundamental causes.[24]

1.   Economic pressures caused by technological changes in publishing

2.   Increased competition for circulation and advertising revenue

3.   Standardization of newspaper content, which produced a loss of individuality and reader appeal

4. A lack of social and economic need for several newspapers in some markets

5. Inept and uncreative newspaper management

6. Inflation and depression, beginning with World War I

7. Planned consolidation

Technological improvements lowered production costs for newspapers with large circulations, but the increased cost of printing equipment required major capital investment. Remaining competitive required large investments in equipment at a time when inflation ate into reserves and pushed interest rates unbearably high. When new presses were needed, many publishers simply closed their doors or sold out.

Newspapers competed not only for readers but also for advertisers, and the advantage went to those with larger circulations and lower costs in each community. Paved highways and city expansion allowed city newspapers to compete for readers in adjacent towns and villages within the range of delivery trucks, often to the disadvantage of the small-town daily or weekly. Magazines, which grew into a major entertainment industry from 1890 through World War II, competed for highly profitable national advertising. Broadcasting took a portion of local and national advertising, reducing profitability and eventually driving many national entertainment magazines out of business. Shopper newspapers consumed a portion of local advertising in many markets.

Increased use of wire service news reports for regional, national, and international news reduced the number of reporters on the payroll and the number of differences among newspapers. Coupled with the rise of syndicated columns, features, and comics, standardized news accounts in competing newspapers gave readers less partisan choice and reduced the need for several newspapers in each city.

Faced with economic, social, and product changes, many publishers were incapable of adaptation. Many held advertising rates down while inflation raised the costs of raw materials, labor, and the amount of capital needed to replace worn-out equipment. Others held to the traditional content formulas. World War I posed a particularly difficult time because it created significant inflation. Inflation and recession preceded the Great Depression in cycles that challenged the financial expertise of every publisher.

The decline hit morning newspapers harder than their afternoon competitors; the number of morning newspapers dropped from 500 to 388 by 1930. The number of afternoon newspapers began growing rapidly after the Civil War because they fit the reading patterns of commuters and the rhythm of small towns growing west of the Mississippi. Small-town publishers, printers, and reporters found the afternoon cycle more in keeping with the flow of news and their readers' day. World War I aided afternoon newspapers because wire news accounts of the battles, fought six to nine hours ahead of American time, reached newsrooms between 2 a.m. and 1 p.m., precisely when the afternoon newspaper was written.

Surviving publishers bought struggling competitors and weak but promising newspapers in other cities, progressively concentrating ownership in chains like those founded by William Randolph Hearst and E. W. Scripps. Some publishers, like Gardner Cowles and his brother John, sought control of a single town: In Des Moines, Gardner Cowles successively bought the *Register*, the *Leader*, the *Tribune*, the *Daily News*, and the *Capital*. With a monopoly assured, he turned the *Register* into one of the finest newspapers in the country. John Cowles bought and merged Minneapolis' newspapers until he held a monopoly with his *Tribune* and *Star*. The Gannett chain, begun with a few small newspapers in upstate New York towns, grew to 16 by 1935.

The Great Depression forced 378 newspapers to close their doors between 1930 and World War II. Had the child labor amendment been adopted, even more newspapers might have gone to their final edition. Shortages of ink and paper, workers and readers, and advertising during World War II bankrupted another 197 newspapers, some of whose worn-out presses simply could not be replaced. Unlike previous wars, World War II produced no circulation records because newsprint was rationed. Newsboys sold out their allotments in half the normal time, and new subscribers were put on waiting lists until someone died, moved out of town, or cancelled a subscription.

Decline of Afternoon Newspapers, 1960–

The postwar period reversed 30 years of decline as newspaper circulations rose dramatically and stabilized profits. Through the 1950s, newspaper circulation grew apace with the economy and the birth rate, briefly stalled by labor strikes and the problems of delivering newspapers into the new rings of suburbs populated by upwardly mobile ex-GIs whose college education and mortgages were part of the GI Bill. But newspapers suddenly confronted a cold new world, one shaped by the electronic age, further suburban development, depopulation of the cities, competition from shopper newspapers, and fundamental changes in life-style. The newspaper industry facing these challenges was mature, somewhat old-fashioned, and slow to recognize the magnitude of the challenge.

FIGURE 2.3 In the Depression, newsboys and newspaper carriers often put bread on the table for their families, despite protests from social reformers about newspapers employing youths. This well known photograph captures the entre-preneurial spirit of the "little merchant" approach to youth carriers and newsboys. Courtesy Library of Congress.

Through the sixties and seventies circulation failed to grow with either the population or number of new households; once great newspapers faded into mergers or died; a new generation of suburban daily newspapers developed; and the life-style of readers became more important for editors, publishers, and circulation managers.

Despite these changes, the number of daily newspapers was the same for 1960 and 1980; 1763. But the apparent stability of those figures is deceptive. The number dropped as low as 1751 and fluctuated annually. Over the 20-year period, more than 275 newspapers died, merged, or converted to less than daily publication; and the same number of new newspapers emerged. The only steady growth came in the number of Sunday newspapers, increasing from 563 to over 700. Sunday circulation in itself underscored the changing nature of newspaper reading, for it attracted readers who had abandoned the daily reading habit.

The victims of these changes were the old giants, the afternoon newspapers that grew strong through two World Wars. Afternoon newspapers of all sizes converted to morning publication, merged with morning papers, or printed their last headlines. Between 1980 and 1982 the award-winning *Washington Star*, *Chicago Daily News*, and *Philadelphia Bulletin* closed their doors. They were followed by the *Cleveland Press*, *Minneapolis Star*, *Des Moines Tribune*, *Atlanta Journal*, *Portland Journal*, *Buffalo Evening News*, and *Tampa Times*. Death in the afternoon became a catchphrase of newsrooms and circulation conventions. Within 10 months of its purchase by the *Los Angeles Times*, the *Denver Post* converted to morning publication, preferring direct competition to the *Rocky Mountain News* to malaise in the afternoon. The *Boston Globe* offered both morning and evening editions, becoming one of a growing number of all-day newspapers planning to survive by straddling the time line.

The nature of changes in the electronic age forced circulation managers to broaden their understanding of readers through marketing studies while directly confronting threats from new competitors for reader time and advertising revenue. One of the most innovative threats came from Gannett Newspapers, which mounted a national daily, *USA Today*. Built from extensive market research and product testing, *USA Today* offered eye-catching graphics, brief articles, and extensive coverage of topics people most often discussed: sports, entertainment, and business. *USA Today* reached more than one million readers within its first year; but more importantly, it attracted single copy purchasers who were also being wooed by daily newspapers as a means of increasing circulation. However, most daily newspapers base their circulations on local residents concerned with local issues and coverage. For regular subscribers, *USA Today* was not an acceptable alternative; but *USA Today*'s graphics, especially its weather coverage, resulted in increased use of color and graphics throughout the newspaper industry.

Electronic Competition

The electronic age began in 1957 with the invention of the transistor, but its roots stretch back to radio and the first commercial television broadcasts in 1948. An age of instant broadcast communication, highly portable receivers, and nonstop entertainment at first posed only a small threat to newspapers. After a flurry of battles over use of wire news in the 1930s, radio and newspapers settled into a comfortable, if competitive, relationship, perhaps because many newspapers owned radio stations. Edward R. Murrow's CBS broadcasts from London during World War II did not appear to hurt newspaper sales, but with rationing no one really knew. Through 1960, radio and magazines suffered most from television's voracious advertising appetite and growing popularity, although newspapers lost some revenue; movies, radio, and magazines lost audiences to television's entertainment fare. Television altered the way Americans used their time for news and entertainment, which fit into a more complex pattern of changes in life-style, including suburbanization, high mobility, a rising number of single adults, and competition for readers' time.

The election of John F. Kennedy as president in 1960 defied political and media tradition: His success rested on his skill with television, whether debating his opponent, Richard M. Nixon, or projecting his image through interviews, news accounts, and specially prepared advertisements. Kennedy did not undermine newspapers, he simply extended his skill to the new medium and demonstrated its power in reaching a national audience. From 1960 through 1980, as tragedy and social upheaval followed each other, Americans grew accustomed to watching news happen on television: a presidential assassination in Dallas, race riots, assassinations of Martin Luther King and Robert F. Kennedy, a Democratic party at war with Chicago police, Vietnam demonstrations, presidential impeachment hearings and a resignation, the shootings of Pope John Paul II and President Reagan, the takeover of an American embassy. Through them all and through lesser, local events, television became an integral part of breaking news stories because it was capable of showing in slow motion the action and its aftermath.

Politicians, public relations experts, and advocates of all causes learned the value of scheduling press conferences for the 6 p.m. newscast. Large numbers of people watched the news, along with all sorts of entertainment, so events that could be scheduled catered to TV crews.

Walter Cronkite, the most credible American, anchored the national news for CBS and encouraged people to read newspapers for the full story. But the issue ran deeper: Television's other content consumed time that might have been spent reading, particularly in the evening.

The readers, of course, moved farther from the central city to distant suburbs, commuting by automobile. Increased distances strained circulation systems, press deadlines, and news gathering. Recreation and shopping followed suburbanites out of the city. Outside the city often meant outside the county and school district and a lessened interest in city political news. Suburban newspapers sprang up like shopping centers, taking advantage of low-cost electronic typesetting and offset printing to service the news and advertising needs of new customers. Metropolitan newspapers responded to the challenge with special suburban sections and supplements inserted into the main newspaper, but the technological advantage went to small-circulation publishers because the new systems were incompatible with the equipment and needs of large dailies. Expanded distances between homes and between publisher and subscribers increased the number of motor routes and, therefore, the need for adult carriers.

Social and Economic Changes Affecting Circulation

Life-style changes, brought on by urban growth, affluence, and low-cost transportation, adversely affected newspaper circulation at the same time that newspapers were facing dramatic increases in energy and raw material costs. The mobility of Americans, a long-standing factor in market changes, posed new problems: Those who moved, particularly the college-educated, middle-class, young professionals, were the most desirable audience but were no more than moderate readers. Lacking roots in the community, they often moved to high-rise apartments and condominium complexes where home delivery was difficult. The growing number of single professionals, whether in their twenties and just beginning a career or in their forties and recovering from a divorce, added another readership problem: They were, as a group, infrequent readers. Major entertainments blossomed for the upwardly mobile: professional sports, movies, concerts, nightclubs, restaurants, and social clubs. These forms of entertainment competed with newspapers for time, income, and attention. A new life-style emerged among young married couples who, with two incomes, could afford entertainment away from home and had little time to spend reading newspapers. Eventually, newspapers remodeled older sections to appeal to this audience, but a new life-style allowed less time for reading.

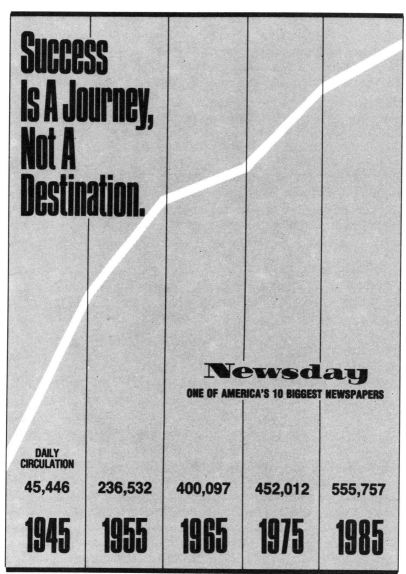

Success Is A Journey, Not A Destination.

Newsday

ONE OF AMERICA'S 10 BIGGEST NEWSPAPERS

DAILY CIRCULATION				
45,446	236,532	400,097	452,012	555,757
1945	1955	1965	1975	1985

Source: ABC Audit, 12-month averages ending Sept. 30 of each year. (1985 figure is 6-month average ending Sept 30.)

FIGURE 2.4   The suburban housing boom that followed World War II triggered a 40-year trend which has revolutionized the market for weekly and daily newspapers. Long Island's *Newsday* broke new ground as a suburban daily, and its rapid growth paralleled the migration to the suburbs. Courtesy *Newsday*, Long Island, NY.

The functional literacy rate itself became a matter of concern to newspapers, as declining reading scores threatened the next generation of subscribers. Florida's legislature allocated special funds for reading enrichment in 1983 in a bill strongly supported by the state newspapers. The *Northeast Mississippi Daily Journal's* publisher, George McLean, pledged $100,000 over 10 years to fund reading aides in the Tupelo school system. But the fundamental problem seemed to be aliterates, those whose parents and teachers can read but do not, thereby setting a non-reading example.[25] The Newspaper Readership Project found that reading was not a daily freetime activity for most schoolchildren, who preferred watching television, listening to the radio, or having telephone conversations with friends.[26] Through the Newspaper in Education Program (see Chapter 3), circulation managers began encouraging newspaper readership among young readers.

Economic factors also affected newspaper circulation. Gasoline prices doubled and tripled following an Arab boycott in 1974. Consumers, faced with drastic increases in automobile, heating, and electrical bills, looked for every economy. Newspapers consume huge quantities of energy to drive their presses and fuel their trucks. They also consume major quantities of newsprint, whose production is heavily energy dependent. Increased costs, passed on to advertisers and subscribers, caused declines in advertising linage and circulation. Advertisers simply bought less space; subscribers purchased fewer newspapers. Almost annual price increases from 1974 to 1982 virtually eliminated duplicate circulation, causing total daily newspaper circulation to level off at about 62 million, where it had been in 1960. Advertisers reacted to declining household penetration and increased prices by shifting some of their budgets to shopper newspapers and direct mail.

Labor costs rose faster than the inflation rate for unionized employees, driving production costs upward. The Newspaper Guild and the Teamsters organized circulation drivers and district managers as early as the 1950s, bringing major salary and work concessions through a series of strikes. Independent news dealers, supported by a favorable Supreme Court decision, organized their own union, the Association of Independent News Dealers, to leverage more favorable wholesale prices. The courts granted independent dealers full control over their route lists and their customers and prevented newspapers from setting a fair market price for the newspapers. Freed from control by publishers, dealers charged what the market would bear. Such developments encouraged newspapers to consider alternative delivery systems, such as the contract delivery agent system discussed in Chapter 8.

Strikes by other unions lowered circulation and taught readers to look elsewhere for their news. A 114-day New York strike in 1963, followed by another in 1965, mortally damaged the *Herald-Tribune*, *World-Telegram*, and *Sun*. Between 1970 and 1978, the newspaper industry averaged 25 strikes per year. The attitude of unions toward newspapers' survival was portrayed for many when striking pressmen beat the *Washington Post* presses with hammers to stop circulation. As electronic typesetting, photographic composition, and offset printing eliminated the need for craft unions and seriously reduced the number of workers, membership of full-time workers in the International Typographical Union dropped from 52,000 to 34,000 between 1960 and 1980. Circulation workers became the focus of union organization activity, because they alone offered the possibility of shutting down the newspaper through a strike. Single copy distributors were added to drivers and district managers as prime prospects for unionization.

Strikes worked to the disadvantage of several unions. The *Janesville* (Wisconsin) *Gazette* hired nonunion employees during a 366-day strike over phototypesetting and offset press installation. After one year and one day, the employees voted the union out. The *Sacramento Bee* took advantage of a strike to redesign its circulation system from mailroom to computerized circulation information system and emerged with a stream-lined, cost-efficient operation.

A reemergence of a failed concept, the shopper newspaper, also took a toll on the economic fortunes of daily newspapers in the 1970s and first half of the 1980s. The first shopper was probably the short-lived *Boston Auction Advertiser* of 1816. Like its successors, the *Auction Advertiser* relied exclusively on advertising revenue, justifying high advertising rates by guaranteeing delivery to every household in a defined territory. The *Cleveland Shopping News* revived the idea in 1921, and by 1933 the American Shopping News Publishers Association represented 255 newspapers with 4,360,000 circulation. Most were owned by independent publishers, although a few were owned by merchants or by newspapers. Virtually all shoppers contained some editorial material and comic strips, but they were not allowed to join the Audit Bureau of Circulations on the grounds that their sole function was to reduce newspaper advertising rates and revenues.

Daily newspapers struck back by creating their own shoppers and by lobbying for antishopper legislation. The *Newark* (New Jersey) *Ledger* delivered their shoppers' guide to 216,000 families not subscribing to the *Ledger*, charging advertisers only 60 percent of the *Ledger* rate for shopping guide insertions. But most publishers sought local handbill ordinances, which forbade blanket distribution of advertising material in autos or yards, on porches, or in mailboxes, thus undercutting shopper distribution. The U.S. Post Office was brought into the fray and forbade delivery of circulars to mailboxes unless they were sent through the postal system. When the Supreme Court upheld the law, shoppers virtually disappeared until the 1960s.

Aided by inexpensive offset printing technology, suburban growth, and advertiser dissatisfaction, shoppers grew into a major competitor of daily newspapers by 1980. The National Association of Advertising Publishers, which replaced the defunct ASNPA, represented nearly 1100 publications out of an estimated 11,000. Shoppers successfully lobbied state legislatures to rewrite the laws limiting publication of legal notices to commercial newspapers; then they began competing for city, county, and state legal notices at lower rates than their competitors. Legislators, persuaded by lower costs, higher household penetration, or antipathy to a traditional nemesis, supported shoppers. Newspapers retaliated by creating their own shoppers. A 1979 ICMA survey found that a substantial minority of surveyed papers published a shopper and many more were planning one.

For circulation managers, competition from shoppers and direct mail meant a major revision of the circulation system and the introduction of computer technology to identify every household address in the primary market area and separate subscribers from nonsubscribers. (Chapter 10 more fully discusses this computerization and its effects.) Circulation districts, which simply grew with the community, were restructured to conform to zip codes and postal routes or to embrace middle-class and upper-class residential areas. Complex insert delivery zones were developed to serve advertisers demanding carefully targeted advertising delivery. Computerized circulation systems, built arduously over several years, allowed newspapers to identify every customer, monitor service complaints, instantly adjust press runs with subscriber changes, and maintain payment records. Circulation conversion proved a costly, time-consuming, frustrating task that might never have been attempted without pressure from advertisers, shoppers, and direct mail.

Postal rates darkened the economic picture through the 1970s. Steady increases in second-class rates made postal delivery increasingly unaffordable, except within the home county of the newspaper. For the *Wall Street Journal*, which relies heavily on postal delivery, the postage rate portion of subscription fees rose from 15 percent to 56 percent between 1971 and 1981. The *Journal* passed the postal costs on to subscribers, offering home delivery in major markets. Dailies raised postal subscription rates and watched mail subscriptions decline. Weekly newspapers had no cheap alternative, particularly if they had extensive rural readership, for postal costs still ran about half the cost of an independent carrier system. Religious and organizational newspapers began reducing publication frequency and raising subscription rates to meet increased postal costs. Centralization of postal processing facilities slowed delivery and complicated newspaper service, and abandonment of Saturday routes service further limited the usefulness of postal delivery.

Almost simultaneously another branch of the U.S. Postal Service began to compete with newspapers by encouraging postal delivery of shoppers and direct mail. By 1983, post offices in major cities had a special department for direct mail services, putting the U.S. Postal Service in the curious position of regulating the delivery rates and practices of newspapers with one hand while competing directly with the other.

NEW LIFE FOR WEEKLIES

Weeklies, which remained relatively stable after the shakeout of the period of consolidation, were rescued from a gradual slide into economic failure by new technology and the brisk energy of suburban development. This return to health was poetic justice: The highways and expanding cities that had driven out many weeklies in the first decades of this century turned into freeways and suburban communities that were so different and so distant from central cities that they needed their own newspapers.

As early as the 1960s, urban growth took people beyond the political boundaries familiar to metropolitan news coverage into different counties and different school districts. Suburbanites created a new market for the

---

TABLE 2.2
U.S. Daily Newspaper Circulation—1986's Top 20

*Average Daily Circulation**

The Wall Street Journal	1,990,205 (morning)
New York Daily News	1,275,268 (morning)
USA Today	1,168,222 (morning)
Los Angeles Times	1,088,155 (morning)
The New York Times	1,035,426 (morning)
The Washington Post	781,371 (morning)
Chicago Tribune	760,031 (all day)
New York Post	751,798 (all day)
The Detroit News	650,445 (all day)

TABLE 2.2 (*continued*)

Detroit Free Press	645,266 (morning)
Chicago Sun-Times	631,808 (morning)
Newsday	582,388 (evening)
San Francisco Chronicle	554,611 (morning)
The Boston Globe	514,097 (all day)
The Philadelphia Inquirer	492,374 (morning)
The Miami Herald	458,759 (morning)
The Cleveland Plain Dealer	454,042 (morning)
The Newark Star-Ledger	452,158 (morning)
Houston Chronicle	425,434 (all day)
Dallas Morning News	390,275 (morning)

*Percentage of Household Penetration In the City Zone[†**]*

119% Times, Bad Axe, Michigan	1,423 (evening)
112% Reporter, Lake City, Florida	4,024 (evening)
108% Sun & Sentinel, Yuma, Arizona	25,378 (evening)
98% Crescent-News, Defiance, Ohio	5,880 (evening)
98% Express, Lock Haven, Pennsylvania	5,682 (evening)
98% American Republic, Poplar Bluff, Missouri	6,929 (evening)
97% American, Somerset, Pennsylvania	2,902 (morning)
96% News-Virginian, Waynesboro, Virginia	8,191 (evening)
96% News, Palatka, Florida	3,743 (evening)
96% Banner, Cambridge, Maryland	4,210 (evening)
95% Leader, Pontiac, Illinois	3,624 (evening)
95% Citizen, Holdrege, Nebraska	2,088 (evening)
95% Journal, Fergus Falls, Minnesota	4,555 (evening)
95% Inter-Mountain, Elkins, West Virginia	3,130 (evening)
94% Times, Bryan, Ohio	3,118 (evening)
94% News-Record, Harrisonburg, Virginia	8,103 (morning)
94% Gazette, McCook, Nebraska	3,202 (evening)
94% Post-Star, Glens Falls, New York	11,239 (morning)
93% Mining Journal, Marquette, Michigan	6,805 (evening)
93% Courier-Express, Du Bois, Pennsylvania	4,005 (evening)

* Audit Bureau of Circulations' FAS-FAX Report—March 31, 1986. This is a six month average.

** Penetration is the ratio of circulation to occupied households in the city zone or newspaper designated market percentages rounded to the nearest whole number, but ranking based on complete percentage figures.

† Audit Bureau of Circulations' FAS-FAX Report—March 31, 1986. This is a six month average.

existing small-town weeklies and for a host of new suburban weeklies. These newspapers thrived on extensive coverage of the four major concerns of their readers: local schools, local government, local taxes, and local community life. As urban growth filled in the fields between formerly distant small towns with tracts of homes and shopping centers, weekly newspapers sprang up. A new phenomenon developed around big cities: rings of weeklies owned by a single publisher and offering special advertising rates for total suburban coverage. These suburban chains offered intense local news coverage and county or regional coverage to readers. With high market penetration in each suburb and access to the entire suburban area, suburban chains offered advertisers two attractive options: Local merchants reached a large proportion of their customers at low cost, and large-scale businesses could reach the entire suburban population or defined portions of it with a single advertising contract. The chains were so successful that metropolitan dailies bought them or built their own, always around some other city.

Technology favored the weeklies as well. In fact, weeklies blazed the trail into electronic typesetting and high-volume offset printing just before suburban newspapers began to emerge. In the early 1960s rural weeklies were facing desperate financial straits. Forced to cut costs in order to survive, they began banding together to purchase common printing plants equipped with the latest labor-saving technology. Because they were nonunionized or were abandoning small union shops, weeklies had few labor problems in this transition. Instead of skilled typesetters, the new plants required only typists. Instead of a score of pressmen, the new offset presses required only a handful. Photochemical plate-making systems replaced composing and stereotyping staffs with a camera and a couple people. The quality of offset printing far exceeded that of letterpress, particularly with photographs and color. The thin plates of offset could not produce more than 20,000 to 30,000 impressions before wearing out, a factor that strongly favored small circulation weeklies and dailies. Plate life has crept higher in the seventies and eighties but still does not favor pressruns typical of big-city dailies.

While central-city dailies struggled with rush hour traffic and press schedules designed to reach far-flung suburban readers, weeklies relied on the postal service and youth carriers. Indeed, in-county postal rates made the circulation system a bargain. Also, institutional newspapers flourished with the new technology, attracted by its low cost, attractive appearance, and operational simplicity. Because these institutional newspapers also relied heavily on postal distribution, the U.S. Postal Service found itself with a flood of new second-class postal customers. The result was close attention to second-class service and rates from newspapers and postal authorities. Every postal rate bill drew close and careful scrutiny from the trade associations representing newspapers.

The National Newspaper Association, founded in 1885 and representing small weeklies and small dailies, monitored the changes and kept both old and new members up to date through *Publishers' Auxiliary*, its weekly newspaper. The Catholic Press Association, like other groups, turned over an increasing amount of its convention time and bulletin space to postal rate issues.

In their adversity, weeklies found the drive for readjustment and revision; and their successes forced daily newspapers to adapt or lose readers. When metropolitan editors found it difficult to cover or print the news of every suburb, weekly editors devoted several reporters and generous play to precisely that news. When daily circulation managers encountered problems serving the outer rings of the urban area, weekly managers sold subscriptions to the local paper and relied on mail carriers. When high prices forced small advertisers out of big dailies, suburban newspapers offered affordable space. As a result, the newspaper industry moves toward the end of the twentieth century as a strong, healthy, and powerful industry substantially different from the one welcomed in 1900. The second largest employer among manufacturers, newspapers went through the recession of the early 1980s more successfully than any other industry. The adaptations that produced healthy earnings in a recession had powerful and far-reaching implications for the circulation systems; sales, distribution, and collection methods had to adapt to new, sometimes computerized realities.

A LOOK AT CIRCULATION TODAY

The history of newspaper circulation is the story of an industry constantly adapting to social and economic changes, new technologies, and the demands of changing life-styles. The economic success of contemporary newspapers is based in part on the large cost savings and simplified printing methods brought by electronic typesetting and related innovations in printing and production machinery. New equipment, discussed in Chapter 7, allows newspapers to provide precisely counted bundles to contractors and carriers, to automatically insert preprints and special sections, and to speed loading of zoned editions into the proper trucks. Computer technology, discussed in Chapter 10, has touched circulation offices as well, providing mailing lists of nonsubscribers for total market coverage publications and swift handling of all the information a circulation department needs. Computers adjust delivery routes and draws, notify carriers and district managers of customer changes, print bills, and adjust the pressrun. In short, computers have touched and changed every facet of circulation except the nature of circulation workers and the uniqueness of a 12-year-old carrier.

While home delivery remains the preferred method of circulation, the 1980s have brought a new concentration on single copy sales as a means of stimulating circulation growth and reaching intermittent readers. Also new is the increased awareness of advertising and editorial staffs of the importance of circulation and its interaction with their efforts.

The changes of the 1980s go beyond a simple shift of emphasis from home delivery to single copy sales. In the past, circulation work was dominantly a manual labor task: delivery and collection coupled with door-to-door and point-of-purchase sales.

To these tasks have been added new concerns about newspaper marketing, collaboration with advertising staff for delivery to targeted areas, alternate products for nonsubscribers, and a series of new managerial challenges created by computerization of circulation records. In many newspapers, district managers have been relieved of manual labor in the delivery and service components in order to devote more time to sales efforts mounted in conjunction with larger marketing and promotion plans.

The transition can be most clearly seen in the work of the International Circulation Managers Association (ICMA), the professional organization. Marketing has been a growing theme, reflecting the new reality: Newspapers no longer sell themselves; and everyone, especially circulation workers, is being called into new roles mandated by changes in American life-style and newspaper readership. Computers, which were once understood as better recordkeepers for traditional circulation practices, have now become contributors to the marketing efforts. In some newspapers circulation is part of a marketing department; in others it is part of a marketing division; in many, the circulation manager sits on a marketing committee. In their search for survival and growth in the final 15 years of the twentieth century, newspapers have turned to marketing for solutions; and circulation practices and perspectives have been significantly altered as a result.

NOTES

1. James M. Lee, *History of American Journalism* (Garden City, N.J.: The Garden City Publishing Co., Inc., 1913), 2.
2. Edwin Emery and Michael Emery, *The Press and America* (Englewood Cliffs, N.J.: Prentice-Hall, Inc., 1978), 4.

3. Postmasters had the franking privilege, which meant they had only to sign their name on the envelope in lieu of a postage stamp.
4. Benjamin Franklin, *Autobiography* (New York: Washington Square Press, 1955), 24. Ben Franklin wrote that he was employed to carry the papers to the community.
5. *Royal Gazette*, 8 November 1773, as cited by Frank Luther Mott, *American Journalism* (New York: Macmillan, 1962), 105.
6. *New York Weekly Journal*, 18 March 1751, 1.
7. "The Yearly Verses of the Printer's Boy, Who Carries the Pennsylvania Gazette to Customers," *Pennsylvania Gazette*, 1 January 1746.
8. Frederic Hudson, *Journalism in the United States from 1690 to 1872* (New York: Harper and Brothers, 1873), 99. Hudson claimed the tradition began with William Bradford in Massachusetts.
9. Hudson, *Journalism in the U.S.*, 33.
10. *Farmer's Weekly Museum*, 21 August 1797, as cited by Frank Luther Mott, *American Journalism* (New York: Macmillan, 1962), 160.
11. Donald J. Wood, *Newspaper Circulation Management—A Profession* (New York: Newspaper Research Bureau, 1952), 2.
12. Alfred M. Lee, *The Daily Newspaper in America* (New York: The Macmillan Company, 1937), 28.
13. Frank Luther Mott, *American Journalism* (New York: The Macmillan Company, 1962), 160.
14. Lee, *Daily Newspaper*, 28.
15. *American Minerva*, 9 December 1793.
16. Lee, *Daily Newspaper*, 56.
17. Lee, *Daily Newspaper*, 258.
18. Mott, *American Journalism*, 160n.
19. *New York Journal*, 17 October 1896, as cited by Mott, *American Journalism*, 525.
20. Lee, *Daily Newspaper*, 288.
21. Will Irwin, "The Fourth Current," *Collier's* 46 (February 18, 1911): 14.
22. S. Bent, *Ballyhoo: The Voice of the Press* (New York: Boni and Liverwright, 1927), 319.
23. Charles O. Bennett, *Facts without Opinion* (Chicago: Audit Bureau of Circulation, 1965), 10.
24. Raymond B. Nixon, "Trends in Daily Newspaper Ownership since 1945," *Journalism Quarterly* 31 (Winter 1954): 7.
25. Robert Duffey, quoted in *presstime*, 3:9 (September 1981): 20.
26. Newspaper Readership Project, "Children, Mothers and Newspapers," privately distributed research report (Reston, Va.: American Newspaper Publishers Association, 1981).

CHAPTER

3

The Marketing Concept and Newspapers

Reflecting significant marketplace changes during the 1970s, newspaper buying and reading habits confronted newspapers with multiple challenges. Circulation growth did not keep pace with the population or with the number of households: Circulation leveled off and household penetration declined. Rising production and labor costs forced prices uncomfortably high for both advertisers and subscribers. With increasing vigor and sophistication, other media and entertainment competed for readers' time, attention, and purchasing power. Together, these market factors affected every newspaper, from the weakest to the strongest, whether independent or publicly owned, commercial or institutional, weekly or daily.

To meet these challenges, newspapers turned to marketing, the basic business function that had helped other companies adapt to changing customers and environments. This chapter examines marketing as a business concept and as a philosophy of management that recognizes that customer needs should determine the newspaper's orientation.

In the 1980s among newspaper people, marketing simultaneously became a watchword and a topic of extensive debate. As newspapers sought to upgrade their marketing efforts, market research and a marketing orientation began to pervade the newspaper business.[1] Some newspapers moved boldly to sophisticated marketing methods while embarking on educational programs for their managers across departments. Others carefully studied the results of such efforts and calculated the value of this approach for their own operations. Journalists feared emphasis on marketing might cause the editorial content to seek the lowest common denominator or the highest popularity, whatever the costs to more serious news coverage of unexciting but important issues. Circulation managers questioned the implications of marketing for established sales, service, and collection practices; yet few denied that newspapers needed to adjust to their readers in order to survive or grow. In adjusting, newspapers changed their management functions as part of the incorporation of professional marketing. The following sections examine the basic components of marketing as they apply to newspapers and highlight the challenges newspaper managers face when they adopt a marketing approach to business.

WHAT IS MARKETING?

The word "marketing" has two distinct uses in common business language: It describes the commercial process, i.e., the relationship between producers and consumers; and it characterizes a particular philosophy or system of business management. Both meanings flow from the same root definition: Marketing is the product planning, pricing, promoting, distributing, and servicing of goods and services needed and desired by customers.[2]

By defining the commercial process from the customer's perspective and making customer needs and desires central to all phases of business, marketing leads to a different style of management, one based on knowing and reacting to customers in product planning, pricing, promotion, distribution, and service. These marketing terms, in relation to newspapers, can be defined as follows:

Customers are those who purchase the newspaper or space within it; they include readers and advertisers.

Needs and desires are the personal, social, and psychological reasons for which the newspaper is purchased, read, or used as an advertising vehicle.

Product planning is the formulation of a newspaper's advertising and editorial ratio, news and feature content, special sections, style, size, format, layout, graphics, use of color, and focus or orientation.

Pricing includes the wholesale, subscriber, and single copy purchase rates; and the retail, national, and classified advertising rates.

Promotion comprises efforts to sharpen the newspaper's image in the community or to bring specific newspaper features, services, or writers to public attention. Promotion may include sponsorship of charitable events, sports teams, concerts, and the like.

Distribution includes the market area covered (RTZ and AOZ); the delivery of the newspaper to wholesalers, retailers, and customers; and allocation of advertising space within the newspaper.

Servicing includes responding to complaints from the middlemen, advertisers, and readers through letters to the editor and in the redelivery of missed or damaged newspapers.

Because marketing assumes that consumer needs and desires change and that production components can be changed in response, it seems particularly appropriate to a rapidly changing and heterogenous society such as post–World War II America, where companies face highly mobile and differentiated consumers from region to region, from age group to age group, and from life-style to life-style. For an intensely localized product such as a newspaper, marketing offers the means to adapt successfully to unique, local customers, spelling the difference between success and failure in solving readership and circulation problems.

Marketing as a Managerial Concept

First developed by the Japanese in the seventeenth century as a philosophy of business management, the marketing concept is based on the principle that a company must first establish what the customer wants, then where, when, and at what price in order to supply the right product at the right time and in the right way. When first widely used in the United States after World War II, marketing was primarily a troubleshooting method to deal with specific problems. Increased attention to consumer needs and satisfaction broadened the role of marketing, making it a separate department in many businesses and a philosophy that permeated management decisions and corporate structure.

Companies managed according to the marketing concept differ in self-definition, corporate goals, and organizational structure from those based on the other common managerial concepts: production, product, and selling. Each concept makes different assumptions about the nature of the commercial process and emphasizes different strategies for success in the marketplace.

Management from the *production concept* builds from the basic principle that consumers favor low-cost, readily available products; and it sets high-volume production and massive distribution as its primary goals. A production-oriented newspaper defines itself as the inexpensive mass newspaper that is for everyone and that has a broad circulation zone. The penny press of the 1830s typified a production concept, emphasizing massive distribution and low-cost production. In the 1980s, emphasis on availability and volume may lead to unprofitable circulation in areas having little corporate, editorial, or advertising value to the newspaper. Increased production costs rendered this approach obsolete, forcing newspapers to evaluate the costs of circulation in fringe areas and the numbers of unsold newspapers against the goals of the company. A contemporary version of the production concept emphasizes massive low-priced circulation (often at heavily discounted rates), which is made profitable only through increased advertising revenues.

Management from the *product concept* begins with the principle that consumers choose products with the highest quality, performance, and features; and it sets product excellence as its primary corporate goal. A product-oriented newspaper sells news and emphasizes high-quality content and printing. The *New York Times* and the *Christian Science Monitor* follow the product concept. In the product concept, journalists, particularly the senior editors, shape the newspaper according to their professional standards. While this editorial insulation from outside pressures enhances independence and produces a product professionals admire, it can threaten the survival of the newspaper if the editor loses touch with customers in the local market. Emphasis on high-quality printing can give the pressroom enough authority to compromise deadlines and press times in pursuit of printing excellence. Managers imbued with the product concept believe circulation will rise with product quality if circulation adequately performs its tasks.

Management in the *selling concept* flows from the principle that consumers do not buy enough products without aggressive promotional and sales efforts, whatever the quality of the product; and it emphasizes multimedia advertising campaigns and constant hard-sell promotions and discounts. Newly introduced newspapers, like *USA Today*, rely on the selling approach to establish themselves; otherwise, the selling concept is limited to highly competitive markets, for example, Toronto, where the *Sun* offers only single copy sales. The burden of increasing circulation falls completely on the salespeople and sales techniques. Combined with a production concept, the selling concept can produce quick, temporary circulation gains through underpriced subscriptions, which prove short-lived and ultimately unprofitable. In a competitive market, the selling concept becomes the required strategy for the newspaper with less circulation. To hang on, the second newspaper may wage an "anything goes" sales battle. One mark of a sales orientation is the ceaseless sales campaigns heavily dependent on discounts, prizes, giveaway games, and promotions.

Because the *marketing concept* begins with satisfaction of customer needs and desires, a market-oriented newspaper defines itself as providing the information customers want and need, when and where they want it. Readership and marketing studies become part of product revisions, price changes, promotions, sales, service, and delivery systems. A market-oriented newspaper precisely identifies its customers and constantly reviews company efforts against the standard of customer satisfaction. Guidelines for production, the product, and selling come from the customers and are based on market studies.

Marketing Management

When the marketing concept merges with principles of sound corporate management, it produces four essential managerial principles.[3]

1. Marketing is customer-oriented, beginning with the establishment of customer needs.

2. Marketing is an integrated management function.

3. Marketing is results-directed, seeking to achieve specific objectives.

4. The marketing concept requires systematic planning.

Customer orientation ranks first among these principles. Marketing management integrates each company function into a system for translating consumer needs and desires into products or services, at prices consumers judge reasonable. Managers similarly devise distribution and service programs to satisfy consumers. In effect, the customers control the company's direction through the marketing unit, which studies their needs, desires, and milieu and translates the results into corporate activity. All production elements from planning through service remain, by definition, flexible enough to accommodate changes in customer needs and desires. In a company completely committed to marketing management, the marketing people effectively run the company, just as accounting people effectively run companies completely committed to cost effectiveness and cost accounting standards or salespeople run companies committed to the selling concept. Many companies will grant marketing a major role but stop short of allowing a single department control of the operation.

As a management system, marketing integrates the efforts of each department in the newspaper by virtue of its relation to consumers. A newspaper organized on a marketing model modifies the rigid departmental isolationism of traditional line and staff structures by refocusing departmental identity on satisfying customers and potential customers, whether readers or advertisers. The result of these softened departmental walls is a company guided by the marketing concept and tightly organized around marketing expertise.

Marketing management measures success in attainment of specific, defined goals and objectives. Because of its customer orientation, the marketing approach allows specification of customer needs and desires to be met in each production area, whether for small groups of customers or a broad cross section. While a net paid circulation figure may be a goal, marketing insists on more precise goals related to identified customer groups and their unmet needs.

Both short-term and long-term planning are essential to skilled marketing management because they extend the link between customer and company into future activities. Two levels of planning derive from the marketing philosophy. The first and broadest is the company's strategic marketing plan, which lays out the basic identity and long-term corporate future, including the acquisitions and diversification essential to a strong, economically balanced corporation. The second level, the marketing plan, details company activity necessary to attain specific marketplace goals. This plan will cover five years or more, and it will be revised and extended at least annually. Both plans force the company to anticipate the market for goods and to look to future customers in order to survive. The belief that customer satisfaction leads to profitable growth underlies strategic market planning and leads management to carefully delineate the customers to be served, their needs and desires, and company adjustments essential to success.[4]

STEPS IN THE MARKETING MANAGEMENT PROCESS

Within a company's operation, several principles of marketing management apply to the marketing management process:

> analyzing market opportunities, researching and selecting target markets, developing market strategies, planning marketing tactics, and implementing and controlling the marketing effort.[5]

Analyzing Market Opportunities

Identifying market opportunities begins with several basic questions: Who are our customers? What is our business? Who should be our customers? It then moves to analyzing unserved and underserved markets within the newspaper's geographic boundaries. The market opportunities may lie in the product or in the market; that is, they may identify what the newspaper could offer readers and advertisers or the kinds of readers and advertisers whose needs could be met by the newspaper. This analysis also looks to the future for both the product and the market. What lies ahead for news and advertising? What lies ahead for this market's economy and development? What competition will face the newspaper in the near future? How are customers changing?

Researching and Selecting Target Markets

A target market is a specific, well-defined audience segment or combination of audience segments that the newspaper seeks to serve with a product. Researching and selecting target markets requires substantial data collection on the general market, on customers, and on specific groups or segments of the market. Following data collection, management selects targets for marketing efforts based on likely profitability and necessity. Research on the target market guides development of particular products (sections, types of articles, design, an entire newspaper) and of price, delivery, and service.

The five marketing options among which management may choose include[6]

1. Single segment concentration. For this the publisher seeks dominance in one demographic or geographic segment. A neighborhood newspaper or special product written and delivered to people in a demographically homogenous group typifies single market concentration because it is a specific product for a specific part of the market. Here weeklies have their greatest advantage over dailies.

2. Product specialization. Here the publisher concentrates on dominance in one topical area or business with reduced regard for specific demographic or geographic segments. Product-specialized newspapers include the *Wall Street Journal*, *Women's Wear Daily*, and the *Chronicle of Higher Education*.

3. Market specialization. For this a publisher seeks dominance in all demographic or geographic segments of a narrowly defined market. Smaller daily and weekly newspapers that provide broad coverage for everyone in a community or county tend to be market specialists, as do suburban ring weeklies.

4. Selective specialization. For this a publisher develops various products, each aimed at a particular segment of the overall market. Zoned editions and special content sections can be specialized when they vary their content for particular geographic areas within a metropolitan area.

5. Full coverage. For this a publisher offers something for everyone,

cutting across segment and product specializations. Major metropolitan and larger daily newspapers with diverse markets fit this category.

Target market selection includes market positioning: Will the newspaper serve a mass audience but emphasize a largely middle-class group with interests in the arts, politics, and business; or will it seek a blue-collar readership more interested in sports, short articles, and photos? Will it compete by concentrating more on families or single people? Because most daily newspapers in smaller markets lack direct competition for readers, market position may be less important than it is in metropolitan areas where position is critical. Yet even the smallest daily newspapers face competition from shoppers, weeklies, other dailies, and other media. Defining the desired market position against these indirect competitors is important. For instance, defining the market position for *USA Today* posed a major task for Gannett partly because it competes with a wide variety of daily newspapers in diverse markets.

Developing Market Strategies

Developing market strategies means spelling out the precise business plan to meet marketing objectives. The plan should include expenditures, the marketing mix, and assessment of such environmental conditions as competition, price, supply demand, raw material costs, advertising revenue, etc. The plan may be revised as conditions change.

The expenditures are a percentage of income dedicated to the project. For circulation projects it may include a cost per subscription allocation. The marketing mix comprises the adjustable elements used to reach the market goals. Although many such elements exist, they fall into four major categories, commonly known as the four Ps: product, price, place, and promotion.[7] The marketing mix is both a description of the controllable options and a plan for allocation of company resources. Because a newspaper serves two sets of customers, the marketing mix becomes somewhat complicated.

As a product, the newspaper is highly perishable, losing its value within hours after printing. It has value because it provides some combination of information, opinion, and entertainment to the reader and because it stimulates business for the advertiser. Value for readers can be found in the packaging, service, and full range of content, from editorials to comics and late news to classified ads. Each content element provides value to some set of readers, though not for all. For advertisers, product value includes the readers, advertising options, warranties, and service.

A key to the future of newspapers is providing an information package that is indispensable.[8] When nonreaders say they have no time for the newspaper, they are saying the product has a low priority, that it is nonessential.

The price variables for both sets of customers include discounts, allowances, payment periods, and credit terms. For readers and circulation middlemen, it comprises subscription, single copy, and wholesale rates. For advertisers it includes multiple insertion rates, long-term contracts, and co-op plans. When Joseph Pulitzer started the *New York World* in 1883, he sold it at one cent to undercut the competing *Herald*. Thus challenged, the *Herald* lowered its price to one cent. The effect was fourfold: The *World* achieved the status of a major competitor; the *Herald* lost anticipated circulation revenue; the *Herald* lowered profits of dealers and distributors, creating circulation problems; and the *Herald* retained a few readers it would have lost to the *World*. Twelve years later William Randolph Hearst started the *Journal* as a one-cent paper, and Pulitzer cut his price to one cent. Pulitzer later mused, "When I came to New York, Mr. Bennett reduced the price of his paper and raised his advertising rates—all to my advantage. When Mr. Hearst came to New York, I did the same. I wonder why, in view of my experience."[9] Pricing is a critical component for a mass-marketed newspaper.

Since 1970, advertising rates and single copy prices have kept pace with the consumer price index.[10] Price increases do not of themselves explain why individual newspapers gain or lose circulation. Price increases led to immediate circulation loss 74 percent of the time for large newspapers but to circulation increases 65 percent of the time for small newspapers.[11] Some newspaper costs have risen faster than inflation because newspapers are heavy energy and natural resource consumers (gasoline, electricity, newsprint). Soaring costs across the entire business spectrum explained the rising prices but did not necessarily appease readers.

Unstable production costs remain one of the major concerns for market pricing plans. If prices of resources and energy remain stable through the 1980s, newspapers will still face labor costs keyed to inflation and high-cost technological improvements. At the core, pricing defines the value of the newspaper and reflects company decisions about how to make the newspaper affordable, competitive, and profitable. For circulation managers pricing also raises questions about which customers pay more and the problem of adjusting vending boxes to accept the proper combination of coins for daily and Sunday newspapers. Carrier morale may suffer if the new price works out to an even dollar sum, thus decreasing collection tips.

The place as part of the marketing mix goes beyond geography to the circulation and advertising efforts that make the product accessible for the desired customers. It includes the circulation distribution system (middlemen, carriers, haulers, retail outlets, boxes, transportation schedules, and the like), advertising salespeople, advertising agencies, and so on.

Promotion includes all efforts to encourage target customers to purchase the newspaper or an advertisement in it; it is discussed in detail in Chapter 4.

Planning and Implementing the Marketing Plan

The tactical plan specifies the activities for each of the four Ps in the marketing mix. It leads to redesign or revision of the newspaper; revised pricing; changes in place; and purchase of promotional material, time, and space. These activities culminate in the final stage, implementation and control, wherein management evaluates the marketing effort against established goals and makes course corrections. Part of the contingency planning involves incorporation of future market research to avoid the kind of marketing myopia that emphasizes products over consumer needs by locking in product development irrespective of changes in the marketplace.

MARKETING IN THE NEWSPAPER STRUCTURE

While newspapers recently have focused their attention on two key elements of the marketing concept, customer needs and desires and systematic planning, they have found that marketing's development as an integrating management function is particularly vexing. Long-standing divisions between advertising and editorial autonomy have not lent themselves to establishing and coordinating product, price, place, and promotion agendas for separate customer groups. The need to serve both sets of customers with different products in the same newspaper has posed a problem for over 100 years. Newspaper economist Jon Udell identified the following three factors as the root cause of strong departmentalization:[12]

1. The intense pace of newspaper operations and concomitant pressures to meet deadlines

2. The complexity of producing a newspaper

3. The belief that democracy needs a press free of internal and external forces

The resulting departmental autonomy leads to the antithesis of integrated marketing: informal planning, autonomous departmental decisions, and prejudice against long-range thinking.[13] Weeklies and small dailies have a different problem: tiny "departments" and neither time nor resources for marketing or long-range thinking.

The introduction of marketing as a formal management system raises the dilemma of positioning marketing in relation to established departments. Beyond this, while advertising and circulation departments may have used aspects of marketing, editorial departments traditionally have not. Resistance to innovative management systems decreased only after the demise of dailies that failed to change in response to market conditions and the success of newspapers committed to marketing management, for example, the Knight-Ridder group.

While not all newspapers fully embrace marketing as a management philosophy, many have established at least a marketing group or committee of department heads and top management that analyzes every phase of the newspaper from a marketing perspective. The latter approach avoids confrontation over editorial autonomy but produces some marketing benefits. Newspaper promotion expert Edward Linsmier predicted that these efforts would become a continuing trend.

> Successful newspapers in the '80s will centralize and maximize their marketing, research and promotion functions. Whether this is a one-person department on a smaller newspaper or 60 specialists on a metropolitan newspaper, the centralized unit should report directly to the chief executive in order to help the newspaper achieve its strategic and fiscal objectives.[14]

Another indication of the growing acceptance of the marketing philosophy is newspapers' involvement in the Readership Council and the Readership Project.[15]

A principal concern of marketing management is the marketing environment within which a newspaper operates, that is, the world outside the newspaper that affects the newspaper's ability to serve its customers. This environment includes the nature of the market, competition, publics, and the broader spectrum of influences: demographics, economics, politics, law, and culture. Newspaper marketing plans depend on a broad range of research sources, from anthropologists to underwriters. Whether employed as a method of understanding the newspaper, the readers and nonreaders, business conditions for advertisers, today's market, or tomorrow's trends, marketing operates through extensive research as the best defense against unprofitable surprises and the best offense for changing times.

MARKETING RESEARCH

Systematic marketing research provides the information that serves as a barometer of an industry's changing conditions, gives vital public feedback, and acts as an early warning system against competitive threats. Whether it concentrates on the marketplace, the customers, the newspaper itself, or how readers use newspaper content (particularly advertising), market research aims at continuous contact with the marketplace and replaces the guesswork and subjective impressions upon which marketing decisions may have been based with more precise data. Research data aids decision making; it is not a substitute for it.

Understanding customers' life-styles has always kept newspapers attuned to their readers' needs and desires. In earlier, simpler days, publisher-editors almost instinctively adjusted the newspaper to fit the community because they were an intimate part of it and knew almost everyone in it. That tradition continues among today's small daily and weekly publisher-editors who maintain a close relationship with a broad cross section of readers. The swelling suburbs and highly mobile urban Americans have complicated that relationship, however, by making it virtually impossible for an editor or publisher of a medium-sized daily to maintain contact with changes among each group of readers. Modern marketing research provides a substitute for the personal insights publishers gleaned from conversations with a cross section of the community and intimate knowledge of its subgroups.

Leo Bogart of the American Newspaper Advertising Bureau declared, "There has never been a time when research was as widely used in the newspaper business as it is at present."[16] Research has gained high credibility among editors of metropolitan newspapers, where identifying and characterizing readers and their interests is most difficult; but large newspapers are not alone in conducting research. While 9 out of 10 large newspapers conducted readership studies between 1977 and 1979, 7 of 10 medium-sized dailies (circulation 50,000 to 100,000) and more than 5 of 10 small dailies (25,000 to 50,000) also surveyed readers.[17] Market research scope includes three main areas: the market, the newspaper itself, and the products sold through newspaper advertising.[18] While the majority of past research has concentrated on market, research on the newspaper and its products has grown significantly in the past decade.

The Newspaper Market

The newspaper market differs from newspaper to newspaper in several ways, but basically it includes the range of conditions affecting the marketplace and two distinct groups: the readers and the advertisers. A newspaper can define its market by geographic, topical, or customer boundaries; or it can combine them for a market/product mix that expresses the company's goals. In practice, editors and publishers define their market with a blend of geography, topic, and readership. Weeklies and small dailies intimately connected to their markets require less research, but they cannot monitor market changes without regular study.

Newspapers acquire market knowledge from two types of research: primary and secondary. Primary research is work the newspaper does for its own purposes. Secondary research is data collected for other purposes, for example, the census. Secondary research is usually less expensive and more quickly obtained than primary research, but it is also less useful because it was constructed for other purposes.

Normally market research begins with an exhaustive review of secondary research before moving to primary research. Sometimes secondary data suffice; other times, secondary data limit the demands on primary research or establish a baseline for comparison. Useful secondary sources include the Bureau of the Census in the U.S. Department of Commerce, the Federal Research System (business indices, sales figures), *Editor & Publisher's Market Guide*, Sales Management's Annual Survey of Buying Power, the Standard Rate and Data Survey volumes on media and markets, and Dun and Bradstreet. Local secondary sources include state, county, and city census figures; commerce analysis; business indices; Chamber of Commerce research; and the Federal Reserve Bank summary of activity. Secondary data provide a portrait of a market's buying power, population, housing, commercial activity in various product and service categories, and general demographics. Computer data bases available through commercial services allow rapid gathering of secondary data from a wide variety of sources. Some newspapers utilize such data for editorial purposes as well; for instance, as a service to its region, the *Rapid City* (South Dakota) *Daily Journal* annually updates a 10-page summary on the Rapid City area.

Two forms of primary research dominate newspaper work: the market survey and the focus group. The survey employs established techniques and careful sampling to gather information by telephone, mail, or face to face from a large number of people representing a market cross section. In 1979 the American Society of Newspaper Editors commissioned a major national survey of newspaper readers, which suggested a variety of reader needs, among them more local coverage. Three Sigma, a national newspaper market study released in 1981, provided advertisers with a number of readership measures (as discussed in Chapter 1) beyond the net paid circulation for 124 daily and 89 Sunday papers through a survey of 54,000 respondents.

Focus group interviews typically involve 8 to 25 carefully selected people who are led through a discussion of specific topics by a trained moderator. To aid subsequent analysis, the interviews are often tape recorded. Focus groups have provided insights on how people use their time and how they perceive various media. Results are then integrated with information about life-style and attitudes. The *Minneapolis Star and Tribune* used focus group interviews to discover how readers used their time on Saturday and Sunday as part of a study on a weekend newspaper to replace the Saturday and Sunday editions.

The two market research methods—survey and focus groups—can be combined in more elaborate studies with far-reaching implications. A series of 10 focus group interviews commissioned by the *St. Paul Dispatch and Pioneer Press* was combined with 1600 individual surveys to establish the market data base for long-range planning and to identify overlooked markets. Both contributed to understanding the changing newspaper market, one through in-depth conversations of a few people, the other through limited conversation with a wide range of people.

Marketing does not view customers as a large, undifferentiated group. Rather, grouping customers into different market segments depending on their needs and desires is a major premise underlying the marketing approach to customer satisfaction.[19] From this perspective, a company's customers comprise a series of homogenous groups, each distinctive from the other groups in basic ways. For newspapers the task becomes studying the customers to identify segments of readers according to their needs and desires, which newspapers can fulfill. Demographic data provide points of similarity among readers and nonreaders, such as income, education, occupation, residential area, age, marital status, hobbies, use of nonworking time, and other measurable traits tending to correlate with audience segments. For example, young, single, college-educated professionals living in apartments tend to want similar things from a newspaper.

For limited purposes customers can be viewed by the frequency with which they buy or read the newspaper, whether by segments or as an all-inclusive group, whether advertisers or readers. Circulation workers most frequently categorize customers by their purchase traits: daily and Sunday, daily, Sunday only, single copy, or nonsubscriber. Circulation records for the Audit Bureau of Circulation describe circulation by area or

FIGURE 3.1   In a campaign targeting different readership groups, blue collar workers received special attention. Courtesy The Journal Company, Milwaukee, WI.

type and can guide marketing efforts to reach one or more sets of customers—for example, by encouraging emphasis on converting single copy purchasers to subscribers. However, such functional groupings are too inclusive to serve as market research segments. Similarity of life-style, attitude, or some other combination of needs and desires linked to newspaper purchase and reading forms the core of market segments.

Customer Needs and Desires

Customers consciously decide to purchase the newspaper through subscription or single copy methods, whether daily, on Sunday, or occasionally. Whatever the frequency, these purchase decisions reflect an attitude toward the newspaper and its ability to meet their own needs and desires. The needs and desires that move humans have been the subject of extensive research in psychology and other social sciences, and these findings have been applied to the way newspapers fit into people's lives. The typical American newspaper has evolved over three centuries into a complex package of material that seeks to fill the needs and desires of a wide range of people, from chess enthusiasts to car fanciers, whose primary need (and reason for buying the newspaper) may not be the latest information from Washington or Rome or any other political capital.

FIGURE 3.2   Malls have become an important gathering place where newspapers help pass the time and guide shopping decisions. Courtesy The Journal Company, Milwaukee, WI.

The entire newspaper is the product people buy, making the entire newspaper subject to market research. Advertising material attracts a significant readership by filling readers' needs. For some readers, advertising content is more important than the editorial or sports page, the comics, or the lead story.

FIGURE 3.3   In mass transit stations, like the Toronto subway stop, newspapers
find a large audience which may use the newspaper for privacy during the
commute as well as a source of topics for discussion at work.
Courtesy the *Toronto Star*.

Marketing management underscores the relationship between the future of newspapers and adaptation to changing requirements of the public. While the press has been the topic of extensive comment and research, readers and potential readers have been only sporadically studied and then only in small, local situations. Instead, the scholarship has concentrated on journalism, politics, and newspapers as institutions. The major and notable exception, the Newspaper Readership Project, began in 1977 as a series of national studies funded by the American Newspaper Publishers Association (ANPA) and the Newspaper Advertising Bureau (NAB). Over a five-year period, the project conducted 36 research projects under the direction of Leo Bogart of the NAB; the results of these studies have appeared in *Journalism Quarterly*, *Newspaper Research Journal*, and *Public Opinion Quarterly*.

These national studies identify major social trends and patterns affecting reading habits and potential readers, but they do not fully explain the dilemma faced by a particular newspaper whose market differs from the national situation. Because a newspaper must adapt to conditions existing within 20 miles of the main office or at most within a region, national studies provide no more than a backdrop, a pattern of information that possibly leads to a clearer understanding of the local problems. Combined with local studies of customers, these national results allow newspaper managers to understand their local readers in the context of American society and note their temporal relation to trends: in the forefront, in the middle, or at the end of cultural changes.

Research on why readers use mass media has found that media satisfy dozens of psychological needs, which can be grouped into the following five major categories:[20]

1. Cognitive needs related to knowledge and understanding, such as news and editorial opinion

2. Affective needs related to aesthetic, pleasurable, and emotional experience, such as enjoyable feature articles, photographs, or human interest accounts to which readers can relate

3. Intrapersonal integrative needs related to gaining confidence, stability, and status, such as self-help articles, material reflecting the reader's values, or advice columns

4. Interpersonal integrative needs related to contact with family, friends, and the world, such as articles that form the basis for conversation (sports or fashion) or business discussions

5. Escapist needs related to easing tension, such as cartoons, crossword puzzles, and light features

In developing marketing plans and designing circulation sales campaigns, the circulation manager needs to know that this research does not mean people buy newspapers for mysterious, hidden reasons rooted in their childhood. Rather, newspaper purchase and use represent a conscious decision, whether habitual or new, made by someone with a particular goal in mind. Knowing what those goals are aids circulation sales. People constantly choose one medium over another hoping to fulfill the needs listed above, but not all these decisions involve a purchase. Television viewing, for example, may be a simple attention decision.

Consumer behavior research provides a variety of models linking the various elements of a purchase decision in ways that allow managers to study their own success and failure with the public. The buying decision process and buying behavior are psychologically complex and beyond the scope of this text. However, research has established that people choose to buy or read newspapers for at least one of the following reasons:[21]

1. To keep informed about the world situation

2. To help make decisions about public affairs

3. To provide fodder for social discussions

4. To feel connected to the outside world

5. To obtain tangible information of practical use
6. To reinforce existing beliefs and find out what others believe
7. To provide relaxation and entertainment

These motivations denote readers' uses for newspapers and the gratifications they receive from reading, but they do not apply evenly across all demographic groups or at all times. Critical to any understanding of customer needs and desires are those factors that separate readers from nonreaders. Knowing the differences helps focus marketing efforts on both retaining present readers and gaining new ones, thereby affecting the overall marketing plan.

As part of a multiple-phase study, the Catholic Press Association examined the motivations of those who purchased and read the 165 Catholic newspapers and 368 Catholic magazines.[22] Like their institutional peers and commercial counterparts, the Catholic publishers found they needed to understand the needs of their member-readers in order to halt declines in circulation and readership. They also turned to the characteristics of their present readers, former readers, and nonreaders.

Characteristics of Readers

While 89 percent of Americans read a newspaper at least once a week, only 47 percent read one daily, usually skipping Monday or Tuesday, when readership is lowest. Research found a 20 percent decline in daily newspaper readers, meaning a reduction in the frequency of reading but not its total abandonment. For over a decade nonreaders comprised 11 percent of the population; in the same period, readership did not increase in any important demographic group.

The people who read less often are most likely full-time homemakers, white blue-collar workers under 35 years of age, and the less educated of all ages living in suburbs and central cities of smaller metropolitan areas. This generalization, based on national data, is but a rough sketch of the problem, a broad portrait. The demographic traits accounting for most of the difference between readers and nonreaders are: age, education, income, marital status, race, community size, mobility, and orientation to news.

Age Age is important because it directly measures the reader's likely activities and interests; and it indirectly measures other key demographic variables linked to it, such as career development, income, freedom from responsibilities, mobility, community involvement, and opportunity to

TABLE 3.1
Percentage of Daily Readers by Age[23]

Age	Read Yesterday
18–24	55%
25–34	59%
35–44	68%
45–54	70%
55–64	73%
65+	67%
18–49	61%

Source: 1985 Simmons Market Research Bureau

read. The percentage of frequent newspaper readers rises with age. At the upper end, particularly among elderly retirees, it may reflect reduced opportunity to obtain the information from coworkers, social contacts, or elsewhere as well as increased time to read. Table 3.1 profiles readership among various age groups.

Age is a complex variable because differences in reading may also reflect the attitude toward newspaper reading developed during childhood, adolescence, or early adulthood. A serious question that marketing raises is whether the present 25- to 29-year-olds will read newspapers as frequently in 20 years as the current 45- to 49-year-olds.

Education Education directly measures literacy and indirectly measures likely interest in current events, social status, occupational level, and income. College graduates are more likely to have white-collar or professional careers in which news and opinion are the currency of conversation; they are less likely to watch television. Education must be paired with age, because a 60-year-old high school dropout, like many of that generation, may have worked to support his family in the Depression and even a high school graduate may never have been able to attend college. Table 3.2 correlates readership habits with education.

Education data immediately raise the question of what the subjects mean by reading. For one, reading "yesterday" may mean looking at the cartoons and sports scores or supermarket ads. Because these data come from self-reports, that is, the interviewer accepts what the subject says, both education and readership may suffer from the "halo effect," which is the tendency of people to put themselves in the best light during interviews. Nonetheless, the relationship between education and readership is clear and powerful—the higher the educational level, the more people read the newspaper.

Household Income Income measures the ability to purchase the newspaper and the likelihood that the major breadwinner will need newspaper information for social or workplace conversations or for success at work. As Table 3.3 shows, income is significantly related to reading at low-income levels.

Marital Status Marital status directly measures stability within the community and indirectly measures stability of life-style, particularly when linked to age. The considerable difference in readership between the

TABLE 3.2
Average Daily Readership by Education[24]

Education	Read Yesterday
Some high school or less	49%
High school graduate	66%
One to three years of college	70%
College graduate	78%

Source: 1985 Simmons Market Research Bureau

TABLE 3.3
Average Daily Readers by Household Income[25]

Household Income	Read Yesterday
Under $10,000	48%
$10,000–$14,999	59%
$15,000–$19,999	63%
$20,000–$24,999	63%
$25,000–$34,999	66%
$35,000 and over	75%
$50,000 and over	80%

Source: 1985 Simmons Market Research Bureau

married or widowed and single or divorced reflects life-style and time at home. The former tend to spend more time at home, indeed to own homes. The recently divorced, struggling through a difficult change in life, often move as an effort to adapt; or they face financial hardship greater than income levels would suggest. Table 3.4 correlates readership and marital status.

Community Size　Community size, which is the population of the place of residence, has some bearing on newspaper readership, particularly if the community is a small city of 25,000 to 50,000. Cities this size lead all others in percentage of frequent readers, possibly because they are large enough to require a newspaper for information but intimate enough to have local news as a constant topic of discussion. Smaller communities can survive on word-of-mouth news; larger communities become fragmented into neighborhoods and suburbs. Many metropolitan suburbs fall into the 25,000 to 50,000 population category. Table 3.5 illustrates the strong relationship between readership and community size in this category.

TABLE 3.4
Average Daily Readership by Marital Status[26]

Marital Status	Read Yesterday
Single	60%
Married	68%
Widowed, divorced, separated	57%

Source: 1985 Simmons Market Research Bureau

TABLE 3.5
Average Daily Readership by Community[27]

Community Type	Read Yesterday
Metropolitan Central City	69%
Suburban	67%
Nonmetropolitan	53%

Source: 1985 Simmons Market Research Bureau

Other Marketing Factors   The effects of *race* on marketing involve complex problems, including the recent waves of immigrants from Southeast Asia, Central America, Mexico, and Puerto Rico; segregation's legacy of inferior education; and the socioeconomic effects of substandard literacy. Race involves unemployment or underemployment, low income, alienation from the political structure, high mobility, family instability, and limited need for newspaper content as the currency of conversation. While 68 percent of whites are frequent readers, only 54 percent of nonwhites fall into the same category. The historical roots of this problem appear in a study of black Americans. In contrast to 82 percent of whites who recalled newspapers in their homes when they were 11 or 12 years of age, only 66 percent of blacks could recall one.[28] Blacks are more than twice as likely to rely exclusively on television for their news. A further problem is geographic: Nonwhites tend to fill the inner cores of metropolitan areas, where newspaper delivery has been abandoned or payments must be in advance to resolve carrier robberies and nonpayment. The result is low penetration.

Mobility   Mobility is the frequency with which people move from residence to residence, thereby measuring the degree of attachment for either a community or dwelling unit. Frequency of readership declines with increased mobility because community attachment and home ownership provide powerful motives for reading local news. Mobility is particularly prevalent among young singles; 48 percent of people in their late twenties moved out of their original metropolitan area and home county between 1970 and 1975. In some apartment complexes dominated by young singles, turnover reaches 20 percent per month and more. Elderly move as well, as the Sunbelt communities well know; but they tend to remain frequent readers despite seasonal migration. The "snowbirds" become residents of two cities, which increases their need for newspapers. Mobility may also interact with geographical differences in reading. Frequent newspaper reading is strongest in the Northeast (79 percent) and North Central (75 percent) areas and weakest in the South (62 percent) and West (67 percent).[29]

Another marketing factor, *orientation to news*, begins with childhood and can be thought of as family background: parental interest in newspapers, parental attitudes, and life-style. Newspaper subscriptions run strongest among families with children at home, reflecting more limited entertainment options, greater interest in local school politics and taxes, and home ownership. Family members, particularly parents, have a greater interest in community affairs and more reason to remain at home. This orientation to news carries forward to children as they mature. Of those who had newspapers in the home when they were children, 67 percent subscribe to at least one newspaper, and 70 percent are frequent readers.[30] Only 49 percent of those who as children didn't have the newspaper at home subscribe, and 56 percent read a newspaper regularly. Clearly, an orientation toward newspapers in the family affects children's subsequent reading attitudes and habits. Family orientation reflects several other demographic traits, principally parental income, education, social status, integration within the community, and interest in the content of newspapers. Because frequent newspaper readers tend to discuss current events with friends and family members, they establish a model of social and intellectual behavior for their children that includes heavy newspaper reading.

Multiple Newspaper Readers and Nonreaders

Marketing research provides information about two distinct groups whose profiles allow greater accuracy in planning: multiple newspaper readers and nonreaders. Multiple newspaper readers, who read at least two newspapers per day, have diminished as newspaper prices have increased. Those who remain tend to be older; college graduates; more affluent; voters; locally active; and heavy consumers of magazine, radio, and television information. In short, they live a life heavily dependent upon news and information.

Nonreaders are the opposite: young, less educated, lower income, nonwhite, single or divorced. They do not read for any of the following reasons:[31]

Just not interested: 30 percent
Not enough time to read: 22 percent
Receive all necessary news from radio/TV: 12 percent
Delivery problems: 12 percent
Paper costs too much: 10 percent
Buy copy at newsstand/read someone else's: 9 percent
News too depressing: 4 percent
Never been asked to subscribe: 4 percent
Dislike newspaper's editorial policies: 3 percent

This portrait was clarified by a *Los Angeles Times* study of dropout readers who said they had no time to read. For one group, the increasing size of the newspaper was so psychologically intimidating that they felt guilty about the stack of unread copies. "Cancellation for these members

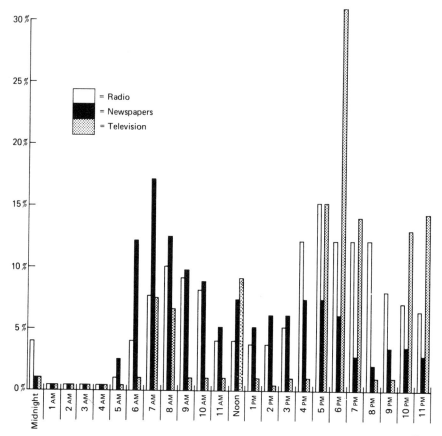

FIGURE 3.4   Percent Exposed at Each Hour to Newspapers, Radio, TV[33]

was a means of alleviating guilt," the study concluded.[32] Others said reading required too much concentration and effort, unlike radio and television; they preferred predigested news.

Customer Use of Media

Competition for reader time and attention from radio and television was studied from several perspectives in order to determine how these media fit into readers' lives. A chronological approach appears in Figure 3.4.

As the graph shows, newspaper reading tends to be somewhat more evenly spread across the day than radio or television attendance; but it competes with radio for morning time and with television for evening time. Because it measures total audience attention, this graph provides only a rough sketch. It doesn't, for example, portray those who listen to the radio or watch television while reading the newspaper; nor does it indicate what content readers seek in radio or television. Furthermore, this graph does not distinguish by demographics. Nonetheless, this profile of media use illustrates the nature of competition among radio, television, and newspapers.

Several related findings clarify the portrait of newspaper usage during the day in competition with broadcasting. Only 53 percent of the public read morning newspapers before lunch, and 15 percent read them in the evening. By contrast, 62 percent read afternoon newspapers before dinner, and 12 percent read them the next morning. The publication hour and distribution efficiency affect these patterns, but a small group read newspapers the morning after publication. Does that mean the readers obtain their news late? It seems not. Radio news is the first news source of the day for 43 percent of the public, newspapers first for 35 percent. The 22 percent for whom TV is the first source tend to be in lower income and education groups.[34] One fourth of the public receives news from all three media daily; 29 percent use a single source. Recent research points to a sharper differentiation, indicating that newspapers remain the dominant regular source of news, while television falls far behind as a regular source.[35]

A key question remains: To what extent does competition from radio and television decrease use of newspapers? Competition from television has contributed to the decline in the number of households purchasing more than one newspaper, but it has not replaced newspapers as a news source. To the contrary, newspaper circulation has risen most in cities where TV news show ratings are highest. Circulation losses for evening newspapers have been heaviest in cities where evening news ratings have dropped the lowest. In some markets, news in any medium faces serious problems. Those who listen to broadcast news are more likely to be frequent newspaper readers (or vice versa; frequent newspaper readers are likely to hear broadcast news as well). Those who watch television news spend more time with newspapers than those who watch very little. The marketing conclusions drawn from these findings are as follows:

1. Fundamental life-style traits affect all news media, whether print or broadcast.

2. Americans seem to have an expandable capacity for news, making use of all media rather than excluding some.

3. The results do not make newspaper managers sanguine, for

broadcasters compete with newspapers for advertising, not just audience.

While they retain a major role in the information-seeking behavior of most Americans, newspapers still face difficult challenges, particularly among three market segments: blacks and Hispanics, women, and the adult population under 30.[36] In each group, the values and interests are changing rapidly enough to warrant constant attention. Each major segment can be subdivided by education, income, occupation, residential area, and other demographic variables in trying to solve these marketing problems. The dilemma for circulation managers is balancing the needs of these readers against the needs of other audience segments and all those needs against the professional judgment of the journalists. As a daily product, a newspaper has multiple opportunities to approach the smaller segments' needs while retaining the traditional function of voicing the community's common concerns. The need to learn steadily about a newspaper's segmented readership is one of many reasons why marketing and marketing research will continue to play a major role in the future of newspapers.

In serving editors and publishers, market research has measured how well newspapers have fulfilled their role as consumer products, which may not directly measure how well they fulfill their public service role in a democracy. A large body of research provides greater understanding of the relationship between newspaper content and readership and the editors' perceptions of the customers for whom the newspaper is designed.

The Newspaper Itself

From a marketing perspective, research on the newspaper itself has been dominated by studies of typography, readability, materials, content analysis, and advertising/editorial ratios. As a group these studies focused on narrow technical questions: How many words will fit if another typeface or size is used? What typeface seems easiest to read? How wide should a column be for easy reading? What newsprint standards do the presses require? What political positions did the newspaper take between 1960 and 1972 on the Vietnam War? Research studies traditionally have not examined the *business* of newspapers nor have they addressed the larger questions raised by a marketing perspective because they were exclusively product centered.

One of the first efforts to gather different kinds of information about newspapers was through the now-defunct Circulation Promotion Research Center, a joint venture of the International Circulation Management Association and the Inland Press Association. Established in the late 1960s, the center generated the first survey data on newspaper carriers and district managers. With the assistance of Belden Associates, a research firm that has studied broadcast and newspaper audiences for 40 years, the center surveyed sales and promotion efforts and reported its findings in regular bulletins. When this effort merged with the Newspaper Readership Project, newspaper product research developed rapidly beyond the traditional readership studies into an examination of various relationships between newspaper content, editors, readers, and related market conditions.

However, readership studies continue to dominate research on newspapers because they provide demographic data of value to advertisers and marketing staff and because they offer a means for understanding the local newspaper market. At their simplest, readership studies provide demographic descriptions of the readers and the relative popularity of content either for specific items (an article or ad or feature) or for type (comics, classified ads, sports, etc.), page, or section. More complex studies go beyond simple descriptions to analyze how various audience segments move through the newspaper, the relationship between readership of one item and readership of other items, and the content types appealing to specific audience segments.

In the typical readership study, subscribers and single copy purchasers are asked either to go through an issue of the newspaper with the surveyor and note what they read and the sequence of reading, or they are given a list of articles, regular features, advertisements, and other elements and asked to note those which they read. At the root, readership studies describe how the product is used by readers and identify the role each content item has in the overall appeal of the newspaper. Such studies have been a staple of newspaper research since the 1950s.

An expansion of this approach for a national study was examination of the newshole, that is, the space devoted to editorial content, either as the number of full pages per week or as a percentage of total page space and its relationship to readership. Every newspaper has a break-even percentage, or the minimum amount of advertising necessary to support editorial content. Because they have more total pages and more advertising, larger newspapers devote more weekday pages to editorial content: Newspapers over 100,000 circulation average 26 pages; newspapers under 10,000 circulation average 10 pages of news. Yet on a percentage basis, the opposite image appears: Newspapers under 25,000 circulation use 49 percent of their page space for news, while those over 100,000 use about 37 percent of their space for news.[37]

Newspapers that gained readers, whether morning or evening, had the greatest increase in both the number of pages devoted to news and the percentage of space devoted to news. Conversely, those that lost circulation devoted less page space to news. But because the number of pages is set by advertising linage and advertising linage is affected by circulation, the relationship is more complex than it first appears. Rising circulation makes it easier to sell advertising and increase the newspaper's size; falling circulation reduces the newspaper's appeal to advertisers. Nonetheless, the link between circulation and newshole is strong.

Children, for whom newspapers, radio, television, magazines, and comic books are major media and upon whom the future of newspaper circulation rests, comprise an important market group. Research found that most children as young as six years of age knew some of a newspaper's content, as Table 3.6 shows.

The data show that children use newspapers for entertainment then change their reading behavior and perspective on newspaper content as they mature. Other studies of children and youth have examined use of newspapers in school, parental discussions about newspaper content, and a wide range of elements that might explain or affect subsequent newspaper reading. The data all suggest that ongoing research remains essential, because each generation experiences media differently. Both the media and the social environment of prospective readers changes continuously, thereby altering the relationship between youngsters and newspapers from childhood through young adulthood.

Exploring reader attitudes toward newspapers in general, without reference to specific content, offers a different perspective on readers and their relationship to newspapers. Such studies proceed by seeking reader reactions to highly positive and highly negative statements representing common observations about newspapers, for example, "I like to get my news from the paper because I can pick it up or put it down whenever I want," or "The news in the paper is stale; by the time I get it I know just about everything I'm interested in." A national market study found that 83 percent of readers agreed with the first statement and 81 percent disagreed with the second. The ability to control when, what, and how much news will be read seems extremely important. Other factors readers strongly endorsed were familiar organization permitting easy access to desired news, predictable delivery or purchase time, and range of news stories unavailable on TV. Obviously, attitudes toward the newspaper reflect experience with the local product, so they will vary from market to market.[39]

Other marketing studies on the reader relationship to newspapers detail the type of paper readers would assemble, given the chance (it would be similar to the one they receive, but with more advice on best food buys, health, nutrition, home maintenance, religion, letters to the editor, travel, and fashions); how a newspaper could more readily fit into their life-style; how it could increase its appeal; and the like. In all of these studies a skilled market research distinguishes between what subjects *say* they would do and what they are likely to do.

These findings and others more specific to the local market led many newspapers to make revisions in the 1970s to adjust to their readers. The *New York Times* changed typography, added new sections, and revised its image of subscribers. The *St. Paul Pioneer Press and Dispatch* totally revamped the newspaper and developed special weekly sections to meet its market. The *Herald-Telephone* in Bloomington, Indiana, a university town, adjusted both the editorial content and the subscription packages to fit the life-style and residential cycle of college students. Newspapers moving from afternoon to morning publishing cycles did so only after substantial market research into reader needs and desires.

The key questions remain: Why do readers purchase newspapers, and why do nonreaders avoid them? The answers lie in both national trends and local market situations, as reliable readership studies demonstrate.

Newspapers as Businesses

Research on newspapers as business enterprises comes from the professional associations and individual newspaper companies. In 1977 the Inland Press Association mounted a study on small newspaper economics to provide a well-researched baseline for publishers. ICMA studies circulation methods and costs for various activities, similar in kind to studies conducted by the associations representing editors, advertising managers, personnel managers, operation managers, and fleet supervisors. With costs spiraling, many newspapers studied their operations to wring out inefficiencies and questionable methods. For example, cost control research identifying each newspaper's value raised questions about circulation practices that generated large numbers of return copies.

Research has found that no matter what the local market conditions, small newspapers spend relatively more on administration and mechanical departments, and large newspapers spend more on circulation and raw materials. The reasons are not complex: Administrators become a higher percentage of the work force as the size of the newspaper decreases because the number of administrative roles does not diminish steadily with the size of the work force. Large newspapers have larger page counts and circulation, leading to economies of scale not available to small newspapers. While reducing mechanical costs, size requires paper and ink in abundance. Further, larger metropolitan newspapers face major distribution problems in reaching outside the immediate community to the distant suburbs and county seats.

As Table 3.7 illustrates, administrative overhead decreases as a portion of costs with rising circulation, but newsprint and ink costs rise with increased circulation. The largest newspaper can afford circulation sales staff and other administrative support and can spread the cost over a large circulation base. However, wastage from unsold copies increases with each single copy outlet; larger newspapers simply have larger single copy operations. Circulation costs rise slowly with increased circulation.

Such research helps newspapers assess their resources and anticipate cost changes when circulation grows or decreases, and it provides benchmark figures for comparison. The latter is perhaps most important for independent, privately owned newspapers.

Journalists themselves became research subjects in the 1970s, when scholars tried to discern how newsroom decisions were made and to

TABLE 3.6
Children's Familiarity with Newspaper Content by Age Group[38]

Newspaper Content	6–8	9–11	12–14	15–17
Sports	17%	44%	58%	52%
Comics	39%	47%	45%	37%
General news	21%	26%	25%	35%
Classified advertising	6%	12%	18%	26%
Local news	3%	11%	18%	22%
Social news	6%	11%	18%	19%
Advertising (general)	12%	18%	19%	18%
Weather reports	6%	18%	18%	17%
Front page	2%	7%	8%	14%
Horoscopes	1%	4%	7%	14%
Accidents, disasters	15%	16%	14%	13%
Personal advice	1%	6%	11%	12%
U.S. news	4%	7%	16%	11%
Foreign news	1%	6%	13%	11%
Movie ads	4%	12%	16%	10%
TV & radio listings	5%	14%	9%	9%
Editorials	—	3%	6%	8%
Puzzles, games	6%	5%	4%	4%

TABLE 3.7
Newspaper Costs by Circulation Sizes, 1976[40]

Department	5,000	25,000	75,000	200,000
General administration	36%	30%	27%	23%
Mechanical	21%	19%	18%	15%
News-editorial	15%	14%	14%	13%
Advertising	10%	9%	8%	7%
Newsprint, ink	10%	17%	22%	28%
Circulation/distribution	8%	10%	12%	13%
TOTAL:	100%	100%	100%	100%
Total average expense:	$400,000	$2,350,000	$8,500,000	$27,000,000

analyze journalism as a profession. These studies found that journalists were not representative of the population at large in significant ways. They were better educated, less traditional, less religiously inclined, less socially involved, and better paid than the average reader, making it difficult for them to understand how the audience reacted to newspaper content.[41] Thus, journalists have lost touch with the reality of their readers' lives. Several books analyzed the internal organization of newsrooms and the definition of news that resulted from the decision-making system.[42]

Advertising Product Research

Advertising product research is a newer field of study than market and newspaper research; it is also more complicated and more expensive.[43] Product research provides advertisers and manufacturers with data on the acceptance or sale of specific products or brands and its relationship to the customers whom the newspaper and advertiser share. Product research was a staple of newspapers until sophisticated national advertising research provided manufacturers with rigorous data on brand acceptance in local markets.

Traditional consumer analyses paid panels of consumers to track their purchasing habits in diaries, listing brands purchased, place of purchase, prices, and related traits. Combined with data from studies on shopping center customers, general consumer patterns, and established market patterns, these analyses provided powerful insights for local merchants as a service of the newspaper. For example, the marketing manager of the *Minneapolis Star and Tribune* sets a merchant's sales history, target customers, and goals against the *Star and Tribune*'s consumer data base and produces a unique market study. With graphs depicting sales cycles, demographic distribution, and the rest, newspaper representatives confer with advertisers to discuss the sales curves. The result is a product research study that allows the newspaper to demonstrate its role in reaching customers. In one instance, a study demonstrated that a clothing store was in the wrong shopping centers for its target customers.

MARKET PLANNING

The marketing research findings come together in the final marketing plan, which guides each newspaper department's activities in a coordinated effort to achieve specific goals. The two dominant traits of all marketing plans, systematic planning and integrated management, can be formalized through interdepartmental marketing committees or through market planning by department heads and top executives. Variations in the marketing perspective can be seen in three distinctly different marketing approaches from the *Toronto Star*, the *Toronto Globe and Mail*, and the *Minneapolis Star and Tribune*.

Toronto Star

The key to market planning at the *Toronto Star* is an action-oriented plan with three main segments: (1) the situation assessment, (2) issue identification, and (3) strategic thrusts.

The situation assessment analyzes the marketplace and the *Star*'s role in it, relying heavily on market research and direct experience. For example, a target market focus study conducted by the *Star* among adult women in Toronto provided basic readership information; data on the purchasing power of female *Star* readers; and identification of light, medium, and heavy use of specific products by these readers. Such data aided the advertising sales component of the marketing plan. Data on the needs and desires that newspapers could fulfill for this population provided another component of the situation assessment.

Identification of key issues flows from the evaluation of readers' needs and desires. The *Star* measures its success in terms of share of the market, reflecting the competition with two other dailies. The key issue is addressing this specific market segment in order to increase the *Star*'s share of female readers in specific age, educational, income, or occupational groups. Having identified the issue, the plan moves to strategies for improving the *Star*'s share in precisely defined segments. These segments can be defined by single or multiple demographic traits (all women; single women age 18–30; professional women age 25–50 living in key areas of the circulation zone; or adult females of all ages in households with more than $20,000 annual income).

The strategic thrusts in product planning, promotion, pricing, delivery, and service that increase penetration in the target segment become part of the overall market plan. Each action plan includes a principal objective, a brief project description, an assignment of responsibility for the plan to specific department heads, and a specific time schedule. For example, the circulation manager may be charged with devising a bonus plan aimed at increasing subscription sales in households within the target area, while a feature editor devises new content appealing to adult females in the same area and the advertising manager develops a program to increase linage from advertisers interested in this segment. As a result, the marketing group brings together department managers in developing action plans from the outset. The primary strength of this approach is a series of working documents that define the company's strategic developments and each department's role. Such integrated management combines the marketing concept with line and staff structure to take full advantage of both.

Toronto Globe and Mail

A different approach is used across town, where one individual heads both the marketing and circulation departments of the *Globe and Mail*. Marketing begins with the premise that circulation is a product to be planned as carefully as the newspaper's layout. As Canada's business daily, the *Globe and Mail* has national marketing problems beyond the stiff competition of the Toronto market, which means planning requires precise definition of location and demographics.

The marketing plan is based on an up-to-date analysis of the competitors' market plans and a forecast of marketplace action. Such planning cannot be reactive, that is, responding only to strategic thrusts from competitors; it must be proactive, anticipating competitors' moves and implementing plans to neutralize those efforts. Competition in this view embraces not only newspapers, but also broadcasters, direct mailers, and shoppers.

Adaptability underlies the *Globe and Mail* marketing plan, so that it can rapidly take advantage of changes in any market across Canada and solidify circulation in Toronto when it has promotional funds. Promotional expenses are product investment for the *Globe and Mail*; thus, income fluctuations determine the level of promotional activity.

With a national marketing plan, the costs of administering rapid, unplanned growth become an important element, lest the newspaper gain too much unprofitable circulation. Cost-efficient orders are one of the ingredients in the market plan. Another is allocation of delivery expense to subscribers, including those in Toronto.

The *Globe and Mail* marketing plan focuses on locations for circulation growth in keeping with its unique content. A major metropolitan daily without national circulation may prefer to absorb higher costs to obtain orders in demographic or geographic groups that major advertisers find powerfully appealing, simply to outflank competitors. Appropriately, the *Globe and Mail* approach fits the customers, as good marketing plans must.

Minneapolis Star and Tribune

The *Minneapolis Star and Tribune*'s circulation marketing plan focuses on specific target audiences. The plan begins with identification of the market variables the newspaper controls (price, promotion, sales, collection, and product) and over which the newspaper has no control (seasonal trends, weather, and the economy). Once objectives have been defined, managers analyze existing practices and requirements. Then short- and long-term circulation goals are set.

Step 1: Management Defines the Strategic Objectives

1. The target audience is defined by some combination of geography, demographics, and psychographics.

2. The newspaper's resources (dollars and people) are precisely defined.

3. A time schedule with review dates and completion date is defined.

4. A percentage circulation increase is set for the required impact, either in six-month averages, quarterly averages, or one-day counts.

5. The policy and operational constraints on methods, e.g., contests, systems, product revisions, and the like, are defined.

Step 2: Market Diagnosis

The goal of market diagnosis is to identify the cause for deviation from acceptable or desired circulation levels of a specific target group. The methods include consumer research on customer needs and desires, circulation studies of existing market conditions for the product, historical trends, and recent changes in any component. The key questions in the step are as follows:

How satisfactory is our present single copy and home delivery service?

Does the product serve community interests?

Do our sales and promotion efforts achieve sufficient reach and frequency?

What is our current pricing for each type of service (home delivery, single copy, motor route, mail)?

How do our product, price, service, promotion, and sales efforts compare with the competition's?

How do the market factors in the area under study compare with those in similar areas?

What are the historical circulation and population trends in the target area? How do they compare with other areas?

Have there been any changes in orders, circulation, service, price, product, or collection procedures by our company or any competitor? If so, what are they and when did they occur?

This thorough field analysis should suggest potential solutions and strategies that need to be discussed and tested in a small area to verify the most likely causes of deviation from expected circulation results. Following market testing, the identified causes lead to development of an action plan and strategic objectives.

Step 3: Marketing Plan Development and Implementation

The plan confirms management's objectives and constraints developed in the first step and identifies the appropriate strategies and tactics. A market plan outline might look like the following:

Desired Impact	Strategic Area	Tactics
Short-term circulation gains	1. Sales	Blitz/phone sales/carrier/direct mail/ etc.
	2. Promotion	Sampling/local newspaper awareness
Long-term circulation gains	1. Product	More local coverage/special sections/other
	2. Price	Discounts/premiums/90-day guarantee/adjust single copy price but not home delivery
	3. Service	Offer choice of porch or tube/add routes/add racks/improve carrier service —tube to door

—mail to tube
—rack to door for apartments
4. Collections Begin office billing for apartments
and high turnover areas

The fully developed market plan then goes to top management for approval and modification. After implementation, it is monitored for performance through regular reports and milestone reviews.

MARKETING AND CIRCULATION

As the preceding material demonstrated, circulation plays a major role in marketing, which integrates company activity around fulfilling customer needs and desires. The standing tasks of circulation departments—sales, delivery, service, and collection—cover several functions explicitly named in the basic marketing definition. Moreover, because circulation workers deal directly with customers on a daily basis, they can provide ongoing feedback from the field and help reshape market plans to accommodate customers. Properly linked to other departments' activities, a circulation department can identify problems before they become serious and monitor the acceptance of product, prices, promotion, distribution, and servicing activities.

While lacking the precision of scientific research, circulation information provides impressions from customer contacts, which in the aggregate aid research interpretation by providing a reality test. The goal of market research is accurate portrayal of the world "out there" to newspaper management, and circulation work takes place "out there" on a daily basis. Some newspapers have formalized the system by having circulation workers notify editors of all content reasons given in subscription cancellations or refusals. Those who have adopted a marketing management philosophy have developed marketing committees of circulation, advertising, editorial, promotion, and production supervisors. The marketing approach to newspapers adds some new tasks and emphasizes the importance of traditional circulation activities in content planning, pricing, promotion, sales, and service.

Content Planning

In the most immediate sense, content planning belongs to editors and advertising managers who control the daily content. From a marketing perspective, content planning involves identifying target markets and preparing products appropriate to them. In this sense, content planning requires the expertise of circulation, production, promotion, and perhaps accounting people. Each unit provides unique expertise on some facet of the product and market.

Circulation's perspective, derived from long experience with customers and the precise marketplace geography, goes beyond considerations of subscription sales, delivery, and collection to aspects of the target market, delivery, and product acceptability. In the marketing approach to content planning, circulation has a strong role, although clearly a secondary one.

Pricing

Price increases immediately affect circulation figures, but the effects may diminish in six months to a year. Research on circulation and price increases found that, among large circulation newspapers, price increases produced circulation losses 74 percent of the time. Between 1973 and 1975 newspapers raised their prices by 26 percent and sold 2.5 million fewer copies daily for a net loss of 4.5 percent.[44] The largest loss was in duplicate readership, that is, households purchasing several newspapers. The effects, nonetheless, were significant.

Discount offers that cut subscription prices also lead to serious circulation losses over the long term. As discussed in the next chapter, a universal principle of pricing is that discount offers create rapid increases but long-term instability by developing an expectation of discounted prices and by debasing the core of paid subscribers.

Wholesalers are the newspaper's customers in some situations; they purchase the newspapers from the publisher and sell to whom they will. Wholesale pricing generally involves incentives for additional sales and rewards for longevity and past sales success, as well as actual costs of materials and delivery, resulting in contract negotiations over price. Pricing in this situation reflects the relationship that the newspaper wishes to develop and the amount of profit it is willing to share with contractors. Legally, the newspaper can only suggest a retail price to contractors, which complicates marketing plans.

Price sensitivity requires that circulation managers help develop pricing strategies in the marketing plan in order to accurately project revenue and evaluate costs. Three managerial practices that aid circulation include: (1) exchanging pricing information with circulation directors of noncompeting newspapers in the region and of similar size elsewhere, (2) closely studying pricing research supported by the ICMA, and (3) balancing circulation and revenue in planning any market strategy involving pricing. Simply passing increased costs along to readers does not yield profitable growth. In competitive situations, the problem is compounded by a competitor's maneuverability and the likelihood of a price war. In general, the economically stronger newspaper can set a lower price to keep a competitor financially hamstrung; but in a battle between equals, direct price competition can financially exhaust both competitors or reduce their financial ability to adapt in other ways to the market.

Promotion

Promotion includes a variety of activities that bring the newspaper content or image to the public mind through advertisements, public activities, or press conferences and releases. Promotional methods may address a specific problem or issue, create or sharpen the newspaper's image in the community, or directly couple with sales activities. From a marketing perspective, promotion is essential to increased sales.[45] Combined with marketing, promotion fits into a planned strategy for appealing to target markets and maximizing sales. In a planned approach, circulation sales efforts interact with a wide range of promotional approaches. Indeed, the promotion unit may provide sales tools, art service, and related aids to the circulation unit in order to closely tie promotion and sales. This area is more fully detailed in Chapter 5.

Sales

Two standing assignments of circulation departments are sales functions: selling new subscriptions to irregular readers and selling as many single copies as possible to people who do not subscribe or cannot be economically serviced.[46] Enmeshed as it is in sales, circulation benefits from marketing in a variety of ways. Ultimately, the success of circulation sales efforts depends on the acceptability of the newspaper's content: The more it meets the readers' needs, the more enduring its relationship with the customer. Experiments with special products, target market appeals, and direct mail come from the relationship between marketing and circulation. Variations in sales techniques for different types of efforts and different age groups reflect a marketing approach.

Sales figures also measure the effectiveness of marketing plans because the final test of customer satisfaction is the exchange of money for product. Given adequate promotion and effective sales efforts, weak response indicates the market plan must be revised to accommodate unexpected elements. The first step, of course, is explaining the weak response. Conversely, strong sales demonstrate the effectiveness of the market plans. Sales will be discussed more fully in Chapter 5.

Distribution and Service

Distributing newspapers to subscribers and single copy outlets or to wholesalers, and customer service in the form of redelivery of missed or damaged newspapers, fielding complaints about employees or delivery, and adjusting bills are among the standing circulation assignments. Maximum newspaper distribution is the focal point of the whole newspaper effort, making it the crucial marketing function for circulation.

Changes are working their way through distribution systems; such changes include special free newspapers for nonsubscribers, carrier delivery of magazines and other goods, experimentation with alternate vehicle fuels, and leased transportation equipment. Major metropolitan newspapers revise their distribution territory in order to reduce unprofitable circulation as part of market planning, and marketing research offers insights into delivery times and printing cycles.

Service fits with distribution as a means of maintaining customers. Circulation service studies, whether formal market research or informal managerial surveys, provide an important element in the marketing program for they monitor customer satisfaction. The goal of such studies is to enable circulation supervisors to pinpoint delivery problems and their causes before they drive away subscribers. Long-range market plans generally incorporate service studies as part of the effort to satisfy customer needs and desires. Service, along with distribution, is covered in Chapter 8.

The development of computerized circulation information systems (CIS) has linked customer service and distribution and enabled newspapers to monitor carrier service and to speed recordkeeping on subscribers and single copy outlets. By integrating a number of delivery and service records, circulation information systems have enabled newspaper managers to develop marketing plans for Sunday-only subscribers, former subscribers, and nonsubscribers. These systems have become essential to large newspapers' distribution control by tying daily starts and stops to pressruns and enabling immediate response to subscriber requests. Through CIS, large newspapers can identify each subscriber by name, address, telephone number, and customer history; monitor performance at the route, district, and zone level; provide sales leads for new efforts; and identify delivery by ZIP code or voting precinct or ward. For marketing, these elements can be combined with demographics to develop precise marketing plots of an entire market. Coupled with focus groups studies, the CIS data lead to much more precise images of the customers. Computerization will be fully discussed in Chapter 10.

NOTES

1. Elise Burroughs, "Modern Marketing Makes Its Mark," *presstime* 3, 12 (December 1981): 9.
2. Jon G. Udell and Gene R. Laczniak, *Marketing in an Age of Change: An Introduction* (New York: John Wiley & Sons, Inc., 1981), 5.
3. Martin L. Bell, *Marketing: Concepts and Strategy* (Boston: Houghton-Mifflin, 1980), 6–8.
4. Ibid., 7.
5. Phillip Kotler, *Marketing Management* (Englewood Cliffs, N.J.: Prentice-Hall, Inc., 1984), 61.
6. Derek F. Abell, *Defining the Business: The Starting Point of Strategic Planning* (Englewood Cliffs, N.J.: Prentice-Hall, Inc., 1980), 13–17.
7. E. Jerome McCarthy and William D. Perreault, Jr., *Basic Marketing: A Managerial Approach* (Homewood, Ill.: Richard D. Irwin, 1984), 46.
8. Elise Burroughs, "Planning Seen as Key to Unlocking Growth," *presstime* 3, 8 (August 1981): 7.
9. Don C. Seitz, *Joseph Pulitzer* (New York: Simon & Schuster, 1924), 214.
10. Burroughs, "Planning Seen as Key to Unlocking Growth," 8.
11. Leo Bogart, *Press and Public* (Hillsdale, N.J.: Lawrence Erlbaum Associates, 1981), 43. This volume is Bogart's summary of two decades of readership work conducted under his supervision by the Newspaper Advertising Bureau, Inc. for the Newspaper Readership Project. The data comes from 28 different studies conducted between 1961 and 1980 and privately circulated among member sponsors in the newspaper industry. The data in this chapter are drawn from these private reports, but for easy access citations are to the figures used in *Press and Public*, except where more recent figures are available. *Press and Public* is crucial reading for anyone who wishes to understand the several aspects of newspaper readers, markets, editing, and circulation.
12. Jon Udell, *The Economics of the American Newspaper* (New York: Hastings House, 1978), 48.
13. Ibid.
14. Edward A. Linsmier, "The '80's: Marketing/Promotion," *presstime* 2, 1 (January 1980): 27.
15. A project coordinated by the American Newspaper Publishers Association, it studied newspaper readers and nonreaders in an effort to develop methods for increasing circulation by adapting newspapers to the audience.
16. Bogart, *Press and Public*, 252.
17. Charles Lehman, "A Survey of Circulation Managers" (New York: Newspaper Advertising Bureau, 1979). This research report was prepared by Response Analysis Corporation and circulated to subscribers of the Newspaper Readership Project.
18. Herbert Williams, *Newspaper Organization and Management* (Ames: Iowa State University Press, 1978), 418.

19. Kotler, *Marketing Management*, 22.

20. Elihu Katz, Michael Gurevitch, and Hadassah Haas, "On the Use of the Mass Media for Important Things," *American Sociological Review* 38, 2 (April 1973): 164–181.

21. Everette E. Dennis and Arnold Ismach, *Reporting Processes and Practices: Newswriting for Today's Readers* (Belmont, Calif.: Wadsworth Publishing Company, 1981), 41.

22. George Gallup, "U.S. Catholics and the Catholic Press" (New York: Catholic Press Association, 1980). The five volumes of research in this study span four years.

23. Simmons Market Research Bureau, Inc., *1985 Study of Media & Markets* (New York: Simmons Market Research Bureau, Inc., 1985), 2. For further discussion of the underlying concepts, see Bogart, *Press and Public*.

24. Ibid., 5.

25. Ibid., 8.

26. Ibid., 17.

27. Ibid., 32.

28. Bogart, *Press and Public*, 75.

29. Ibid., 59.

30. Ibid., 100.

31. Ibid., 62.

32. Times-Mirror public relations department correspondence with author, Sept. 16, 1983.

33. Newspaper Advertising Research Bureau, *"The Daily Diet of News: Patterns of Exposure to News in the Mass Media"* (New York: Newspaper Advertising Research Bureau, 1978), 14, 24, 35.

34. Ibid., 117.

35. Lawrence Lichty, "Video Versus Print," *Wilson Quarterly* 6, 5 (Special Issue 1982): 49–57.

36. Bogart, *Press and Public*, 255.

37. Ibid., 143.

38. Thelma Anderson and Albert Gollin, "Children, Mothers and Newspapers" (New York: Newspaper Advertising Bureau, 1978), 14.

39. Bogart, *Press and Public*, 129.

40. Inland Daily Press Association, "Study of Costs of Operation for Daily Newspapers" (Chicago, Ill.: Inland Daily Press Association, 1978), 18.

41. See, for example, John Johnstone, Edward Slawski, and William Bowman, *The Newspeople* (Urbana, Ill.: University of Illinois Press, 1975); Everette E. Dennis and Arnold Ismach, "A Profile of Newspaper and Television Reporters in the Metropolitan Setting," *Journalism Quarterly* 55, 4 (Winter 1978): 739–743; Stuart Schwartz, "Inner Directed and Other-Directed Values of Professional Journalists," *Journalism Quarterly* 55, 4 (Winter 1978): 721–725; and Michael Burgoon, et al., "Newspaper Image and Evaluation," *Journalism Quarterly* 58, 2 (Spring 1981): 411–419.

42. See, for example, Chris Argyris, *Behind the Front Page* (San Francisco: Jossey-Bass, Inc., 1974); Herbert Gans, *Deciding What's News* (New York: Pantheon,

1979); Leon Siegal, *Reporters and Officials* (Lexington, Mass.: D.C. Heath, 1973); and Gaye Tuchman, *Making News* (New York: Free Press, 1978).

43. Williams, *Newspaper Organization and Management*, 427.

44. Bogart, *Press and Public*, 42.

45. Linsmier, "The '80's," 27.

46. Leo Bogart, "Circulation: The Key to Successful Newspaper Marketing," address to the International Circulation Managers Association convention, New York City, 21 June 1982. See also three other monographs by Leo Bogart: *Circulation Department Practices* (New York: Newspaper Advertising Bureau, Inc., 1980); *Circulation: Key to Successful Newspaper Marketing* (New York: Newspaper Advertising Bureau, 1982); and *Fifteen Case Histories in Circulation Management* (New York: Newspaper Advertising Bureau, Inc., 1982).

CHAPTER

4

Promotion and Circulation Sales

Promotion and sales, although closely related components of an overall marketing strategy, differ in purpose, function, and strategy. The purpose of promotion is to create and maintain accurate public information and impressions about the company and its products. The purpose of sales is to maintain the present customers and develop new ones in an exchange of money for the product or service.

Promotion functions through a wide variety of public contacts ranging from sponsorship of civic events and advertising campaigns to internal communication and creation of sales campaigns and materials. Internal promotion generates unity, loyalty, and understanding among a newspaper's employees and their families. External promotion, on the other hand, is aimed at a newspaper's customers—both readers and advertisers. External promotion, the focus of this chapter, is the broad-scale effort to create a favorable sales environment by establishing awareness among noncustomers and solidifying the relationship with customers. All successful promotional efforts generally aid sales by increasing product identification, name awareness, and corporate image. Newspaper promotion broadly defined merits a book in itself; this chapter limits discussion to newspaper promotion as it applies to circulation sales, unless otherwise indicated.

From the public's perspective, a coordinated promotion and sales effort presents the clearest portrait of the company, the newspaper, and the reasons for reading it. This is accomplished through image advertising, product advertising, and traditional public relations activities. However, coordination of promotion and sales efforts requires planning among three departments: advertising, circulation, and promotion. Often, editorial is the fourth unit involved. Uncoordinated efforts produce a weak, confusing portrait of the newspaper, but even the confused and hazy image created by uncoordinated promotion and sales efforts can increase sales simply by raising awareness of the newspaper or curiosity about its contents. Most newspapers have found that ongoing promotion is essential in the contemporary newspaper market to hold present customers and gain new ones. In marketing-oriented newspapers, promotion remains a vital link between the overall marketing strategy and sales, whether of advertising space or newspapers.

WHAT IS PROMOTION?

The word promotion has several connotations, ranging from the broad notion of publicity to specific techniques like discounts and from unscrupulous flamboyance to skilled product advertising.

The irony of newspaper promotion, as Edward Linsmier, former executive director of the International Newspaper Promotion Association, pointed out, is that although newspapers play a major role in the promotional efforts of other companies, they fail to promote themselves to either their public or employees. Few newspaper employees, let alone members of the general public, can define the role of the free press in a free society. Even journalists are poorly informed about the newspaper business.

The size of promotional budgets points up the problem: In 1980 very few newspapers allocated even 2 percent of their total budgets to promotion, research, public relations, and community service. The newspaper space purchased by broadcasters exceeded that which newspapers used for self-promotion.[1] Broadcasters are not the only newspaper competitors who promote their services using newspapers; cable systems, direct mailers, shoppers, national newspapers, and outdoor advertisers all compete with newspapers and promote their services to the public at large or their target markets. Although they derive 70 to 80 percent of their revenue from advertising, newspapers do not recognize the need to promote themselves.

For newspapers, external promotion can be defined as any identifiable effort on the seller's part to persuade buyers to accept the seller's information and store it in retrievable form.[2]

Elements of Promotion

The following four separate components stand out in the definition of promotion:

1. An identifiable effort by the seller
2. Persuasion of buyers
3. Acceptance of information
4. Storage of the information so that it can be recalled

Each of these steps bears strongly on the overall promotional strategy.

Identifiable effort implies that the newspaper takes positive, active steps to project an image and provide information to the public. The absence of promotion does not mean the public receives no information or forms no image; it means the newspaper has no control over the information and image. Identifiable efforts include the full range of advertising and public relations activities. An example is a promotional campaign built around a slogan and featured on billboards, radio and television spots, posters and flyers, and in-newspaper advertisements. Special events, employee speeches to civic groups, or sale of promotional products (mugs, T-shirts, posters) can be specifically linked to the theme. Apart from special campaigns, newspapers actively promote their image by supporting charities, local improvement projects, and related activities that fit the newspaper's image.

Persuasion of buyers means that a newspaper appeals to reason and emotion to reach its promotional goals, which may include changing, affirming, or creating opinions. In other words, the newspaper increases public knowledge, counters inaccurate impressions, and redefines its own image through persuasive techniques. This persuasion can be direct, as in an advertising campaign, or indirect, as in cosponsorship of civic projects and consistent public relations activity. It always seeks to influence the public's opinion, even if it induces no immediate action. The buyer includes those currently buying the newspaper and those possibly buying it in the future; these buyers can be grouped by their media use, media behavior, or demographics; or they can be an undifferentiated public.

Acceptance of information is the result of successful persuasion. Acceptance implies that the persuasion has been successful, but also that the message itself appropriately addresses the entire audience or a targeted segment. Both the message content and the presentation style must contribute to acceptance, the content by being forthright and important to the audience, the style by fitting the audience's interests and abilities and the medium's characteristics. Note that the public accepts the seller's information but does not commit itself to action, making promotion substantially different from sales.

The information accepted by the public includes specific facts, ideas, and impressions that inform the people about newspapers in general, the newspaper in the local community, the newspaper industry, the newspaper company, or a specific newspaper. The facts relate to the newspaper content (columnists, special features, news achievements, or advertising coupons), to newspaper services (classified ads, coupons, home delivery), to the people and processes (editors, reporters, executives, carriers, news flow, printing techniques), to the community's acceptance of the newspaper (readership figures, endorsements), and to the price or value. The ideas embrace broad concepts like democracy, news judgment, an informed public, the First Amendment, or freedom of the press, or narrower concepts like local investigative efforts, the newspaper's concern for good local service, or the newspaper's self-defined role in the community. The image is that of the newspaper (your window on the world), its staff (your watchdog on government, your sports experts), or the company (an information expert). Overall, promotional information includes whatever the company decides is valuable and necessary for the public to know and feel about the newspaper.

Storage of information so that it can be recalled means the promotion must be structured for recall and be but one of a series of efforts to bring the newspaper and public together. This step underscores the long-term character of the informational relationship, which may subsequently link with promotional efforts; circulation sales campaigns; public speeches by executives; special news ventures; or innovations in content, design, or services. Here, too, the information includes facts, ideas, and images, but particularly those designed for easy recollection and reference. The memorable slogan around which a large promotional campaign develops is one aid to recollection. Redesign of the newspaper logo or nameplate offers an opportunity for creating a memorable redefinition of the newspaper by linking it to a strong visual device. In coordinated marketing efforts, the sales campaign relies on this recollection of information.

Purposes of Newspaper Promotion

Paul S. Hirt, a nationally recognized expert on newspaper promotion, used the concept of the "whole newspaper" as the basis for promotion. The "whole newspaper" includes every form of content and service tailored to the needs of the local market.[3] From this perspective, newspaper promotion takes the following forms:

1. To relate the newspaper to its various missions, to its changing market, and the array of competitive media

2. To seek out untapped areas of editorial, advertising, and circulation potential, and to create and coordinate "total newspaper" programs to extend the newspaper's services to these areas

3. To isolate, dramatize, and advertise current values that make the newspaper worthy of reader appeal

4. To help coordinate all departments in decisions affecting the selection of goals and strategies to achieve them

Together, these four roles make newspaper promotion primarily responsible for internal and external communication and put promotion at the service of other units, particularly advertising, circulation, and editorial. In the first role, promotion crystallizes the self-definition for the company and the public. Part of this process develops from marketing strategy, and part of it reacts to the promotional efforts of other media. In the second role, promotion studies aspects of the newspaper that, through promotional efforts, could improve circulation, advertising sales, and editorial interest as well as public understanding of the newspaper's service. Market research and internal evaluation provide data for these promotional efforts, resulting in a formal public relations and advertising effort. In the third role, promotion produces product advertising that informs the public or reminds them of ways in which the newspaper can please them and be useful. Here, promotion acts as an in-house advertising agency. The fourth role places promotion in service to other departments, providing knowledge and skill for specific sales campaigns and other marketing efforts.

These roles mark newspaper promotion as a complex set of tasks involving internal and external communication, public relations, advertising, and publicity. Not surprisingly, about 80 percent of newspaper promotion professionals consider themselves both marketers and promoters. The promotion role dominates on smaller papers (under 100,000 circulation), while the marketer role dominates on larger newspapers.[4]

The Promotion Department

Promotion tasks require artists, copy writers, and public relations and advertising experts, whether employees or professional consultants. The newspaper's size determines the number of people to be hired specifically for promotional work. In a small newspaper promotion may be one of several responsibilities borne by each department head. In a larger newspaper, the advertising department and the circulation department may have their own artist and promotion specialist who comprise the promotion team, leaving internal and external public relations tasks to others.

Promotion departments tend to be tiny. On newspapers under 100,000 circulation the typical promotion staff comprises four people; those over 100,000 circulation employ an average of seven promotion people.[5] In addition, newspapers of all sizes may purchase public relations and advertising services from outside agencies, either for part of a project or for an entire campaign. Outside contracts can prevent overworking the newspaper staff, provide special media expertise (radio, television, outdoor ads, multimedia shows), and provide a fresh perspective on the newspaper and its market.

Promotion departments most often report to the chief executive officer (publisher or president), a general manager or executive vice-president, an advertising director, or marketing director. Very few promotion managers report to the circulation manager; but on a day-to-day basis they work more regularly with circulation managers than with any other department or executive, with advertising directors ranking second and editors ranking third.[6] Others with whom promotion managers work include the publisher or general manager, marketing manager, art depart-

How to spot the truly knowledgeable Bulls fan.

The fan on the left isn't just screaming his head off. He's offering an informed commentary on the game, based on the sound, timely statistics, in-depth analysis, and behind-the-scenes insight you get when you read Chicago Tribune Sports.

Chicago Tribune

A great city deserves a great newspaper.

FIGURE 4.1

FIGURE 4.2

FIGURES 4.1 and 4.2   These powerful advertisements were part of the promotional efforts for the *Chicago Tribune* (left) and the *Central New Jersey Home News* (above). The Home News promotion announces a new Monday section and aims to convert single-copy buyers to subscribers. Both ads are part of larger campaigns promoting a number of special sections or features. Courtesy *Chicago Tribune, Central New Jersey Home News* and INPA.

ment, sales director, market research department, and classified or retail advertising manager.

PROMOTIONAL EFFORTS TIED TO CIRCULATION

How promotion departments contribute to sales of national, classified, and retail advertising; assist marketing research and the news staff; provide internal communication; and project the company image is less important for this text than how promotion contributes to circulation efforts. On the broad scale, every promotional effort aids circulation by making the newspaper familiar to nonsubscribers and reinforcing the purchase decision of present subscribers. More specifically, circulation benefits from such promotional activities as carrier promotion, sales promotion, product advertising, and the Newspaper in Education (NIE) program.

Carrier and Sales Promotions

Carrier promotion comprises recruitment, training, and retention, a particularly troublesome set of tasks when the carriers are youths and the climate imposes difficult winter delivery. Booming economic times increase the problems, whether the carriers are youths or adults. More will be said of these activities in Chapter 8, but the promotion department plays a major role in encouraging carrier applications through advertising campaigns and rewarding good carrier performance through public recognition. The promotion department may also produce training manuals, slide shows, and other materials.

Sales promotion links promotion and circulation departments in developing and implementing subscription sales campaigns. The goal of such campaigns is to increase circulation or to prevent cancellations following price increases, strikes, or product redesign.

A hybrid form of promotion, sales promotion includes

> those marketing activities other than personal selling, advertising and publicity, that stimulate consumer purchasing and dealer effectiveness, such as display shows, and exhibitions, demonstrations, and various nonrecurrent selling efforts not in the ordinary routine.[7]

Essentially, sales promotions comprise a one-time project, production, or offer designed to bolster sales. A sales promotion may link selling with the company's broader promotional efforts; but it typically includes such devices as rebates, games, point-of-purchase displays, bonuses, brochures, and similar attention-getters, making it seem like advertising.

The sales promotion sets increased sales as its primary goal and aims at short-term effects; it is not necessarily part of a strong promotional effort. Promotion, in general, sets an informational relationship with the public as its primary goal and aims at long-term effects.

Product Advertising

Product advertising can be part of the marketing plan but independent of circulation sales campaigns. The purpose of such advertising is to announce new content, contributors, or services; to highlight elements that appeal to target groups; or to inform the public about the range of content and services the newspaper provides. Virtually everything and everyone connected to the newspaper can be part of product advertising: news features; syndicated services; special sections; standard sections and departments; local columnists and personalities in the newsroom or the press room, in circulation, or in the executive suite. As a regular product and service, a newspaper offers virtually unlimited topics for promotion. All product advertising aids circulation sales, whether or not it is keyed to a subscription drive.

The promotional devices that aid sales promotion and product advertising include, in addition to the major advertising media (radio, television, newspaper, and magazine advertisements), a wide range of printed materials and techniques, reflecting the range of contacts between the newspaper and its public. Some promotional possibilities are listed below.

Carrier/delivered

Flyers announcing new services or special offers
Sample newspapers for a two-week trial period with sales follow-up
Tear sheets or copies of ads promoting special features or sections

Public placards

Posters and cards for newsstands, vending boxes, outlets
Signs for trucks and company cars
Transit ads
Window decals for store outlets
Billboards

Company giveaways (or sale at cost)

Preprints of special sections or features

Sports schedules, calendars, maps
Free classified listings for the unemployed
Placemats with full color reproductions of notable page designs
Souvenir items with company nameplate, pages, slogan

Direct mail

Subscription offers to former subscribers
Offers to newly married, new home buyers
Offers to school dormitories, apartment house managers
Offers to nonsubscribers

Newspaper in Education Programs

Newspaper in Education (NIE), pioneered by C. K. Jefferson of the *Des Moines Register and Tribune* in the 1930s, has long been a major promotional effort aimed at educators and schoolchildren. The American Newspaper Publishers Association Foundation developed NIE into a major educational program with teacher education and specific, detailed curricular approaches and materials for every grade level from 1 through 12. For some newspapers NIE is the only promotional effort aimed at increasing circulation.

NIE operates on the local level as a tie between newspapers and schools; teachers learn to use the newspaper as a classroom supplement, usually in special seminars or short courses sponsored by the newspaper. The newspaper also provides teacher aids and instructional materials along with bulk rate copies of the newspaper on special delivery arrangements timed to fit the school calendar. More than 500 local newspapers, both weeklies and dailies, participate in NIE programs in the United States and Canada.

The goals of NIE are as follows:[8]

1. To help students become informed and involved citizens who can determine and guide their own destinies in a democratic society

2. To help students develop skills of critical reading, by teaching competence in newspaper reading

3. To provide educators an economical, effective, and exciting teaching vehicle for lessons in writing, history, mathematics, current events, consumer affairs, ecology, and scores of other subjects

4. To convey an understanding of the free press as an essential institution in a free society

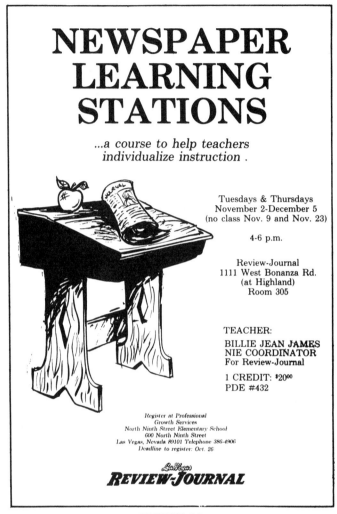

FIGURE 4.3

FIGURES 4.3, 4.4, & 4.5   Some of the most creative promotions are built around Newspaper In Education (NIE) programs. The *San Jose Mercury News* and *Las Vegas Review-Journal* ads seek teachers for NIE training workshops. The *Times-Picayune States Item* ad informs readers and offers several ways to contact the NIE Coordinator. Courtesy *San Jose Mercury News, Las Vegas Review-Journal,* and *New Orleans Times-Picayune States Item.*

Exercise Your Mind
with the Newspaper

Reading — it's necessary for survival, for enrichment, for enjoyment. But before students will read, reading must make sense in their lives!

That's why more and more educators have discovered that the newspaper is one of the most versatile and relevant tools available for teaching this vital life skill.

The newspaper presents us with information — entertainment, features, news and reports that keep us in the know. And with each new edition, we have the opportunity to learn something new.

Students of all ages and their teachers are finding that the newspaper is a valuable part of their learning experience, an up-to-date textbook that can be used to teach every subject from math and English to career education and economics.

March 3 through March 7 is Newspaper In Education Week.
The Times-Picayune/The States-Item joins the Louisiana Reading Association in its annual celebration.

Make reading The Times-Picayune/The States-Item a part of your students' training. Call Caroline Monie, NIE Coordinator, at 826-3126 for information, educational materials and low-cost classroom subscriptions.

NIE Week - March 3 - 7, 1986

The Times-Picayune
The States-Item

FIGURE 4.4

FIGURE 4.5

5. To foster students' personal growth through use of the newspaper, which provides information, entertainment, and skills necessary for modern life

In a study of NIE programs, Edward De Roche, dean of the College of Education at the University of San Diego, found six direct effects.[9]

1. It affects teachers' attitudes toward newspapers as educational tools and toward newspaper personnel.

2. It improves students' competencies in reading a newspaper.

3. It influences students' interest in subject matter and improves current event knowledge.

4. It encourages students to continue reading the newspaper as adults.

5. It improves reading development in vocabulary and comprehension.

6. It improves the quality of students' verbal interactions in the classroom.

Educators have promoted NIE as a bridge between the classroom and the real world. While NIE may boost circulation sales slightly, the primary goal is to promote the use of the newspaper. The *Orlando* (Florida) *Sentinel* combined NIE with the CBS Reading Program in a regional effort and gained about 2400 circulation per week through the school year. The program extends as far as the public schools in St. Petersburg, where a special drop of the state edition is made from the regular run. There, NIE provides circulation and competitive presence. The *Chicago Tribune* has long made NIE a major promotional activity in the schools within its circulation area. However, because NIE has overtones of competition and profits, many educators have been leery of close association with one newspaper in a competitive situation.

To reduce duplication of effort, Wisconsin newspapers pooled their resources in 1960 and established a summer course at the University of Wisconsin–Madison as part of a unified statewide NIE program. As part of the agreement, local schools were provided with the local newspaper. Harold Schwartz, then vice-president for circulation of The Journal Company, publisher of the *Milwaukee Journal* and *Milwaukee Sentinel*, said the agreement was based on the recognition that "a student anywhere in the state who learns to read a newspaper and be comfortable with it in school will continue as a newspaper reader all his life, no matter where he lives."[10] The cooperative effort enabled greater reach into the schools because school officials were no longer put off by competitive sales approaches from several newspapers. The pooled resources also allowed expansion of the program's resources, and newspaper executives demonstrated that their goal was educating young readers, not merely selling the schools more newspapers.

CIRCULATION SALES

Circulation sales activities have one specific goal: to increase the number of newspapers sold by directly stimulating purchase decisions. This call to action is what distinguishes sales efforts from promotional efforts. The target audience for these activities includes nonbuyers, irregular buyers, and regular single copy buyers, whether they live or work in the community, are passing through, or are spending a vacation there. Although everyone who can read and afford the newspaper is a potential customer, circulation sales activities focus on buyers because the major goal is increasing purchases. Increasing readership is at best a secondary goal.

This does not mean circulation sales will not increase readership or that circulation salespeople are unconcerned about readership; rather, the focus on buyers recognizes the difference between readers and purchasers and sharpens the focus of sales campaigns to those likely to purchase a newspaper, typically household heads, office managers, and businesses with visiting clientele (restaurants, physicians, lawyers, repair shops).

As highly perishable products that change daily, newspapers have mixed sales problems. Like other mass market goods, they appeal to a large, variegated audience. But unlike almost every other product, newspapers (with the exception of weekly newspapers and special sections of the Sunday newspaper) have a shelf life measured in hours rather than days or months.

Home delivery and single copy street sales have assured rapid delivery for over 300 years, with modifications for technology and local conditions; but changes in the industry and society have created unique sales conditions for each. Home-delivered subscriptions now face the problems of urban congestion; crime; and high-rise apartments with difficult access, high turnover, and population density. Single copy sales face the problems of freeway commuting, sales locations, and predictability. (These problems are further discussed in Chapters 8 and 9.) Circulation managers must devise sales campaigns that motivate their salespeople, allow supervision, integrate door-to-door and telephone sales, provide promotion, and stay within the budget. Successfully managing circulation sales requires a firm grasp of psychology, sales tactics, personnel management, and organization.

Newspaper Buying Motives

As discussed in Chapter 3, audience studies have shown that people read newspapers to fulfill several types of needs: cognitive, affective, personal integration, social integration, and escapist. But how do these psychological needs translate into the practical decision to purchase a newspaper, particularly on a regular basis? Under what conditions will people alter their buying and reading habits? These questions underlie the development of effective sales campaigns, and they are closely tied to the marketing strategy.

The spectrum of buyers includes those subscribing to help the young carrier win a trip to Disneyland, to save money by clipping coupons, or to satisfy a crossword puzzle habit. It also includes regular readers, sporadic readers, and bored airplane passengers trying to pass the time. In general, people purchase newspapers for reasons related to the content, to noncontent use of the newspaper, and to the sales techniques or sales-person's skills.

Customers who buy the newspaper for its content are generally responding to one of the five sales appeals listed below.[11] Each item includes the general thematic line that a sales appeal would employ.

1. Social acceptance. This includes news of families, neighborhood, community, organizations, sports, and other special topics, enabling people to converse with their friends and neighbors. Buying the newspaper helps you know what the community is discussing. This is particularly effective for weeklies.

2. Prestige. This includes major news stories of state, national, and international scope, allowing an individual to maintain informed conversation among people at work, particularly superiors, or to remain an expert in a particular topical area like films or politics. Buying the newspaper keeps you ahead of the pack. Big dailies have an advantage here.

3. Personal profit. Stories and features for improving one's financial status and investments or allowing advantageous spending for normal consumer goods, such as food and clothing, fall into this category. Most advertising content, including coupons, fulfills this need. Buying the newspaper saves money.

4. Entertainment or escape. Content that amuses or informs about amusement fits this group, which includes comics, movie articles, and advice columns. The newspaper brightens your day.

5. Habit. Newspaper reading is a powerful habit, stimulating continued and even increased purchase of a familiar and satisfying product. The newspaper is a comfortable and reliable old friend.

Curiosity about the newspaper will produce single copy sales but seldom a subscription. Even travelers and newcomers who purchase a few copies simply to sample the newspaper may be compelled by habit, social acceptance, and prestige. Promotional advertisements can include appeals to these motives and may combine social acceptance and entertainment appeals in featuring a sports columnist or advice columnist.

Not all purchases directly relate to content. Noncontent uses provide some sales, particularly of single copies. Studies indicate some subway commuters purchase newspapers to hide behind, that is, to protect their privacy during the commute. Studies have also indicated that some regular readers use the newspaper to isolate themselves from family members. Others may purchase prestigious newspapers for the sake of appearance, reading very little of them. Or customers may order the newspaper from a youth carrier as a means of helping a young person. Obviously these noncontent uses produce sales, and sometimes serve as the basis of a sales campaign.

Successful salespeople create sales through their ability to persuade others to a product's value or to sense and exploit other sales-producing motives, such as the simple desire to get rid of the salesperson. High-pressure sales techniques sell new subscriptions for a short time; but if the content isn't appealing, the subscriber will be a short-term customer. Some people agree to subscribe simply to avoid seeming rude or to end the sales pitch; but they typically cancel their subscription quickly, particularly if given an opportunity in a sales verification phone call.

Whatever the mix of reasons for which someone purchases a newspaper, the goal of circulation subscription sales is to entice nonsubscribers to try a three-month subscription, giving the content a chance to make its own appeal and making newspaper reading a daily routine. After 12 weeks in the home, the newspaper should be able to sell itself through its content. For single copy sales efforts, the goal is to create enough curiosity and interest through advertising to entice nonreaders to try the newspaper and to convert irregular readers to more frequent purchasers.

Subscription Sales Techniques

The need for constant sales efforts in today's newspaper markets causes some circulation salespeople to feel that they are constantly reselling the same short-term customers. The mobility of today's newspaper customers in every market, coupled with competition from other media and sources of leisure, forces circulation managers to develop ongoing sales efforts in cooperation with promotional efforts. Even managers in small towns have to mount regular sales efforts to maintain circulation penetration.

Subscription sales efforts use door-to-door canvassing, telephone sales, and direct mail. In today's complex market, no single sales approach reaches every customer group or produces sufficient circulation increase. A survey found that about three out of four newspapers with circulations over 100,000 used at least two of these sales methods. About one in six relied on a single sales approach, overwhelmingly carrier sales.[12] Carrier sales remain the stable backbone of newspaper circulation sales in general: Ninety-two percent of the newspapers studied relied on them. Door crews were used by 69 percent and telephone solicitors by 68 percent. Only 8 percent of the newspapers used direct mail, attesting to its recent application to newspapers, relatively low yield, and difficult implementation.

A study of Canadian newspaper practices produced comparable

results.[13] Carriers sold for 98 percent of the newspapers, telephone solicitors for 78 percent, and boy crews for 53 percent. Over 40 percent of Canadian newspapers used direct manager crews for door-to-door sales, a significant variation from the role of district managers in American newspapers, where they supervise carrier sales rather than sell extensively. About 23 percent of the newspapers contracted for sales crews. Direct mail and other approaches were used by 33 percent of the newspapers studied.

Door-to-Door Canvassing Door-to-door canvassing is accomplished by the carriers or special sales crews. The carriers, whether adults or youth, canvass everyone without a full (daily and Sunday) subscription on their routes. This door-to-door approach remains the most successful method of contacting homeowners. Carriers who canvass nonsubscribers or Sunday-only subscribers on the route can make the most powerful pitch because they provide the service. Also, newspaper route lists change daily; therefore, carriers know who the likely prospects and the poor customers are. In a full-blown sales contest, carriers may be limited to their own routes and districts for the first segment, then allowed to sell anywhere in the circulation zone. This strategy reflects the sales power of carriers on their own routes. However, not all carriers sell well; therefore, specially trained sales crews may augment sales efforts by canvassing intensively door to door.

Youth carriers require special training and supervision, but they offer the advantage of numbers. A newspaper using youth carriers has small routes and many carriers who, if properly mobilized, will meet the goal of frequent sales contact with every household in the community. Youth carriers also offer sales advantages beyond their sheer numbers. Emotionally volatile and energetic, they can be easily stimulated by a good motivational presentation and will hit the streets with contagious enthusiasm. At the same time, a string of rejections can quickly undermine a youth's confidence; so district managers typically organize canvassing teams of carriers. In this way, district managers can bolster sagging confidence and monitor carriers' sales pitches to locate the weaknesses.

Cash prizes motivate youth carriers less than do merchandise awards, such as basketballs, radios, bikes, watches, and jackets. Companies specializing in prizes for sales contests provide special catalogs with the merchandise most popular among specific age groups. Of course, a big trip, whether to Disneyland or London, is an ever popular and powerful motivational tool.

Youth carrier sales meetings revolve around teaching selling techniques, including the newspaper's merits and quick responses to standard buyer objections. Role-playing the sales approach proves an effective method for simultaneously motivating and educating. Another technique is the content quiz in which carriers challenge each other's knowledge of the newspaper's columnists, stories, and other content. At the root, these sales meetings provide a group mentality about selling that generates enthusiasm and the right selling attitude. However, while some young people can sell a newspaper on its merits, most can only be effective by asking the prospect to help them win a prize, an approach known as the *begging appeal*.

Adult carriers readily learn to sell the benefits of the newspaper, but they have neither the appeal nor motivational traits of youths. Adults are harder to motivate. They prefer cash incentives over prizes, unless the prizes are impressive; they, too, can work hard for a trip to the Bahamas or London. The *St. Petersburg Times*, which uses adult carriers exclusively, spends substantial time on sales training and emphasizes the *obligation* to sell that comes with the job.

Adult carriers usually have large motor routes with 200 or more customers, meaning fewer carriers to canvass door to door than with youth delivery. Moreover, many adult carriers have another full-time job and family responsibilities, which make it more difficult for them to spend many evenings canvassing. In part, the effectiveness of adult carriers depends on whether they are employees of the newspaper, paid to sell as well as deliver and collect, or independent contractors, who have far more freedom to decide whether or not they want to sell. Some newspapers have increased their emphasis on other sales approaches because adult carrier sales have been only moderately productive and other sales approaches more cost effective.

For all carriers, the key to circulation sales lies in motivating the district managers and carrier supervisors. To develop an aggressive, sales-oriented district manager force, the *Rocky Mountain News* began using a personality screening test to identify applicants exhibiting the traits common to successful salespeople. This test is also used for subsequent performance evaluations during periodic employee reviews. The *News* also encourages district managers to polish their sales skills by selling door to door at least one evening a month.

In addition to youth and adult carriers working individually or in a group, newspapers sometimes use crews for circulation campaigns. Door crews are groups of carriers, former carriers, or others trained to sell the newspaper door to door by using a variety of sales techniques and the newspaper's merits. Because they work strictly on commission, these crews use high-pressure sales techniques; but they do produce substantial sales. With a good-sized commission fee attached to every subscription sale, employee sale verification is essential. Newspapers often require cash with each door crew order, which yields 100 percent reliability but decreases the number of orders. They may also withhold payment until the orders are verified by telephone or carrier.

Common among newspapers with adult carriers or generally inadequate sales production, door crews can be internal, operating under an employee's supervision, or external, operating on contract for services. Internally supervised door crews offer the advantages of higher reliability and greater control of appearance, behavior, and sales tactics. An employee supervisor means an internal crew begins with a fixed labor cost, which expands with each additional employee. The management question is whether or not the results justify committing a full-time employee to what might be irregular sales efforts.

Outside door crews have a history of generating unreliable sales and unpredictable dress and behavior. Newspapers have far less control over the outside crews, but external or contract crews can be terminated at any time, do not require direct employee time, and provide subscriptions at a very predictable cost.

Telephone Sales Telephone sales offer access to mobile city dwellers, particularly newcomers and residents of high-rise apartments and condominiums. Small-town newspapers have found commissioned telephone solicitors valuable additions to the door-to-door sales force for reaching rural residents and apartment dwellers.

Telephone sales are not universally favored, because they create verification problems and can irritate subscribers. Telephone sales typically yield most results during early evening hours, but daytime sales efforts can be effective in metropolitan areas. Telephone sales crews, like door crews, can be either internal or external, with the same assets and liabilities. Internal salespeople normally receive a minimum salary (as defined by state and federal laws) plus commissions scaled to increase productivity. External sales personnel receive a commission only.

Random dialing, the basic telephone number generation system, involves dialing every number from 0001 to 9999 in a single prefix area (e.g., 331). Inevitably, such a system locates subscribers and unlisted numbers, so several sales strategies, such as the service check, must be devised to avoid irritation. In this system, the salesperson identifies herself or himself as a service checker for the newspaper and asks if the paper is delivered on time and in good condition. Selling begins only if the respondent does not subscribe. Telephone numbers of former subscribers also constitute a list of likely prospects.

Telephone sales rooms, known as *boiler rooms*, require experienced supervision. Control of telephone salespeople's time per sale and general presentation are constant supervisory challenges. People can be far more rude toward a salesperson on the telephone than in person, so salespeople need support and encouragement, particularly after a string of unsuccessful phone calls. Repetition can make the sales approach monotonous and ineffective within a few weeks, requiring retraining.

The *Houston Post*, which converted a contract crew to an internal one, provides extensive simulation training. Its phone room produced 1.32 new subscriptions per solicitor per hour, a respectable figure, at a cost of $3.00 per order. The *Bloomington* (Indiana) *Herald-Telephone* provides telephone solicitors with a short, simple guide to telephone sales in its area coupled with tape recorder training sessions. These include questions about specific local activities that people might like to follow in the newspaper. *Herald-Telephone* salespeople average 2.2 orders per hour at $2.55 per order. The *Herald-Telephone* manual is a model for small-town newspapers and small telephone sales crews. The *Tampa Tribune* also provides its internal telephone crew with a telephone sales manual, which is a model for metropolitan newspapers and large telephone sales operations.

Direct Mail   Direct mail selling produces far smaller circulation gains than do carrier, door crew, or telephone methods; but it has been used by large and small newspapers with cost-effective results. With a well-designed and well-written set of materials, direct mail is an inexpensive and effective method for generating subscriptions in areas where door-to-door and telephone methods have generated few results.[14]

Historically the major problem for circulation managers has been developing a prospect list; but computerized mailing lists, whether purchased or generated internally, simplify the matter. Nonsubscriber lists can be augmented with classified advertiser lists, nonrenewal or cancellation lists, marriage announcements, or any similar newspaper list; however, the lists should be culled for subscribers because direct mail to subscribers wastes postage and printed material. Apart from names and addresses, the major components of a direct mail campaign are the sales letter, an easy method for subscribing, and at least one follow-up mailing.

The sales letter is critical to direct mail success and should include the following:[15]

1.   The material must look interesting in form and words.

2.   It must be written to attract the reader's attention, interest, desire, and action.

3. The writer must use the *you* viewpoint as much as possible, avoiding an emphasis on *we* or *I*.

4. The letter should contain *one* special offer to stimulate immediate action.

The direct mail piece should include a postage-paid return envelope or postcard or list a phone number for easy reply. Many prospects lack the motivation to locate an envelope and a stamp or write a letter. A second direct mail piece should be sent to those not responding to the first letter to remind them or to offer a better reason for replying (greater discount, premium offer).

Just as door-to-door sales are measured by number of sales and telephone efforts are measured by sales per person per hour, direct mail efforts are evaluated by the percent of new subscriptions based on the number of letters mailed out. A 5 percent success rate (or 50 subscribers for every 1000 letters) is considered good for newspapers. Costs per order are calculated the same for each of the three systems: The total cost of the sales effort is divided by the number of verified subscriptions.

The *Bloomington* (Indiana) *Herald-Telephone* offered a discount of one dollar per month for a two-month subscription in one of its direct mail appeals to nonsubscribers. It yielded 11.67 percent return, an exceptionally good yield for direct mail. The first letter was followed by a second letter offering the same discount but appealing strictly to sports fans and featuring the sports columnist's photograph. It gained 5.1 percent response.

Single Copy Sales Techniques

The goal of single copy sales is to increase the number of purchases among those not buying each issue of the newspaper. This means enticing nonbuyers to begin at least irregular purchase and moving irregular and infrequent purchasers to regular, frequent buying. This consumer group, including the newcomer, the tourist or traveler, and the former subscriber, must be reached by a combination of advertising and maximum access to points of purchase.

Advertising Advertising includes all media, with generally more emphasis on non-newspaper ads. Some newspaper advertising may prove valuable, for nonbuyers are not necessarily nonreaders; however, the sales campaign should concentrate on other media, particularly radio and television.

The *Wall Street Journal* has purchased radio time, particularly in the early morning hours, to feature a compelling story and digest of interesting material from the most recent edition. Other newspapers have done the same, focusing on morning and evening driving time audiences and news programs to highlight some part of the newspaper's content. Regular radio and television presence leads the audience to identify the newspaper's ads with a particular time on the broadcast schedule. To introduce *USA Today*, Gannett purchased massive amounts of radio and television time to stimulate single copy sales at a time when it could not offer home delivery.

Outdoor Advertising   Outdoor advertising includes billboards and bus cards. While capable of only limited content, these advertising vehicles have great visual power and can be used to emphasize the sales campaign theme, create presence, and provide images of the newspaper. *USA Today* used outdoor advertising in which the blue nameplate, shaped like a press cylinder, dominated the space. The image replicated part of the television, newspaper, and magazine ads, thereby creating presence and recalling the name of the newspaper.

Point-of-Purchase Displays   These displays are either rack cards or posters. Rack cards, which are placards affixed to the vending boxes, can simply call attention to a particular story by rephrasing the headline in very large type or make a verbal sales pitch. Usually simple in design and content, rack cards catch the pedestrian's eye and raise curiosity about a particular story. Posters, on the other hand, can be hung from the roof of a newsstand, placed in the window of a retail outlet, or plastered on the wall near a vending box. Colorful and more elaborately designed posters can reinforce the sales theme or make their own appeal for readership and purchase. A lesser but essential point-of-purchase display form is the simple sign informing pedestrians and drivers that the newspaper can be purchased inside a retail outlet. Whether taped in the window, hung above the door, or nailed to the wall, these signs create sales.

Sheffield Newspapers, Ltd., in England, has a point-of-sale package that has greatly increased the public's awareness of their newspapers. This leaflet, like a small catalog, is given to all distributors and newsstand outlets. It pictures 12 different point-of-sale items obtainable from the newspaper. Some of the items are as follows:

1.   Shelf strip—a self-adhesive strip in two colors, containing a message promoting the newspaper. It's affixed to shelf edges.

2. Wobblers—specially designed mobiles for inside use. The hanging portion moves in an eye-catching fashion with any breeze or air current. A sales message is printed on both sides.

3. A self-adhesive vinyl message, in three colors, for fastening to the inside of a store window.

4. Booklite—a freestanding or wall-hung illuminated indoor sign, using only a 75-watt bulb.

5. OPEN and CLOSED sign for the store's door promoting the newspaper.

6. Litter bin—a triangular waste receptacle with newspaper promotion on all three sides.

Maximum Access   Maximum access means that anyone who wants a newspaper need not go out of his way to find one. It also means distributing 15 to 20 percent more copies than can be sold in order to supply single copy outlets with enough newspapers to prevent sellouts. More will be said on this in Chapter 9; but from a sales perspective, increasing the number of places the newspaper can be purchased decreases the number of sales lost through unavailability. The single copy outlets include retailers such as drugstores and supermarkets, newsstands, mechanical vending boxes, and newsboys. A campaign for increasing single copy sales includes possible increase of the number of points of purchase along with a major advertising campaign.

Special Offers

Circulation sales provide 20 to 30 percent of the revenue for most newspapers not locked in intense competition, which means a newspaper can afford to make a subscription more attractive by shaving the actual subscription cost and passing the cost on to the advertiser. Particularly in competitive situations, newspapers use a variety of special offers to promote sales. In the Pulitzer era, this was known as forcing sales and at times resulted in almost giving the newspaper away. Common special offers used today are discounts, premiums, money back guarantees, and games.

Discounts   Discounts are extremely successful at generating sales. Discounts are limited to subscription sales and often involve half-price offers for a few months or three months for the price of two. The important element, in the view of discount systems, is getting the newspaper into the home for a trial period in order to increase the newspaper's chance of selling itself. The discount can be taken off the price for the subscription period at the time of sale, or the new subscriber may receive discount coupons given to the carrier at the time of collection. Small price reductions for long-term prepayment, for example six months or a year, are not discounts in this sense.

The sudden burst of circulation that a discount offer brings can turn into a precipitous decline when the discount period ends. Before it died, the *Washington Star* used half-price offers to build circulation; but circulation dropped so dramatically when the offers expired that circulation fluctuated by as much as 75,000 copies, and advertisers began to question the newspaper's circulation figures. The *Toronto Star* uses its computer system to wean subscribers from the discount midway through the subscription period. The first renewal offers about a 10 percent discount; each subsequent renewal offer increases the discount until the final offer, sent with the cancellation notice, offers a 50 percent discount. Faced with two competing newspapers in Toronto, the *Star* cannot afford to lose a subscriber.

Some circulation managers oppose discounts because they degrade the newspaper and cut essential revenue as well. The complexity of the *Toronto Star* system underscores the quicksand character of massive discounting; it is extremely difficult to extricate oneself, particularly if a group of subscribers comes to expect discounts. Nonetheless, discounts remain widely used because they rapidly increase circulation.

Premiums Premiums have a century-long history in newspaper sales, beginning in the Pulitzer era in New York. While premiums do not reduce the subscription price, they involve an exchange of a gift for cash. If the gift is large enough, anyone will pay a small price for the newspaper. The advantage to premiums is that they do not perpetuate themselves; however, premiums effectively reduce circulation income and shift the sales pitch from the newspaper to some other item. Another problem is that a newspaper's low price severely limits the range of premiums that can be offered. Some involve inexpensive items carrying the newspaper's logo, historical front pages, or other graphic designs. Companies that provide newspaper premiums have sprung up to help promote this sales offer.

Money Back Guarantees These guarantees have become a popular sales offer because they do not directly reduce subscription prices. In this offer, every subscriber is guaranteed that if the newspaper proves unsatisfactory during the subscription period, it can be cancelled for a full refund. Given the subscription price, few people are motivated to seek a refund. Moreover, having received the newspaper, most subscribers would feel uncomfortable about demanding their money back. The guarantee does not have the selling power of a discount, but it aids circulation sales.

Games Games have long been a popular circulation booster, as described in Chapter 2. In essence, the games involve puzzles, hidden words, game boards, or lottery-style numbers printed in the paper. The customer with the winning solution, word, pattern, or number claims a merchandise or cash prize. A full-blown Wingo or Bingo game can cost $500,000; and if it produces an increase of 30,000 net paid circulation, the cost per order is $16.66. A major problem with games is that people will steal whole stacks of newspapers from vending boxes and newsstands in the search for winning numbers. Games must also adhere to all state and legal requirements. Beyond that, subscribers gained on games tend to disappear as quickly as those gained on discounts. The hope is that by steadily increasing the time between games, the newspaper can hold an increasing number of the subscribers on the newspaper's merits.

Circulation Sales Monitoring

Special offers signal the need to boost circulation because they create additional costs. Those not affecting the purchase price (money back guarantees and games) are added to departmental overhead as internal costs; those reducing the purchase price (discounts and premiums) become external costs. Because the Audit Bureau of Circulations closely monitors external costs, the difference is significant.

In line with its founding philosophy of making circulation figures comparable and credible for advertisers, the Audit Bureau of Circulations closely monitors sales contests and campaigns for evidence of giving the newspaper away. ABC insists that the subscriber exchange some money for the newspaper alone as proof of readership, and its standards carefully define the line between a net paid subscriber who receives an offer and the unacceptable giveaway. It is important to note that the ABC concerns itself with the individual sale, that is, the external cost, rather than the overall sales effort and the internal costs per order. If a buyer exchanges money for the newspaper, the ABC is unconcerned about internal costs.

The definition of acceptable offer flows from the basic definition of a net paid sale, which is a newspaper copy for which a customer (other than a wholesale dealer) pays at least 50 percent of the basic price for a single copy, monthly, quarterly, or annually. Any discount exceeding 50 percent of the basic purchase price produces sales uncountable as net paid circulation. The same applies to premiums: Their value cannot exceed 50 percent of the subscription price for the period.

The ABC rules set the premium's fair retail price as the wholesale price plus 25 percent, and this figure is used to determine whether the premium falls within the 50 percent rule. Printed material valued at less than 15¢ and directly related to the newspaper is not considered a premium, nor is a back copy given without requiring a subscription. With an average three-month subscription costing about $22, premiums must be valued at less than $10. Any combination of discount and premium must also fit within the 50 percent guideline.

Special rules govern the sale of combined subscriptions of morning and evening newspapers. The 50 percent rule applies; but unless the full price is collected, it is considered a forced combination, which removes net paid classification. If the prices differ between the two publications, a special formula applies to insure that at least 50 percent of the full value of each newspaper is charged.

Most circulation sales involve credit; the newspaper begins delivery without having cash in hand. The Audit Bureau regulations set a three-month limit for continuing circulation without payment. Noncollection without cancellation beyond three months removes the subscription from the net paid category. This prevents newspapers from using the unpaid subscriptions as a ruse for giving away the newspaper.

The Sales Campaign or Contest

To focus attention on sales, newspapers periodically mount sales campaigns and contests. Some newspapers have two major campaigns in the spring and fall, when circulation tends to fluctuate most. Others prefer a series of three- and four-week campaigns throughout the year, usually because their market produces smaller but regular fluctuations. Circulation managers who produce two major annual campaigns go to great lengths to find a campaign theme and stage an exciting kickoff for district managers and carriers.

Whether massive or modest, the campaign links every element to the theme to focus attention on the contest itself and its purpose: sell, sell, sell. The kickoff, the prizes, the slogan, and the promotional materials all try to maintain enthusiasm; however, the theme cannot be so elaborate as to detract from the fundamental goal, increasing sales.

Ken Davis, who has analyzed management of circulation campaigns, developed a comprehensive list of questions that summarize the complex elements in a sales campaign.[16] Davis groups the questions into 11 sequential categories, illustrating the chronological sequence, as follows:

CIRCULATION CAMPAIGN CHECK CHART

PRELIMINARY

1. Why have a contest?
2. What do we want it to do for us?
3. What specific results do we want?
4. How much can we afford to spend to get these results?

PARTICIPATION

1. How many carriers, carrier helpers and carrier substitutes are eligible to participate in the proposed contest?
2. Any other people?
3. Are the families of the carriers and any others eligible to participate?
4. Can our office force be put into the picture so that both carriers and DSMs [District Sales Managers] will feel their eyes are on them?
5. How will quotas be determined?
6. Are they fair?
7. Do the DSMs know they are fair?
8. Can we insist on the DSMs making their quotas?
9. What special care should we take to bolster any known weak spots among our carriers? After all, individual attention is absolutely necessary to group success.

TYPE OF CONTEST

1. Should it be competitive?
2. Should we use teams or groups?
3. Should we use a quota winner plan or a tournament?
4. Perhaps club offers would be best, such as trips of which there are three types—educational, sporting events and recreations.
5. Perhaps we should use merchandise, such as clothing, games or food.
6. Then again, cash might be best or honor pins, plaques and certificates.
7. Serious consideration is always given to special novelties.

BEFORE WE DEFINITELY DECIDE ON ANY TYPE OF CONTEST,
WE ALWAYS CONSIDER THE FOLLOWING:

1. Is the contest designed to bring out the best in the tail-enders rather than cater to "hot shots"?
2. Is it simple?
3. Does it give a change of pace and scenery?
4. Is it built to do a constructive, educational job, as well as make participants work harder?
5. Does it teach better ways to sell and reward those who put these methods into operation?
6. Will it "click"?

THEMES, TITLES AND SLOGANS

1. What kind of theme will we use?
2. What will we call the contest?
3. Does the theme tie in with the contest?
4. Does the theme fit our business?
5. What about the slogan?

SCORING PLAN

1. What kind will we use?
2. Is it simple?
3. Has everyone a chance to win?
4. Should we use teams?
5. Will there be a qualification contest?
6. Should there be a special reward for completing a goal ahead of time?
7. Shall we use a "spurt"?
8. How much can we afford to spend for prizes?
9. Who gets the prizes?
10. What prizes shall we offer?
11. When shall prizes be awarded?
12. Will winners be announced and prizes awarded without delay?

SELLING TOOLS AND INDUCEMENTS

1. Shall we use a special order form and selling folder?
2. Are we planning on using a subscriber inducement?
3. Is it directed at getting immediate action?
4. What kind of carefully detailed plan are we going to give the men so they can effectively sell this campaign to their carriers?
5. Have we skipped any opportunity to use showmanship?
6. Does the plan make it easy for the carrier and field man to sell a large volume of business?
7. Does our appeal to the prospect break down resistance?
8. Are our incentives and plan for action presented attractively and compelling?
9. Do we make it easy for people to buy?

ANNOUNCEMENTS AND TEASERS

1. Should we use a teaser?
2. Do advance announcements carry detailed rules with exact starting and finishing time?
3. Does it give the whole story in clear, unmistakable language?
4. Does our opening announcement tell all the rules, encourage, include personal message, list and sell awards—sell the newspaper?
5. Is our announcement sufficiently spectacular to jolt carriers into 100 percent cooperation?

LENGTH OF CONTEST

1. How long will it be?
2. Will there be ample time to properly promote it?
3. When is the best time to start?

MEETINGS

1. Are we going to fire the opening gun at a special meeting?
2. Have we planned the meeting so it will move swiftly and surely to one goal?
3. Will there be comfortable seating arrangements so that everyone can see and hear?
4. Will there be proper ventilation?
5. How about a "stretch" period?
6. Will we use charts or other visual aids?
7. Are the charts large enough for all to see?
8. Has preparation been made so that the men can take notes?
9. Will we hold any special meetings during the contest?
10. Can we get any unusual publicity?

FOLLOW-THROUGH PLANS

1. Do our follow-through plans induce progress?
2. Sell the newspaper?
3. Ask for more effort?
4. Picture the finish of the contest?
5. Will it be a series of surprises to keep it alive from beginning to end?
6. Have we arranged for progress reports to be used at frequent intervals?
7. How many mailing pieces will we use?
8. Are bulletins, letters and standings tied in so they will be received at the most favorable moment?
9. Will we write frequent, personal letters, commenting on standing and showing we are keenly aware of the rate of progress?
10. Is there a surprise in every mailing?
11. How frequently will we send progress reports?
12. Have we provided an effective check up and control system?
13. Are we reminding every man that every new subscriber added to their circulation puts more money in their carrier's pocket?
14. Does our closing bulletin make the winner feel good and the losers, if any, wish they had tried harder?

Designing a campaign begins after these initial questions have been answered. The key concerns are duration and motivation. Within the traditional cycle, the campaign may be somewhat longer or shorter according to the need for new subscriptions or the value of the prizes. For some, duration and timing remain virtually identical yearly. Motivation is the heart of the strategy; and it involves the type of prizes, amount of cash, and even staging productions for exciting and informing circulation staff. Popular prizes include cash and trips; weekly prizes might be steaks, games, and record albums.

Examples of successful sales campaigns include the following:

The *St. Petersburg Times and Evening Independent*'s "Battle of Orders" campaign, which divided carriers into teams
The *Sacramento Bee*'s 50-page prize catalog to motivate carriers for short- and long-term contests
The *Denver Post*'s "Number One at the Post" contest, which allowed everyone from carriers to department heads to earn cash and merchandise prizes

Circulation Sales Efforts Evaluation

Several standard measures test a subscription campaign's value and success: the cost per order, order production, verified orders, and retention rate.

Cost per Order   Cost per order indicates the cost of each new subscription and can be calculated for both internal and external costs. Based on daily subscriptions, Sunday subscriptions, or both, the total budget divided by the number of new subscribers yields the cost per order. Prorating for daily and Sunday subscriptions is somewhat more complicated; but if the system is designed in advance so that each new subscription is listed separately, each type of subscription can be assigned a different point value, such as 1 for a Sunday only, 2 for a daily, and 3 for a daily and Sunday.

Order Production   Order production is simply the total of new subscriptions, and it means less by itself than as a percentage of total circulation. Prior to computerized circulation information systems, it was extremely difficult to determine whether the subscribers gained in a contest were new or simply nonrenewals from previous sales efforts. Within the newspaper, order production alone can be a deceptive figure if not compared to previous campaigns and understood in the context of particular districts' penetration and demographics. An established, high-penetration district yields low production, while a rapidly growing area yields more.

Verified Orders Verified orders are those that the newspaper knows to be valid due to subscriber contact. With substantial prize money, commissions, and net paid circulation at stake, the newspaper must guard itself against dishonest carriers, door crews, and telephone solicitors. Most often a newspaper verification system will spot-check new orders from every district and salesperson. While verification of every new order can be ideal for some purposes, it is costly and offers subscribers a chance to cancel their subscription. Spot-checking effectively monitors sales. Verifiers must be taught to resell reluctant subscribers on the telephone, just as service people are taught to resell when cancellations are telephoned into the office. Some newspapers avoid the internal verification system by insisting on cash with each new subscription. Advance payment eliminates verification problems, but it seriously reduces the number of new subscriptions.

Retention Retention measures the percentage of new subscribers renewing after the initial subscription period. Without a full subscriber list, a circulation manager can only estimate retention by plotting circulation figures on a graph beginning with the campaign's first day and continuing through the normal renewal period. This system is imprecise because it assumes that nonrenewals and cancellations occur among subscribers gained during the contest. As carriers and district managers know, it is largely true but not completely accurate. Computerized circulation systems allow precise tracking of new subscribers, including correlation with service complaints and delivery errors, for a more accurate understanding.

Special Sales Problems

Special sales techniques have been developed to reach those eluding or complicating the traditional sales approaches or to limit cancellation after a price increase.

Multiple-Unit Dwellings Metropolitan newspapers face exceptional difficulty with the transiency and high security in multiple-unit dwellings. Transiency is more common to middle-priced units, and ultra-high security is nearly universal in higher-priced dwellings. Business office towers, which can offer subscription possibilities, also require a unique sales approach.

Apartment turnover rates can run as high as 30 percent per month, a rate that aggravates every phase of circulation: sales, service, and collections. For sales, identifying new tenants for limited sales efforts is so difficult that the turnover may justify monthly canvassing, which irritates present subscribers and landlords. Newspaper theft creates sales problems among subscribers, and uncollectible bad debts undermine carrier motivation. Security systems preventing entry into a lobby or central courtyard except by key exclude door-to-door canvassing. If the building manager gives the carrier a key to the complex, only the carrier can canvass; but building managers or owners' associations are increasingly refusing passkeys to youth and adult carriers. Some tenants object to the noise of delivery or canvassing. Many landlords or building managers forbid all sales solicitors, even the newspaper carrier.

The *Ottawa Citizen* has a special apartment sales unit that established business-to-business relations between the newspaper and the apartment owners and managers to resolve delivery and sales problems. The *Citizen* agrees to assume all responsibility for carrier abuses or accidents (such as a broken window). Apartment managers receive a free subscription to the *Citizen* for handing out a *Citizen* sales promotion folder to each new tenant and providing the *Citizen* with a monthly list of new tenants. The *Citizen* folder includes a direct mail solicitation and a response postcard. The carrier receives a list of new tenants and a weekly allotment of sample newspapers. At the end of the week, the carrier collects response cards and makes a sales pitch if necessary. Every returned postcard nets the carrier 50 cents. Each month the names of apartment managers who provided lists are put into a drum, and the winner of the drawing earns a free dinner for two at a high-quality restaurant. To keep up with apartment construction, the *Citizen* lists all new multiple-unit dwellings advertising in the newspaper and contacts the owners and managers. New subscription retention from this effort runs 75 percent in the suburbs and 35 percent in the city, where transiency decreases the retention prospects.

In St. Petersburg, Florida, transiency is a way of life as snowbirds flock south with the first frost to wait out the northern winter. A former apartment and hotel manager was hired to head a multiple-dwelling unit program at the *Times* and *Evening Independent*. This unit, having the power to immediately exclude door crews and carriers from buildings when managers object, has responsibility for over 123,000 households in mobile home parks, apartments, and condominiums and has produced a 51 percent penetration rate. The unit's five employees sell in nonsolicitation buildings through wine and cheese or tea and cookie parties in the community room. An editor or columnist, the district manager, and carrier make a very low key sales appeal; and four-month subscriptions are sold at half price. In other buildings, managers provide new tenants with a special package of materials, including an informational guide to services and recreational facilities in the area complete with telephone numbers, a map of the county, a mail subscription card at a 33 percent discount, a promotional flyer for the newspaper, and a tabloid apartment section with selected articles pulled from recent copies of the St. Petersburg newspapers.

The *Dallas Times-Herald* identified a unique element among apartment dwellers in its market: A large proportion of them spent their week on the road and did not wish to have home delivery during the week. So, the newspaper sells a special weekend package (Friday, Saturday, and Sunday) to apartment and condominium dwellers.

Newcomers In booming cities like Houston, newspapers face the mammoth task of making newcomers familiar with the newspaper and locating sales prospects. The *Houston Post* established a newcomer program that included a relocation seminar for Houston corporations. Completely sponsored by the *Post*, the seminar featured the following topics:

Community Identification in a Boom Town
Exploring Houston through Art and Culture
Houston Business News
Another Look at Relocation
Advertising as a Source of Information for the Newcomer
Corporate Uses of the Newspaper
Orienting the Newcomer to Houston
Tour of the Post *Facilities*

Participants in the seminar, which rapidly oversubscribed, received a sample newcomer folder, which the *Post* offered to provide at no charge for every employee being relocated to the Houston area. The folder contained a two-week sample offer, a directory to Houston, and subscription material. However, the seminar's focus was the problems newcomers face in relocation and the approaches personnel officers might take to alleviate them. Newspaper solutions were offered where useful, but the *Post* established a broader perspective in an effort to help both the corporations and their relocating employees. The *Post* also offered to send the Sunday edition (weighing up to 5 pounds) free to prospective employees and relocating employees to help them develop a feel for Houston and, of course, to identify the *Post* with Houston and vice versa.

College Students In many cities a college or residential school offers the prospect of increased circulation but also the problem of adapting to the school calendar. The *Bloomington* (Indiana) *Herald-Telephone* offers Indiana University students one- or two-semester delivery in the dorms with a premium for advance payment. The student renewal rate runs 55 percent from the first semester to the second. By tailoring delivery to the school calendar, the newspaper avoids delivery and collection problems and reduces sales resistance. Many newspapers in college towns offer half-price subscriptions to college students for a school year with advance payment. The newspaper begins the first day of classes, stops at term break, begins again the first day of the next term, and ends with commencement. The students thus receive a price break through the discount and the precise delivery times, and the newspaper gains net paid customers.

In Minneapolis–St. Paul, newspapers offer students at the University of Minnesota subscription payment through credit cards, billed either in a lump sum or monthly through the school year. Other newspapers set up major sales solicitations at registration for each semester, offering precisely timed delivery at a discount for the term, whether the student lives in a dormitory or apartment or at home.

Price Increase Cancellations   With the steady rounds of price increases over the past decade, circulation managers have developed sales campaigns called "Stop Savers" to reduce cancellations (a cancellation is known as a stop). Each price increase can cause 3 to 5 percent of subscribers to cancel, so the campaign is built around two strategies. The first is to promote renewals at the present rate prior to a price increase. The second is a combination door-to-door and telephone sales effort to reach every canceling subscriber with a renewal pitch. Carriers and district managers who hold sales receive particularly large prizes.

While internally expensive, stop saver programs with large cash and merchandise prizes have proven effective in minimizing circulation losses. When it raised the price of daily and Sunday subscription by 50 cents, the *Rocky Mountain News* mounted a "Price Change" sales campaign. The campaign began with letters to carriers and their parents from the circulation manager, specific campaign instructions for the carriers, and major prizes. Beyond stemming losses, the price change campaign produced a gain of 21,357 net paid circulation. No matter how well-designed the campaign, though, each subsequent price increase over a three-year period decreases the possibility for holding circulation even.

As a constantly challenging activity, circulation sales must be linked to regular, effective promotion for maximum impact. Placed in an overall marketing plan, sales efforts can be tailored to special target groups, whether geographic or demographic. In both promotion and sales, the critical managerial skills are planning, budgeting, motivation, control of activities and image, and regular evaluation.

SUMMARY OF PROMOTION AND CIRCULATION SALES

Promotion and sales are complementary activities that take the newspaper into the community and should be part of a marketing plan for maximum effectiveness.

Promotion is a broad activity designed to provide facts and ideas about the newspaper in a memorable fashion. Within the company, promotion addresses employees to improve interdepartmental communication, unify the efforts, and establish the basis for a well-defined image. Beyond the company, promotion uses various media to project a sharply defined image with product and image advertising, support of community events, traditional public relations methods, and especially the Newspaper in Education program.

Companies must promote themselves to remain identifiable in today's marketplace; but despite their role in the promotions of others, newspapers have been seriously underpromoted. The four major roles of newspaper promotion are: (1) to relate the newspaper to its missions, market, and competition; (2) to seek and exploit areas of untapped potential in the major departments; (3) to identify and advertise newspaper features that readers value; and (4) to help each department select and attain its goals. In a marketing program, promotion organizes all departmental promotions to ensure consistency with the overall plan.

The circulation department works most closely and frequently with the promotion manager, owing to its continuing need for carrier promotional materials. Even general product advertising and image advertising improve circulation sales efforts but more substantially if they are coordinated.

Circulation sales activities seek to increase the number of customers and put the newspaper in the reader's hands long enough so that the content will sell itself. The decline in penetration has led to studies of buying motives, such as social acceptance, prestige, personal profit, entertainment or escape, and habit. These motives, plus the available sales methods, nature of the newspaper, and nature of the market become major components in the design of sales campaigns. The techniques available for subscription sales include door-to-door canvassing, telephone sales, and direct mail. Youth carriers, adult carriers, internal crews, and contract crews offer different advantages and disadvantages, forcing the manager to select those suiting the newspaper's philosophy and needs.

Single copy sales efforts require different methods, including advertising, particularly on radio; point-of-purchase displays; and maximum access through increased outlets. All sales efforts can be boosted with discounts, premiums, money back guarantees, and games for which the Audit Bureau of Circulations has developed specific regulations. Discounts and games, which increase sales most rapidly, yield equally rapid declines when the full price must be paid or the game ends.

Each newspaper has established its own pattern of circulation sales contests, ranging from many short (3- to 4-week) ones to major (12- to 14-week) campaigns. Whether massive or minor, the contest must be designed for the available sales forces, the newspaper, the market, and the budget. The contest must also motivate the entire sales force—from youth carriers to adult telephone solicitors and supervisors. The contest is measured by the cost per order, the production of verified orders, and the retention rate among new subscribers.

Special sales techniques have been developed to increase penetration among apartment dwellers, newcomers, and college students and to diminish the circulation decline accompanying price increases, typically linking public relations and sales efforts.

NOTES

1. Edward Linsmeir, "The '80's: Marketing/Promotion," *presstime* 2, 1 (January 1980): 27.
2. Jerome B. Kernan, William P. Connermuth, and Montrose S. Sommers, *Promotion: An Introductory Analysis* (New York: McGraw-Hill Book Co., 1970), 9.
3. Paul S. Hirt, *Promoting the Total Newspaper* (Reston, Va.: International Newspaper Promotion Association, 1973), ix.
4. Jack Hines and Robert Silvy, INPA Newspaper Promotion Department Profile Study (Reston, Va.: International Newspaper Promotion Association, 1983), 14.
5. Ibid., 7.
6. Ibid., 15–16.
7. Ralph S. Alexander et al., *Marketing Definitions: A Glossary of Marketing Terms* (Chicago: American Marketing Association, 1960), 20.
8. American Newspaper Publishers Foundation, *The Newspaper as an Effective Teaching Tool* (Washington, D.C.: ANPA Foundation, 1977), 3.
9. Edward De Roche, "Newspapers in Education: What We Know," *Newspaper Research Journal* 2, 3 (April 1981): 59–63.
10. Harold Schwartz, address to the Southern Newspaper Publishers Association, Atlanta, Georgia, 29 September 1976.
11. Cyrus H. Favor, *Ideas About Circulation* (New York: American Newspaper Publishers Association, 1978), 8–9.

12. "A Survey of Circulation Operations," *Louisville Courier Journal and Times,* 1976, p. 7. This private research report was conducted for members of the ICMA.
13. Catherine Russell, *The CDNPA/CCMA 1981 Survey of Newspaper Circulation Departments* (Toronto: Canadian Daily Newspaper Publishers Association & Canadian Circulation Managers Association, 1981), Appendix A–25.
14. See, for example, Bob Stone, *Successful Direct Marketing Methods* (Chicago: Crain Books, 1979) and Robert S. Hodgson, *Direct Mail Order Handbook* (Chicago: Dartnell Corp., 1978) for more information. A short course in direct mail through the Direct Mail Association located in Chicago or a university is useful as well.
15. Herbert Williams, *Newspaper Organization and Management* (Ames, Iowa: Iowa State University Press, 1978), 225.
16. Ken Davis, *District Sales Manager Training Programs* (Columbia, S.C.: Intellexi Enterprises, 1979), 111–114.

CHAPTER
5

Circulation Within the Newspaper Organization

The historical changes in the newspaper industry—its appeal to the masses, technological developments, and changes in delivery patterns—have shaped the role of the circulation department within the corporate structure. Circulation not only provides the primary link between the newspaper and its customers, but as a revenue-producing department, it is an essential part of the newspaper's business structure.

Newspaper companies' goals and their organization to accomplish those goals form part of the corporate culture. The corporate culture, or "the way we do things around here," permeates every company; and it may be powerful enough to determine a company's success or failure. The culture is defined as

> a cohesion of values, myths, heroes and symbols that has come to mean a great deal to the people who work there. Whether weak or strong, culture has a powerful influence throughout the organization; it affects practically everything—from who gets promoted and what decisions are made to how employees dress and what sports they play.[1]

Changes in culture usually occur slowly. The corporate culture sets the quality standards by which performance is judged and establishes the basic balance between the newspaper's public service and commercial roles.

The circulation department's organization varies widely from one newspaper to another. Among other factors, the type of ownership and the company structure as elements of the corporate culture play powerful roles in establishing the parameters within which circulation departments operate. Marketplace elements affecting circulation include labor, demography, climate, geography, life-style, and competition; each factor influences decisions on how to deliver newspapers, sell subscriptions, locate single copy outlets, service customers and dealers, and collect money.

TYPES OF NEWSPAPER OWNERSHIP

Ownership more powerfully shapes a newspaper's corporate culture than any other element except, perhaps, the chief executive officer's philosophy. The competing demands from their commercial and public service roles make newspapers highly sensitive to ownership variations because the publisher or majority stockholders set the commercial and news goals of the company. Ownership policies thereby limit the range of solutions to the inevitable conflicts between the two roles. Although the chief executive officer and top managers create the profits, direct the internal allocation of resources, define the style of news coverage and the general editorial content, set the guidelines for advertising content, and establish the relation between the newspaper and its community, the owners ultimately judge the results. Through their judgments, owners maintain, reform, and redirect the corporate culture in the most fundamental area—the very definition of the purpose and character of the newspaper as a business and a public service.

Two aspects of ownership, the type of stock and the number of newspapers in the company, combine to form the four basic types of newspaper ownership. Stock is either public or private and the newspaper is either an independent or part of a group; therefore, the basic newspaper ownership patterns are the privately owned independent, the privately owned group, the publicly held independent, and the publicly held group. Each type of ownership has unique advantages and disadvantages, affecting flexibility, economy, and control in all departments.

Private ownership means the stock or shares in the newspaper are bought and sold outside the purview of the stock markets, most often in transactions between individuals. Just as the stock sales can be kept private, all aspects of the company's financial condition can be kept secret, including profitability. Stockholders decide who may purchase shares and at what price. This is a legal status with significant implications for the Securities and Exchange Commission.

Public ownership means the company's stock is traded on the open market, generally through the major stock exchanges, and is thereby subject to the financial disclosure requirements of the Securities and

Exchange Commission. One individual or family may hold the majority of the stock in a publicly owned company in order to maintain control; but all stock transactions must occur in the public arena, subject to public supervision, and anyone may purchase shares. Share prices are set by the market forces.

Independent ownership means the newspaper has no corporate ties to a newspaper in another market; it stands alone as a strictly local business. A few independent newspaper companies own morning and evening newspapers in the same market, but they remain independent of financial ties to other newspapers in other markets.

Group or chain ownership means the newspaper is one of several owned by the same person, family, or company. The terms *chain* and *group* differ only in connotation: Chain suggests corporate control of both business procedures and editorial content; group suggests central business control and local editorial autonomy.

Private Ownership

Historically, private owners have been editor-publishers like Benjamin Franklin, Horace Greeley, or William Allen White; but they also include partners, families, friends, private investors, newspaper employees, foundations, and educational institutions. To maintain control, privately held companies can require that any stock for sale must first be offered to the present owners; and they can forbid stock sales without approval of the other shareholders.

A quasi-private ownership occurs among newspapers owned by religious denominations, unions, fraternal associations, and political interest groups in that they cannot be bought or sold publicly and share the advantages and disadvantages of private ownership.

The foremost advantages of private ownership are control and financial secrecy. The degree of control varies with the amount of stock any individual possesses in relation to other shareholders. A private owner can establish any level of profitability or public service, can choose to forego profits in order to invest in new equipment or expand news coverage, or can acquire additional properties with minimal concern for the effect of such decisions on the value of the stocks. The history of American journalism runs strong in publishers who prized fearless news and editorial content over strong profits. It also includes many profit-dominated newspapers that subordinated public service to cashflow.

Private owners need never reveal the financial condition of the newspaper, except to tax officials, which is a major advantage in competitive situations. With no need to account to outsiders, private owners have full policy and fiscal control, allowing them to run the newspaper according to a uniquely personal vision.

The major disadvantage of private ownership is limited ability to generate capital. Private owners must rely on their personal financial resources, company reserves, or the loan market when improving the physical plant or expanding or paying inheritance taxes. The number of private owners has steadily declined in this century largely because the costs of business moved beyond the financial capability of private owners and because heirs are unable to maintain the success of the founders. Inheritance taxes have become the greatest problem in recent decades, forcing owners to sell the newspaper to pay the taxes when the owner dies or passes shares to a descendant.

Today most privately owned newspapers are either owned by a special interest group or are newspapers with small circulations. The Ellsworth, Maine, *American*, with a circulation of about 8000, is an example of a privately owned newspaper; James Russell Wiggin is its sole owner, as well as publisher and editor.

Public Ownership

Although some publicly held companies give the company or the stockholders the right of first refusal when stocks are sold, anyone willing to risk cash for a possible share in corporate growth and profits can be one of the owners. Shareholders also purchase a voice, however small, in the operation of the company. Public ownership provides access to large amounts of cash but also results in the disadvantages of public supervision and reduced control.

In exchanging ownership for investor money, the publicly held company can obtain large amounts of money, varying according to the rise and fall of the stock's value on the market. The Securities and Exchange Commission requirements automatically force financial disclosure and regular accounting audits by independent firms on all publicly held companies.

Concern for the unknown public stockholders is part of the corporate culture because the executives are accountable to them for policy decisions, stock value, and dividends. A publisher has less flexibility in working for a publicly held company because the stockholders, many of whom care far less about the newspaper's quality than the dividend check's size, become the judges of managerial ability. Public ownership puts a large thumb on the commercial side of the balance scale. Conversely, the capital generated by public ownership purchases improvements and increases the survival prospects. Simultaneously, public accountability may improve the effectiveness of management and insure that the company will not long suffer at the hands of incompetent business executives, whatever the newspaper's quality.

Independent Ownership

Whether publicly or privately owned, the independent newspaper measures its performance and success in only one market: its home territory. Most independent newspapers are either weeklies or small community dailies like the *Janesville* (Wisconsin) *Gazette*. Like other independent newspapers, the *St. Petersburg Times* and *Evening Independent* have but one marketplace to serve. An independent newspaper's economic fortune depends on the conditions of one locale, wedding the newspaper and community in a close relationship. The independent newspaper will be rewarded for paying close attention to its local market, although not necessarily for investigative work that makes local politicians, unions, businessmen, or popular figures uncomfortable. Whether the newspaper chooses to develop a sweetheart relationship with local power figures or a watchdog relationship,[2] its independent character forces the corporate culture to reflect local conditions. The major advantage of independent ownership is that the elements of flexibility, economy, and control rest in the local market; therefore, the newspaper can quickly adapt to local conditions.

The drawbacks of independent ownership are limited managerial and financial resources. Those promoted from within have little chance to test their managerial skills and gain experience on smaller newspapers with the same corporate culture; those hired from the outside must quickly learn the corporate culture, which can become eccentric. Financial and professional resources needed to keep the newspaper abreast of the market must come from inside the newspaper or be purchased from the outside. Outsiders, as long as they lack sensitivity to the nuances of the local market and the corporate culture, operate at a disadvantage, which can produce inadequate and erroneous decisions. Another drawback of independent ownership is the need for diversification, which has led many once-independent newspapers to acquire other newspapers.

Chain or Group Ownership

A chain or group newspaper is one of several owned by the same person, family, or company, such as Knight-Ridder, Gannett, or Thomson. Chain ownership offers several major financial and managerial advantages. Income from several newspapers allows a profitable property to offset the bad economic conditions of another market. Large chains can provide loans and financial expertise to help a floundering newspaper restructure its finances and its entire production system with the assistance of employee experts in every area.

Large chains have the resources and the need for internal management training, permitting rapid development of young talent in the corporate culture. Groups with newspapers of different sizes can use smaller newspapers as managerial farm teams for the large newspapers; this opportunity for advancement attracts people who prefer moving ahead in a large business to moving slowly in a local business. Young publishers of the Daniels newspapers in North Carolina meet regularly to discuss their business problems with more experienced publishers and the corporate executives. Knight-Ridder offers marketing courses for young managers in its Miami headquarters, and Gannett can move bright young managers among nearly 100 properties from coast to coast.

Variations of Ownership Types

Several variations of the four major patterns produce somewhat different corporate cultures. Family ownership, which dominated American media through 1900, was generally a form of private ownership. High technological costs led to public incorporation and the decline of family newspapers, either through outright sale or conversion to public ownership with majority control by the family. Federal inheritance taxes have further reduced family ownership. The *Nashville Tennesseean* passed from family to chain (Gannett) control when the heir was unable to otherwise produce $16 million for inheritance taxes, despite three years of explorations; only a chain could pay $75 million for the newspaper. A major and public fight in Louisville's Bingham family forced the sale of their *Courier-Journal* and the *Louisville Times*. Gannett bought the papers for $306.9 million in 1986. Still, family-owned newspapers include groups like the McClatchey papers of California.

Family ownership brings the promise of a strong corporate culture through several generations beyond the founder; but bankruptcies caused by inept heirs, intrafamily conflicts, and divided obsession are also found in the history of family newspapers. Some families have been able to maintain the founder's vision and managerial ability across several generations, and family control of publicly owned newspapers has permitted talented nonfamily members to lead the corporation to success.

Employee ownership embraces several different legal structures, but it creates a unique corporate culture in which the managers are accountable to their subordinates as well as to each other. Some systems limit ownership to current employees; others allow employees to keep their stock after leaving. Another system puts all stock in an irrevocable trust in which employees can purchase shares, which earn dividends and grant a voice in policies. Employee ownership on papers like the *Milwaukee Journal* and *Milwaukee Sentinel* establishes permanent ownership, strong corporate identity, and employee commitment. While not preventing the sale of the newspaper nor guaranteeing profitability, employee ownership increases the likelihood that workers will be as concerned about the future of the company as they are about their incomes. The problems of employee ownership include capital generation, employee access to shares, resistance to change from senior employees unconcerned with dividends and stock value, and inbred eccentricity.

Foundation and institutional ownership, while not commonplace, exists beyond university-owned student newspapers. The *Christian Science Monitor*, the *Houston Chronicle*, for many years owned by a charitable medical foundation, and the *St. Petersburg Times* and *Evening Independent*, owned by Modern Media Institute, exemplify this small group. If nonprofit, the foundation pays no taxes and has greater revenue to return to the newspaper for investment. As long as the controlling group remains committed to quality journalism, the newspaper has great independence and increased financial resources. Modern Media Institute, established by publisher Nelson Poynter to prevent sale of his newspapers to a chain, provides newspaper management education to the industry; and the profits support the newspapers.

THE EFFECTS OF OWNERSHIP PATTERNS

The type of ownership affects a newspaper's allocation of resources, adaptability to change, response to the local community, and possibility of expansion. While each type of ownership has specific advantages and disadvantages, in general assets and limitations can be categorized in terms of two factors: autonomous locality and developmental resources.

Effects on Autonomous Locality

Autonomous locality is the combination of two related characteristics—the degree to which decisions about the local situation can be made by local executives and the extent to which management must be concerned with the local market. Managers with high autonomous locality make all decisions, particularly ones involving major resource allocations, in response to the local market alone. Those with low autonomous locality have their decisions reviewed by corporate executives outside the local market and evaluated against conditions and needs beyond the newspaper's community.

The lack of strong locality can prove fatal to a newspaper, particularly in today's competitive market, because newspapers are intensely local products that must adapt constantly. Inadequate response to local needs can lead to failure. When Gannett acquired several newspapers in central Minnesota, it consolidated printing in a new plant in St. Cloud, a county seat. When readers learned that *The Little Falls Transcript*, a daily based in the seat of the adjoining county, was being printed in St. Cloud, they instantly felt that the *Transcript* had become a St. Cloud newspaper, whatever the news content. They shifted their loyalty to a local weekly shopper, which soon ran most of the local advertising, including the county and city legals. The *Transcript* circulation dropped 60 percent, then became a local page in the St. Cloud daily. Low autonomous locality, once known to the readers, ruined the newspaper's standing in its own community. This problem is particularly acute in smaller communities, where survival depends upon mutual support.

Effects on Developmental Resources

Developmental resources are those financial and managerial assets within the company that allow successful expansion, improvement, and adaptation, such as educational programs, cash, research, experimental projects, and technical expertise. A newspaper with high developmental resources can call on specialists already immersed in the corporate culture to solve problems or to allocate substantial funds for circulation campaigns, and it provides growth opportunities for employees.

Combined into Table 5.1, autonomous locality and developmental resources apply to the four ownership types in the following fashion: This flexibility—in the allocation of human and financial resources and in the ability to experiment with change—is a key advantage of newspapers with strong developmental resources. This table points out the balance of advantages and disadvantages accompanying each ownership pattern, making it clear why few publicly owned independent newspapers exist and why groups have come to dominate American journalism.

A publicly owned, independent newspaper has no structural advantages unless the community members own a controlling block of the stock, which enhances autonomous locality but does not increase access to resources. A publicly owned newspaper is accountable to the SEC, which can lead to a uniform accounting system but also yields some control to outsiders. Unless the local publisher has stock in the local newspaper, a compelling element in autonomous locality disappears. Top

TABLE 5.1

Degree of Autonomous Locality and Developmental Resources Affecting
Four Ownership Types

	Autonomous Locality	Developmental Resources
Private group	High	High
Public group	Low	High
Private independent	High	Low
Public independent	Low	Low

management in public groups, accountable to stockholders, will likely encourage profitability of the group, whatever the implications for a particular local newspaper. When harsh economic conditions affect one segment of the group, profitability can make it impossible for circulation managers elsewhere to promote deserving individuals or mount a full-blown circulation campaign. Such tight control severely limits a local newspaper's adaptability, and stockholder pressure emphasizes the business role over local responsiveness.

Group newspapers permit rapid advancement from smaller to larger newspapers within the group in order to develop young managers, but the system also undermines managerial response to local conditions and forces newspapers into a standardized model. Few communities reveal their innermost complexities to newcomers in one or two years, even if young circulation managers could grasp them. The interests of the group and individual manager run counter to the community's need for a knowledgeable voice in the newspaper. One response to this problem is to maintain a permanent local publisher; another is transfer policies requiring five-year minimum stays. Yet a third approach is ignoring the local situation.

The privately owned independent newspaper suffers from a shortage of developmental resources because it has no financial or managerial companions with which to pool profits and expertise. For this reason, informal associations among private independent newspapers emerged as a means of information exchange. Noncompeting private independents rely on informal relationships among themselves as an alternative to experimentation and limited expertise. Private independents tend to proceed cautiously, changing slowly and carefully in order to preserve capital. Another problem is the tendency to promote exclusively from within, limiting a company's access to bright talent from elsewhere in the newspaper industry.

Circulation management is directly affected by the ownership pattern. Group ownership can dictate procedures for circulation accounting, carrier systems, collection policies, prices, and the circulation manager's and district managers' roles. Corporate policy can control staff size and salaries; distant corporate executives can veto plans for local circulation efforts. On the other hand, the circulation manager of an independent newspaper can have the power to develop a unique circulation system, one perfectly suited to local conditions, which are the sole concern. At the same time, this circulation manager has less money for experiments and changes. Across the spectrum of circulation activities, circulation executives find that ownership plays a significant role in defining their problems and options.

INTERNAL ORGANIZATION OF NEWSPAPERS

The corporate structure contributes to the corporate culture by establishing a management style that may not be fully discernible to outsiders. The number and types of newspaper departments vary by the company's size; but whatever the size, certain tasks must be accomplished. In a newspaper the three major work categories are editorial content creation, advertising sales, and newspaper sales. Others include newspaper production, accounting, purchasing, promotion, personnel, and computer services. Given their small staffs, weeklies and small dailies have corporate culture without large-scale organization. Still, the required work is parcelled out among the available staff; and while simple, the organization is observable.

Coordination of the three major departments poses the greatest structural challenge because their distinct functions and intense professional differences carry them away from each other. Editors and reporters tend to avoid contact with advertising and circulation employees out of fear that their integrity as newspeople will be compromised. However myopic, this attitude is a professional ethic rooted in the overt control of stories exerted by advertisers at the turn of the century and reinforced by each attempt to obtain favorable coverage for advertisers. Editorial employees bristle at the suggestion that they concern themselves with advertising or circulation, and yet their product has little value if it doesn't reach readers. This attitude exists as much among weeklies and small dailies as among big dailies, though perhaps it is somewhat softened by working together in smaller quarters.

Because they served different customers and employed different types of people, advertising and circulation departments traditionally seldom interacted; however, with the growing dependence of advertisers on the total market coverage and zoned delivery that circulation departments offer, interaction is becoming more common.

The number of employees performing circulation work varies with the newspaper's size and its circulation philosophy, but circulation emerges as a separate department for newspapers with circulation above 5000. This number of subscribers justifies a separate person responsible for sales; service; collections; and supervision of the carriers, drivers, and dealers. On a small newspaper like the *Goldsboro News-Argus* in North Carolina, one person is both business manager and circulation manager; but he or she has an assistant circulation manager and supervises a number of full- and part-time employees. On a metropolitan daily, a vice-president possibly supervises a circulation unit with hundreds of employees and thousands of carriers and agents. In some newspapers, circulation is part of a marketing division or department; in others, marketing is part of the circulation unit. These variations in size and structure reaffirm the point that newspapers are local businesses guided by very different people and are highly local in nature.

As will be discussed in Chapter 7, some circulation departments take charge of the newspaper in the mailroom, where papers are bundled for shipping as soon as they leave the presses; others only take charge after the newspaper leaves the delivery truck. The truck fleet and drivers are either under the circulation department or supervised by another department head. Even the garage and vehicle maintenance employees are found in some circulation departments. If the newspaper produces its own total market coverage product, the circulation department employs writers, advertising salespeople, and a layout staff; or it simply delivers the finished product. Maintenance of subscriber and nonsubscriber files (see Chapter 10) in a computer system also sometimes falls to circulation employees. Some circulation departments increase profits by delivering magazines and free samples.

Whatever the mix of these extended tasks, most circulation departments share responsibility for three traditional functions: sales, service, and collections. Sales means selling subscriptions and single copies. Service includes two distinct activities: (1) delivery of the newspaper to single copy outlets and subscriber homes and (2) service for customers forgotten by their carriers or cursed with damaged newspapers. Collection means taking in circulation revenue from subscribers and single copy outlets. Each of these functions, discussed in greater detail in Chapters 8 and 9, includes an array of tasks and responsibilities that can be easily defined but difficult to accomplish across the department.

As one department, circulation also has corporate connections and responsibilities; but as a functional unit, circulation works in the world of subscribers and readers rather than in the corporate world. Circulation workers drive the streets, walk the sidelines, meet readers while delivering and collecting, and try to persuade nonsubscribers to try the newspaper for only a few weeks. Observing the life of the community as they work, circulation workers are the scouts of community change, the eyes and ears of the newspaper across the circulation territory. Their familiarity with the readers and community provides a unique, invaluable set of reports for circulation management. As a department, circulation connects the newspaper to the readers.

The circulation department most closely works with production and promotion employees because circulation begins where production ends and circulation campaigns depend on skilled promotion. Efficient circulation begins with a dependable production system, which produces the right amount of newspapers on deadline. In devising sales campaign materials and motivating salespeople, promotional expertise from a department or talented individual is essential. The movement to computerized circulation information systems, as discussed in Chapter 10, has brought circulation and computer services closer together and integrated circulation data with advertising needs.

Departments' relationships with each other is, in part, a response to the newspaper's corporate structure. Organizational charts for 11 newspapers are presented with the case studies in Chapter 11. The internal organization of newspapers, that is, the way employees and managers relate to each other, falls into one of four forms: pyramid, functional, staff and line, and organic, each of which allocates different authority to department heads and uniquely integrates the departments. Size, of course, is a critical element. Weekly and small daily staffs tend to have more personal and less formal structures.

Pyramid Style

The pyramid managerial structure follows the military model, with authority increasing as it moves upward toward the commander-in-chief. With precisely defined grades of authority, the pyramid permits direction of the largest number of people toward a single goal with minimal loss of effect. Weak leadership in any area can be remedied quickly because everyone knows which rank has the highest authority, and everyone of a particular rank holds authority over all subordinates, whatever their unit or specialization.

The pyramid structure does not suit a newspaper with highly specialized employees and different professional groups. Newspapers reach their goals through the success of journalists, advertising salespeople, circulation workers, printers, typesetters, designers, artists, photographers, computer operators, and accountants. A common chain of command makes little sense with highly specialized departments.

Functional Style

A functional organization assigns responsibility to the level of work and ultimately to the individual worker; supervision goes to the most skilled worker. Highly developed by trade and craft unions, the functional organization works well only where a single type of labor prevails. The different skills of a newspaper require separate, competing departments, each vying to bend corporate goals to its own labor goals: print the newspaper, sell advertising, write well, sell the newspaper. The internal conflict of such a system would destroy the newspaper if this system were employed.

Staff and Line Style

The staff and line structure combines elements of the pyramid and functional structures by creating a chain of command within each functional area or department. For a newspaper, the staff and line works efficiently because it encourages each functional unit to pursue its own goals under the leadership of an area expert but in keeping with corporate goals. Department managers in this system control activities within their area of competence, but they have no general authority over employees in other departments. Rank alone does not command obedience, nor are departments set against each other by function. Staff and line structure insulates each unit and encourages it to perform according to its goals; however, each department becomes a separate entity linked only at the highest executive level, and considerable tension and segregation arise from different professional perspectives.

A circulation department in a staff and line structure has considerable freedom to organize itself as needed, fitting form to function. The traditional functions allocated to the circulation department—newspaper sales, delivery, collection, and customer service—are developed without interference from any other unit and with primary concern for efficient departmental operation. To fit the market, the manager combines or separates functions.

Staff and line structure is functional in practice when each department plunges toward its own goals with little regard for the other line departments. Internal divisions among professionals make newspapers particularly prone to this isolation, with writers and editors concerned only about news coverage and circulation workers focused solely on their tasks. In the process, corporate goals become hazy and interpreted in the frame of departmental goals.

Organic Style

Newspapers faced with massive market problems have begun moving toward an organic structure in which departments interact at several managerial levels to develop cooperative responses to market pressures. The *Chicago Sun Times* developed a model of organic structure that illustrates how departments are linked through their concern for the customers: advertisers, readers, nonadvertisers, and nonreaders. At the core of the model are the secondary departments—accounting, purchasing, mechanical, computer, personnel, and promotion. These departments interact with each other on a task basis. The three major departments—editorial, circulation, and advertising—are linked through their concern for the paying and potential customers, thereby bridging the departmental isolation of staff and line structure without attacking departmental integrity. It is a system most typical of weeklies and small dailies, ideal for small staffs.

A major impetus for integrating an organic model lies in potential advertisers and readers who find the current product unsatisfactory in some way. Nonadvertisers are possibly seeking readers of a different content type than reporters are willing to provide. Or, they may want a different circulation pattern, providing selective distribution in a target zone. Nonreaders are perhaps attracted by new approaches identified by market research as more suited to their concerns and life-style or by alternative circulation sales and delivery options. Newspapers that converted from afternoon to morning publication typically began with internal marketing committees, which represent an organic approach to newspapers' problem.

THE EFFECT OF LOCAL MARKET
FACTORS ON CIRCULATION

The organic organizational model underscores the effect of the local market on the structure and operation of circulation departments. The newspaper is a highly perishable commodity whose sales potential for most readers lasts but a few hours but whose reading value can last for days. Speedy, reliable delivery service forms the basis of a strong circulation department because a newspaper unable to provide reliable delivery soon alienates customers, carriers, and middle managers. Efficient daily delivery leads to complex delivery systems in which efficiency far outweighs structural tidiness. As a result, circulation managers have a high tolerance for the kind of organizational and operational diversity that defies rigid systematization. What works in Omaha may be disastrous in Abilene or foolish in Miami. Further, what works well on Omaha's north side may be unnecessary in the western suburbs or shade into an entirely different system as it approaches the downtown area.

Districts in the two county Columbia Metro area are defined primarily by Zip Codes.

FIGURE 5.1   This map of the circulation zones of the Columbia, S.C., newspapers illustrates the various circulation zones, including the mail-only zones. Zip code zones define circulation zones in the metropolitan area, which facilitates TMC service and matches advertisers' direct mail strategies. Advertiser pressure revolutionized circulation systems and methods. Courtesy Columbia Newspapers, Inc, Columbia, S.C.

Six local conditions affect a circulation department's organizational structure: labor conditions, demographics, geography, climate, life-style, and competition.

Labor Conditions

The local labor market affects newspaper circulation just as it affects other labor-intensive industries. No youth carrier system can survive where children are scarce, nor will labor be inexpensive in highly unionized regions. A strong work ethic, particularly one that respects manual labor, affects worker availability and the quality of work completed. Other labor conditions include transitory workers, unemployment rate, minimum wages, state unionization laws, and income taxes. One of the most striking differences occurs between strong and weak union states. In the Northeast, unionized circulation departments raise labor costs, affect delegation of responsibility, and constrain the ability to alter the system. In weak union states of the South and Southwest, wages and working conditions exist that would be impossible with unions. For example, mailroom workers in Minneapolis earn $17.265 per hour; their colleagues in Los Angeles earn $9.16 per hour.[3]

The *Ottawa Citizen* found that the influx of Southeast Asian immigrants created a major pool of youth carriers who worked tirelessly in the inner city. The St. Petersburg papers employ only adult carriers, many of them retirees. The number of girls carrying newspapers has risen steadily with the declining population of youth. The unemployment rate is particularly important for circulation managers because low rates mean high carrier and district manager turnover while high unemployment rates mean a steady work force.

Thus, labor conditions do affect the type of delivery system a newspaper uses and also influence circulation costs.

Demographics

Demographics are statistical snapshots of the local population and are essential to marketing. The elements of particular value to newspaper circulation include illiteracy, home ownership, apartment vacancy and turnover rates, age, family status, and education. Produced by federal, state, regional, and local governments and by newspaper researchers, demographics provide a key to understanding community changes that can be useful in planning.

For election analysis and other reasons, local demographics are broken down to the ward or block level, which assists rebuilding circulation districts for zoned editions and explains variations within zip code or telephone prefix zones. A circulation manager with these data can effectively compare household penetration and collections among circulation districts and establish a baseline for success in circulation sales campaigns.

School district demographics project the availability of youth carriers over the next decade and the movement of families with children. Properly understood, demographics also offer circulation managers a major tool for analyzing circulation sales in a diverse market.

Research has demonstrated that newspaper readership rises with literacy, income, home ownership, age, and education. Married couples with children are regular subscribers; young singles and childless couples are not. Circulation problems rise rapidly with apartment turnover rates, and high vacancy rates throw penetration figures into a different light.

Geography

Geographic conditions affecting circulation include competition from nearby newspapers, housing density, urban spread, transportation system, political units, and energy costs.

A newspaper locked into a market by newspapers from other county seats or metropolitan areas faces problems that are different from those of a newspaper without major competition nearby. The location of competing newspapers shapes the circulation territory the department serves and the character of sales promotions.

A delivery system working well in a community of single family homes can frustrate carriers and customers in an area of high-rise apartments. New housing divisions may require extensions of motor routes then conversion to youth carriers if the population increases. If the territory extends across county lines, revised distribution routes and additional zoned areas for suburban sections may be essential. In rural areas, motor routes and postal delivery can prove cost efficient but alter press times or drop sites.

Mountains and other terrain problems require special circulation adjustments. A far-flung circulation territory requires regional offices, supervisors, and transportation connections. Circulation information moves more slowly and less accurately through a large distribution system.

Climate

Climate effects go beyond weather conditions, which are significant, to the movement of vacationers and part-year residents. Rainfall can mandate almost daily use of plastic bags or careful attention to weather forecasts in different areas of the circulation territory. Snow and ice require delivery to protected areas but also specially equipped vehicles and skilled drivers, affecting the entire transportation system and raising costs. During the winter, windchill factors can limit home delivery in the North. Substations need heat in cold climates, while open-sided shelters and trailers work well in the South.

As vacationers move north and south with warm weather, climate and life-style interact to create special circulation challenges. Seasonal routes are a regular component of circulation systems in resort areas, creating sharp seasonal fluctuations in circulation. Florida newspapers provide special accounting and collection systems for the snowbirds who swell winter circulation, and they encourage mail subscriptions to part-time residents living up north. Northern newspapers reopen delivery routes to lake homes during summer months, and some newspapers use special trucks as mobile substations to serve vacationing residents.

Life-Style

Life-style generally refers to the manner in which people use their time and money and spend their days; but for newspapers it refers to how they obtain their information, how and when they use newspapers, and where they will purchase them. Life-style embraces climate and geography, in part; but it also includes community working patterns, mobility, transportation, affluence, entertainment, and family life.

The newspaper adapts to the timing of community life, setting its clock by the reading times of residents. Cities moved by factory whistles require different delivery times than those moved to the quiet hum of smokeless industry. A blue-collar community breakfasting at 5 or 6 a.m. and returning home to read the newspaper at 4 p.m. differs substantially from a white-collar community laboring from 9 to 5 and returning home for the evening television news. Long commutes by car clog freeways in one community as early as 5 a.m. and in another as late as 6 p.m., affecting the scheduling of circulation truck departures from the printing plant.

Small-town life moves with a different rhythm and pace, less hectic and less complex. A single industry can determine the workday of a small town, but no one industry can control a major metropolitan area. The growth of all-day newspapers is one response to the more complex pattern of urban life, just as the dominance of afternoon publishing in smaller cities fits the rhythm of those communities.

The mass transit system, which carries commuters, increases the possibility for single copy sales just as automobile commuting limits reading time. It is significant for newspapers that only 5.5 percent of Americans walk to work and another 6.3 percent use public transportation. A poor transportation network increases travel times, frustrates delivery truck timing, pushes press deadlines back, and otherwise complicates circulation.

Mobility, that is, the rate at which people move from one dwelling to another or from one community to another, is an aspect of life-style concerning circulation managers because high mobility rates create difficulties throughout the circulation system. High residential mobility complicates every phase of home delivery from recordkeeping through collections. High intercommunity mobility creates the need for constant sales promotion to reach newcomers. Because highly mobile residents lack roots in the community or neighborhood, they read less often and purchase fewer newspapers. Another aspect of mobility concerning advertisers more than circulation people is the willingness of residents to drive to other parts of the city for shopping, work, or recreation. Areas like southern California and Texas, where long drives are common, have different newspaper readership traits than areas like New England.

Competition

Perhaps the most compelling market condition is competition between newspapers and among all media for audience and a share of advertising expenditures. Competition was once among local newspapers; but the growth of the electronic media, shoppers, newspapers with national circulation, and small community newspapers has greatly altered the character of competition.

The Rosse Umbrella Model,[4] shown here, illustrates the new pattern of newspaper competition for circulation. The new competition is multilevel, with each level having certain advantages and significant disadvantages. The metropolitan newspaper has the financial resources to reach the entire audience and provide something of interest to everyone.

Satellite city newspapers can emphasize their town and county news to attract a large percentage of local readers, whereas the big-city daily must thinly spread its news resources over many small communities and several counties in addition to giving full coverage to its central city and home county. In densely populated urban areas, newspapers 20 miles away from each other now compete for the same readers in at least some part of their circulation zones. Satellite city weeklies, like neighborhood and community newspapers, compete less directly and serve a supplementary function. Such competition has forced newspapers to develop special news and advertising sections for readers in satellite cities and

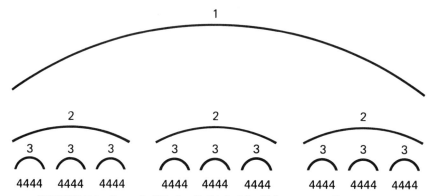

FIGURE 5.2   Rosse's "Umbrella" Model of Newspaper Competition
Courtesy Knowledge Industry Publications.

Key:

Level 1 — Newspaper in large metropolitan center
Level 2 — Newspapers in satellite cities
Level 3 — Local dailies
Level 4 — Weeklies and other specialized media

adjacent counties. Not limited to major metropolitan areas, this competition extends to smaller county seat newspapers as well.

A metropolitan newspaper's circulation territory overlaps the territories of a number of competing newspapers, including those of distant dailies. One need only look at the number of newspapers serving high-density urban areas (17, for example, in Washington, D.C.) to grasp the complexity of this new circulation competition. Away from such areas, new newspapers and old compete, some by being extremely local, others by being more regional.

Competition has been fueled by freeways and expressways, the life-style of commuters who have a foot in each of two communities, and urban sprawl, which embraces once-separate towns. The simplicity and low cost of production made possible in the 1960s by offset printing and electronic typesetting increased the profitability of small newspapers. Some newspapers pooled their funds to purchase a common production plant, allowing them to become sufficiently competitive to survive. The simplicity and price of small newspaper technology have allowed virtually anyone with a few thousand dollars to become a publisher. Today's readers can purchase newspapers fitting their particular interest, whether narrowly local, highly specialized, or metropolitan.

Competition has become a battle of marketing strategies more than of circulation. Pricing, promotion, and product design are crucial. In a competitive situation, a weaker newspaper is at a significant disadvantage because it usually lacks the resources to mount and continue major circulation promotions and must follow the lead of the stronger newspaper in pricing. The stronger newspaper can hold the price down by slightly shaving its profits, thereby insuring that the weaker newspaper must choose between the circulation loss of a price increase and the inadequate income of lower prices. With financial strength, the stronger newspaper can develop special sections, zoned coverage, and special advertising programs to take advantage of the competitor's weakness. These techniques work less well against a nearby city's daily having its own strong base and seeking the majority of the circulation in a shared zone. Competition here is not head to head, but it affects the corporate culture and shapes circulation efforts nonetheless.

Newspapers also compete with other information and entertainment media for reader time and interest. A wide range of information sources, from professional newsletters and publications to electronic data systems, now fill part of the needs once met by newspapers. Television, films, professional sports, and shopping malls compete for free time. The recreation an affluent society can afford sharply limits the time in which a newspaper can be read. Circulation sales campaigns must therefore take advantage of the newspaper's strengths in the local market and wage a different competitive battle for reader time and attention.

Of all the market factors, competition can most directly and strongly affect circulation because it demands reaction and adaptation. A newspaper must respond to competitive challenges in the marketplace or risk extinction.

NOTES

1. Terrence Deal and Allan Kennedy, *Corporate Cultures, the Rites and Rituals of Corporate Life* (New York: Addison-Wesley Co., 1982), 3.
2. William Rivers, *The Adversaries: Politics and the Press* (Boston: Beacon Press, 1970), 47.
3. *Editor & Publisher 1986 Yearbook* (New York: Editor & Publisher, 1986), VI43.
4. James Rosse, Bruce Owen, and James Dertouzous, "Trends in Daily Newspaper Industry 1923–1973." *Studies in Industry Economics*, No. 57 (Stanford, Ca.: Dept. of Economics, Stanford University, 1975). Illustration from Benjamin Compaine, *The Newspaper Industry in the 1980s: An Assessment of Economics and Technology* (White Plains, N.Y.: Knowledge Industry Publications, Inc., 1980), p. 102.

CHAPTER
6

Laws Affecting Newspaper Circulation

The press is the only business in America specifically protected by a constitutional amendment. The First Amendment declares that "Congress shall make no law ... abridging the freedom of speech, or of the press...."[1] The goal of the first amendment is the protection of public expression and the free flow of information, not the maintenance of the newspaper business' financial health; the amendment does not guarantee that the press will make a profit nor does it exempt the business component of the press from fair and reasonable legislation.

Contemporary American law is based on Anglo-Saxon common law and further developed by statutory laws specifying common law or addressing problems not foreseen by common law. This chapter examines the federal, state, and local laws affecting newspapers as business enterprises, particularly those laws influencing circulation practices.

FEDERAL LAWS AND REGULATIONS

Federal laws—and the regulations of federal agencies established to implement those laws—affect circulation practices by defining employees and their rights in collective bargaining and by setting standards for wages and hours, child labor, civil rights, interstate commerce, monopolistic practices, and fair trade policies. Also influencing circulation practices, especially for weekly newspapers, are postal regulations, which are further explained in Chapter 8, Home Delivery.

Passed by Congress, federal laws apply with equal force in all states and U.S. territories. They are enforced by federal agencies through administrative hearings or through the federal court system.

Who Is an Employee?

Of the many laws affecting newspapers, those governing employer-employee relations merit the greatest attention of circulation managers because they substantially affect the rights and obligations of all persons involved in the circulation process.

The definitions of employee and employer vary with different laws. As a general proposition, a newspaper is liable for the actions of a distributor acting as the newspaper's "servant." Servant here means one employed to perform services, whose physical conduct is subject to the direction and control of the employer.

Courts usually weigh several factors in determining whether a distributor is an employee of the newspaper or an independent contractor, with particular emphasis on the degree of control the newspaper has over the distributor's activities. The courts have consistently identified the following factors as significant in determining employee status:

1. The contract explicitly details the newspaper's control.
2. The newspaper pays the distributor a weekly wage.
3. The newspaper establishes the distributor's retail price.
4. The newspaper requires the distributor to "porch" the paper.
5. The newspaper defines the delivery sequence for the distributor to follow.
6. The distributor may not deliver any other publication without the newspaper's consent.
7. The newspaper can terminate the distributor at any time without notice.[2]

A circulation manager wishing to establish a distribution system using independent contractors should minimize control.

Newspaper circulation managers most frequently confront the issue of employee status under the National Labor Relations Act (NLRA), passed in 1935 and amended in 1947 and 1959. The "employee" status of a newspaper distributor is determined on a case-by-case basis by the National Labor Relations Board (NLRB) based on three criteria:

1. the entrepreneurial aspects of the relationship, including the right to control;
2. the distributor's risk of loss and opportunity for profit; and
3. the distributor's proprietary interest in the distributorship.

The NLRB's "right to control" test results in a finding of employee status when the employer controls the manner and means by which the desired objective is achieved and independent contractor status when control is limited strictly to the result sought. Although each case is judged independently, the NLRB has concluded that the following 18 elements of control indicate a finding of employee status for newspaper workers:

1. Control and selection of the scope of a distributor's territory
2. Employer's unilateral control of the newspaper's retail price
3. Newspaper's assistance to the distributor in obtaining new subscribers
4. Newspaper's requirement that a distributor service certain subscribers whether or not the distributor wishes to do so
5. Newspaper's insistence that a distributor place the newspapers in a tube or other designated place
6. Newspaper's requirement that the distributor insure that the newspaper is protected from weather conditions
7. Distributor's ability to return unsold newspapers to the employer
8. Newspaper's replacement, without cost to the distributor, of newspapers lost in delivery
9. Newspaper's control of the subscriber billing procedures
10. Newspaper's retention of advanced payments made by the distributor's subscribers (thus depriving the distributor of immediate possession and use of such funds)
11. Newspaper's reservation of the right or power to pass on the qualifications of substitutes
12. Newspaper's precluding a distributor from delivering any other publication
13. Newspaper's possession and exercise of the right to terminate at will the distributor-employer relationship
14. Newspaper's unilateral right to designate the drop-off points at which the distributors will pick up their papers
15. Newspaper's right to unilaterally impose a delivery deadline time on the distributor
16. Newspaper's handling of the distributor's subscribers' complaints
17. Contract between employer and distributor indicating employee status
18. Newspaper's subsidization of insurance coverage for distributors

These criteria do not carry equal weight, and no single variable determines employee status. Moreover, since an independent contractor customarily bears the risks of loss as well as controls the opportunities for profit, the NLRB studies this aspect of the relationship as well. As the U.S. Court of Appeals for the Ninth Circuit has observed: "An independent contractor will make all essential business decisions and his opportunity for profit will be limited only by his own initiative, efforts and policies."[5]

A more liberal definition of employee, the broadest found in any statute, is used in the Fair Labor Standards Act, enacted as part of the New Deal legislation of the 1930s. The act seeks to protect the health, well-being, and efficiency of workers whose products or services are used in interstate commerce. Provisions of the FLSA govern minimum wages, overtime, and the use of child labor.

The FLSA defines an employee as "any individual employed by an employer."[6] To employ means "to suffer or permit to work,"[7] and employer includes "any person acting directly or indirectly in the interest of an employer in relationship to an employee."

Stated simply, an employee is one who works for compensation and regularly performs essentially routine tasks that are part of the normal operations of the employer. Persons considered to be independent contractors under other laws are considered employees under FLSA if their work resembles that of an employee and they remain economically dependent upon the employer. To clarify the issue of employee status, federal courts frequently have focused on the following five factors:

1. Whether or not the work takes place on the company's premises
2. Whether or not the company exerts a great deal of control over the worker
3. Whether or not the company has the power to fire, hire, or modify the employment conditions of the worker
4. Whether or not the worker does *not* perform a "specialty job" within the company
5. Whether or not workers are forbidden to either refuse to work for the company or to work for other companies[8]

Affirmative answers to the above five inquiries would support a finding of employee status.

Employee Exemptions Congress deliberately and specifically exempted 66 categories of employees from the FLSA. The following four exemptions are particularly significant for newspaper circulation managers:

1. Partial minimum wage exemptions[9]
2. Complete minimum wage, equal pay, and overtime pay exemptions[10]
3. Minimum wage, equal pay, and child labor exemptions[11]
4. Overtime pay exemptions[12]

Under partial minimum wage exemptions, a circulation manager can employ apprentices and the handicapped at wages below the FLSA minimum; however, both the apprentices and the handicapped must meet established requirements. For apprentices, the employer must first establish an apprenticeship program with a recognized apprenticeship agency, then enter into an apprenticeship agreement, which is sent to the apprenticeship agency and the Regional Office of the Wage and Hour Division of the U.S. Department of Labor. The federal code also establishes standards for qualified apprenticeship programs. In general, the code requires the program to be in a skilled trade, require two or more years' work, have a progressive wage scale averaging at least 50 percent of journeyman scale, list a work schedule for experience, obtain agreement to the program from the bargaining agent, respond to a need in the community for the number of apprentices, provide facilities for training and supervision, and make related instruction available.[13]

A handicapped worker is one whose age or physical or mental deficiency or injury impairs his or her earning capacity for the work he or she is performing. In this definition, one who is handicapped for most work but not for that which he currently performs would not fit the FLSA exemption. A circulation manager must demonstrate that the sub-minimum wage is necessary to retain the worker, and that the worker's earning or productive capacity is limited by a defined handicap. As with apprentices, the circulation manager must obtain a certificate from the Wage and Hour administrator allowing subminimum pay.

Under complete minimum wage, equal pay, and overtime pay exemptions, Congress set up 11 categories of employees exempted from all but the child labor provisions of FLSA. Among these the local newspaper exemption and the white-collar exemption are the most significant to the newspaper circulation personnel.

The local newspaper exemption excludes any employee of a weekly, semiweekly, or daily newspaper with less than 4000 circulation, the majority of which is in the county of publication or in its contiguous counties.[13] Legally, a shopper fits the definition of newspaper only if it has the appearance of a newspaper and includes a substantial amount of news. Circulation means the number of copies sold. For publishers with several different newspapers, the circulation of each is considered separately, as long as they are not the same newspaper in actuality.

Under the white-collar exemption, Congress sought to exclude managerial personnel, specifically executives, administrators, professionals, and outside salespeople.[14] To qualify as executives, individuals must manage a business or department, supervise at least two people, have the power to hire and fire or exert substantial influence on such decisions, exercise authority, and spend over 80 percent of their time performing management functions as depicted above. Furthermore, their salaries must be more than $155 per week.

In addition to the normal executive exemption, there is also an exemption for high-paid executives. Specifically, an employee paid more than $250 per week qualified for the executive exemption by satisfying only the requirements of possessing managerial duties and directing other employees.[15] By utilizing this exemption, a circulation manager can exempt a working foreman who is not otherwise qualified because of the 20 percent nonexempt work requirement.

Administrative employees also have been granted exempt status under the FLSA.[16] In order to qualify for this exemption, the administrator must primarily perform office or nonmanual work directly related to managerial policies or operations; or must regularly and directly assist a proprietor in a capacity requiring the exercise of independent judgment; or must perform specialized work under only general supervision; or must execute special assignments and tasks, and also spend not more than 20 percent of the workweek on nonadministrative tasks. Routine clerical work does not qualify as administrative in character; however, advising, planning, negotiating, representing the company, purchasing, promotion work, and research do not satisfy the administrative office work requirement. Assistant managers, functional department heads, executive secretaries, and sales promotion employees all fall within this exemption. In addition, a special exemption exists for administrators who are paid a minimum of $200 per week and whose primary duties consist of managerial work necessitating the use of independent judgment.

Consequently, a circulation manager may exempt circulation department employees conforming with any of the above definitions of administrative employees. The circulation department employees exempted most frequently are the assistant director and the city and rural circulation directors. In addition, exemptions may be available for employees who plan circulation drives or who otherwise perform a specialized job function in the circulation department.

The minimum wage, equal pay, overtime pay, and child labor exemptions apply to all employees who are "engaged in the delivery of newspapers to consumers."[17] The legislative history giving rise to this exemption indicates that Congress intended to restrict the scope of this exemption to newspaper boys, and subsequent judicial decisions remain faithful to this original intent. The Wage and Hour Administrator has interpreted this exemption to include carriers delivering newspapers to homes as well as those selling on the street. Haulers are usually excluded from the definition of carrier. Those servicing racks and boxes are likewise not defined as carriers unless they also sell on the street or deliver newspapers to homes. Shopper carriers must meet one of two criteria to be exempted from FLSA: (1) The shopper must have the general appearance of a newspaper and contain news of general interest; or (2) it must be inserted into a newspaper. Employees who solicit door to door as well as deliver to the same territories are similarly exempted from the FLSA.[18]

Children as Employees While the legislative history of the FLSA suggests that Congress specifically designed certain exemptions to apply to newspaper boys, the Child Labor Section of the act establishes criteria circulation managers must follow in using youths as newspaper carriers.

The Child Labor section prohibits employers from using "oppressive child labor" in interstate commerce and prohibits producers, manufacturers, and dealers from doing business with anyone who employs "oppressive child labor." This latter prohibition is known as the "hot goods" provision.

"Oppressive child labor" entails the employment of anyone under the age of 16, or the employment of anyone between 16 and 18 in an occupation declared hazardous for children by the U.S. Secretary of Labor. The hazardous occupations of particular concern to circulation managers include driving a motor vehicle and operating power equipment.

A circulation manager may not hire anyone under the age of 16 for any job other than newspaper carrier unless a specific exemption, as outlined in the previous section, is applicable. Moreover, those between the ages of 16 and 18 may not, without a specific exemption, work as drivers or drivers' helpers or operate power hoist equipment.

Who Is a Supervisor?

Like independent contractors, supervisors are not considered employees under the National Labor Relations Act; however, because supervisors are considered extensions of the employer, the employer is legally accountable for their actions. This means a supervisor's violation of the law translates into a violation committed by the employer.

Section 2(11) of the NLRA defines a supervisor as follows:

> The term "supervisor" means any individual having authority, in the interest of the employer, to hire, transfer, suspend, layoff, recall, promote, discharge, assign, reward, or discipline other employees, or responsibility to direct them, or to adjust their grievances or effectively to recommend such action, if in connection with the foregoing, the exercise of such authority is not of a merely routine or clerical nature, but requires the use of independent judgment.[20]

Supervisory status is determined by the employee's duties rather than title. The following three-point test applies:

1. The person must have supervisory authority, i.e., the power to hire, fire, etc. Whether the power actually has been used is irrelevant.
2. The person must have authority over other "employees." For example, a district manager who supervises independent contractors as opposed to employees does not meet this test.
3. The person must have the authority to exercise independent judgment. A person who merely carries out orders does not perform a "supervisory" function.[21]

In the event that a given situation defies easy application of the three-point test, the National Labor Relations Board has used two additional criteria to help determine supervisory status: the presence of substantial wage disparities and an examination of the employee-supervisor ratio.[22] Both criteria are assessed on an ad hoc basis; thus, at some newspapers district managers will be considered supervisors; while at others, using the same criteria, they will be classified employees.

Employees' Rights

Federal laws protect employees' rights to organize, to receive a fair wage, and to avoid discrimination. The application of employee status often determines a worker's protection under the law, particularly in regard to labor practices; that's why it's so important for circulation managers to understand the legal definitions of employee.

The Right to Form Unions The National Labor Relations Act provides federal protection to employees' rights in the following words:

> Employees shall have the right to self-organization, to form, join or assist labor organizations, to bargain collectively through representatives of their own choosing, and to engage in other concerted activities for the purpose of collective bargaining or other mutual aid or protection, and shall have the right to refrain from any or all such activities. . . .[23]

The right to self-organization means that employees can form, join, or assist any organized group, as long as one of the group's purposes relates to wages, hours, or other employment conditions. Employers are specifically forbidden by law to interfere with organizational efforts, to dominate a union or financially support one, or in any way to discriminate in employment on the basis of union membership.

Newspapers can control union solicitation and literature distribution within the plant to some extent, but only under carefully defined conditions. Employers have a right to protect their property and maintain reasonable employee discipline, while employees have the right to organize; and competing interests must be reconciled. As in other cases where legal questions arise, circulation managers should consult an attorney or review the *ICMA Legal Manual*.

A newspaper may have greater latitude in prohibiting nonemployee solicitation or distribution on company property, but only if two major conditions are met. First, rules prohibiting nonemployee solicitation or distribution must not discriminate against unions but must deny this privilege to nonemployees of any and all groups. Second, if employees are inaccessible to nonemployee organizers during work hours and on the premises, the organizers should have some form of access to the employees, for example, by permitting the organizers to communicate with and distribute literature to employees in company-owned employee parking areas.[24]

Employers may not lawfully question employees about union organizing except, as a rule of thumb, where the questioning constitutes an isolated incident and is conducted in a nonthreatening, noncoercive fashion. Polling the employees as to their union affinities is treated less favorably because of the greater "chilling effect" systematic polling theoretically has on free employee expression. Consequently, in order to pass legal muster, employer polling must satisfy a strict five-tiered test:

1. The poll's purpose must be to objectively assess the union's claim to majority membership.
2. Employees must be informed of this purpose.
3. Employees must be assured there will be no reprisals.
4. The poll must be conducted by secret ballot.
5. The employer must not engage in unfair labor practices or otherwise create a coercive atmosphere.[25]

Employers may present their views on unionization with some restrictions, none of which seriously limit their freedom of speech.[26] Employers can utilize speeches, slide shows, films, or bulletin boards to their advantage so long as they do not either threaten retaliatory or punitive action or promise benefits to employees. While this always remains a subjective determination, an employer's speech generally is considered threatening when it predicts consequences over which the employer has control and nonthreatening when it merely states objective facts. For example, an employer may, without running afoul of the NLRA, compare working conditions in union and nonunion newspapers, or even predict that unionization will produce adverse economic consequences if such a prediction is premised on objective facts.

During an organization effort, the employer must conduct "business as usual" as far as benefit dispensation is concerned. Planned increases may not be withheld lest they seem to be retaliatory, nor can benefits be enhanced without substantial business justification.[27] For example, annual increases falling due within the midst of an organizing campaign in many cases must be granted, but sizable and unexpected benefit grants appear to buy employee loyalty.

To insure an autonomous union, employers are forbidden to dominate the union in any way (for example, by establishing an "in-house" union).[28] Moreover, employers may not interfere with the union by allowing supervisors to represent union members, to collect authorization cards, or to otherwise engage in internal union affairs or activities. An employer may not provide financial or other substantial support to the union. This does not mean that an employer and union must remain adversaries; courts have observed that cooperation between the parties should be encouraged so long as an arm's length relationship is maintained.

An employer may not discriminate against an employee on the basis of union membership, either to encourage or discourage membership.[29] Unlawful discrimination may be evidenced by an employer's unequal treatment in punishing union and nonunion employees for the same misconduct. These protections against discrimination extend to job applicants as well as actual employees. Furthermore, an employer may not demote, transfer, deny overtime, or unfairly require undesirable work on the basis of union membership.

Central to the National Labor Relations Act is the goal of peacefully defusing labor disputes via collective bargaining. The act clearly states that "(e)mployees shall have the right to bargain collectively through representatives of their own choosing."[30] Once a union has been recognized as the exclusive bargaining representative for a unit of employees, the employer is obligated to negotiate with that union in good faith over wages, hours, and terms and conditions of employment. This obligation is a sophisticated one and best left to experts; however, circulation managers and supervisors need to understand that, basically, employers may neither interfere with the selection of a bargaining team nor support surface, or "bad faith," bargaining.

The NLRA also protects employees' rights to engage in "concerted activit(ies)," including strikes and boycotts, in pursuit of economic demands or to protest an employer's commission of unfair labor practices.[31] Such activity is lawful if it meets four criteria established by the NLRB and the courts:

1. The activity constitutes a work-related grievance or complaint.
2. The activity furthers some group interest.
3. The activity seeks some specific action.
4. It is lawful and proper activity.[32]

Slowdowns, incidents of sabotage or vandalism, and boycotts directed against other employers are all examples of unprotected activities for which individual employees can be disciplined or discharged.

If the National Labor Relations Board finds that unfair labor practices have been committed, it normally issues a "cease and desist order," which mandates that the unlawful acts in question be immediately stopped.[33] Such cease and desist orders require enforcement by a federal court if challenged. Other remedies available to the board include the reinstatement of unlawfully discharged employees—with or without compensatory backpay—and, in extreme cases, the issuance of a bargaining order requiring that the employer recognize the bargain with a union that, due to the employer's unfair labor practices, has had its ability to be chosen by a majority of employees within a bargaining unit unduly interfered with.

The Right to a Fair Wage The Substantive Rule Section of the Fair Labor Standards Act establishes a minimum wage; the section also expands adult employment opportunities by increasing overtime costs and limiting child labor.[34]

The minimum wage provision defines wages, establishes rules for pay periods, and provides for permissible deductions.[35] Congress can adjust the minimum wage at its discretion. The minimum pay period is 1 hour; however, pay can be averaged over the workweek to compute an average hourly wage if the pay is based on piecework, commission, or a combination of wage and commission. Nonetheless, the average hourly wage must at least equal the established minimum wage.

An employer may lawfully deduct withholding taxes, social security, and unemployment insurance from the wages paid and may also subtract voluntary deductions such as credit union payments, insurance, savings bonds, and the like.

Civil Rights Four federal laws specifically prohibit discrimination.

The *Civil Rights Act of 1866*, established to provide the newly freed slaves with property and contractual rights, applies to all employers and employees in the United States.[36] In fact, section 1981, requiring equal treatment of all racial groups, covers not only employees but also supervisors and independent contractors.

To qualify for redress under section 1981, a person must prove discrimination in wages, hours, or other terms of unemployment in comparison to a white person. Proof of actual intent to discriminate, bad faith, or evil motive is not required and may be supplanted by circumstantial evidence.

Title VII of the Civil Rights Act of 1964 also prohibits discriminatory treatment relating to wages, hours, and conditions of employment. It applies to any employer "engaged in an industry affecting commerce who has fifteen or more employees for each of twenty or more calendar weeks in the current or preceding year."[37] The phrase "industry affecting commerce" is broadly defined; therefore, most newspapers with more than 15 employees fall within the scope of the law. Like the Civil Rights Act of 1866, this law protects any individual, not just employees; however, the protected status of independent contractors remains questionable.

Title VII forbids any discriminatory practice affecting wages, hours, or other terms and conditions of employment based, even in part, on race, color, sex, religion, or national origin. The discrimination need not be deliberate; a nondiscriminatory intent does not excuse a discriminatory effect. A two-part test measures "operational" or de facto discrimination:

1. Does the present practice perpetuate, directly or indirectly, past discrimination?
2. If so, is the present practice justified by a showing of business necessity? Without business necessity, the employer behaves illegally if employees continue to suffer the repercussions of past racial discrimination.[38]

Title VII specifies several unfair, discriminatory practices, including any hiring, firing, wage, or work discrimination; any employee classification or segregation that limits employment opportunity; any discrimination based on employee opposition to an unlawful employment practice or involvement in Title VII cases; and the use of any discriminatory language in an employment ad.

If job requirements discriminate against people protected by Title VII, they must be clearly job-related to survive scrutiny. Consequently, virtually no requirement can be imposed for unskilled labor positions. Some traditionally suspect requirements are: high school diploma, particular sex, particular marital status, nonpregnancy, number of children, arrest record, and dress or appearance codes.

All working conditions must be provided on an equal basis, including wages; hours; and other terms and conditions of employment such as leaves, insurance, and work locations. For example, it is unlawful to limit black district managers to predominantly black circulation districts if the assignment is based on racial considerations. Circulation managers have an obligation to devise transfer and promotion criteria premised on performance and ability alone.

For circulation department personnel, the important exceptions to Title VII are the bona fide occupational qualifications (BFOQ) and bona fide seniority system exemptions.[39] A BFOQ is one essential to job performance. A driver must have a driver's license; a typist must be able to type. A manager must be able to show that those excluded by such qualifications are unable to perform the job safely and satisfactorily. Furthermore, discriminatory treatment of employees performing similar work is lawful if a bona fide seniority system requires it. However, such systems may not include informal arrangements or understandings; thus, acceptable seniority systems are limited to those expressly mandated or authorized by collective bargaining or some other written agreement.

The *Equal Pay Act of 1963*, an amendment to the Fair Labor Standards Act, forbids wage discrimination on the basis of sex unless such discrimination can be justified by a seniority system, a merit system, or some other neutral factor.[40] Essentially, the act requires that equal pay be provided for men and women performing equivalent work. The jobs subject to comparison need not be identical but only substantially equal in skill, effect, and responsibility.

The *Age Discrimination in Employment Act of 1967* prohibits the same discriminations based on age that the Civil Rights Act of 1964 forbids on the basis of race, religion, or other factors.[41] Two narrowly defined exceptions in the age discrimination act cover bona fide occupational qualifications and bona fide employee benefit plans. Based on objective data about driving safety and age, for example, a circulation manager can lawfully set age limitations for a job involving driving. Moreover, unequal benefits to older workers are lawful if the actual amount of payments to all workers is equal.

The age discrimination act protects employees, supervisors, and job applicants between the ages of 40 and 65. Thus, the act does not expressly prohibit employers from discriminating, on the basis of age, among people under 40.

Laws Affecting Business Competition

Beginning in 1890, the federal government enacted antitrust legislation to encourage free and open competition in business. Each of the four major laws in this area—the Sherman Antitrust Act, the Clayton Act (1914), the Robinson-Patman Act (1936), and the Federal Trade Commission Act—has provisions affecting newspapers.

The Sherman Antitrust Act This law, the backbone of antitrust law, prohibits restraints on trade and the monopolization or attempted monopolization of trade. Section 1 forbids any contract, combination, or conspiracy that unreasonably restrains interstate or foreign trade or commerce.

Some business actions are by their very nature illegal restraints on trade, or illegal per se. These include price fixing, allocation of market areas, the tying of the sale of one product to sale of another, and collective refusals to deal (or "group boycotts").

To help assess the legality of particular business arrangements, the courts define business relationships as either horizontal (between or among competitors) or vertical (buyer-seller). Horizontal agreements automatically are suspect under antitrust law because of their intrinsic potential for stifling competition and injuring the consuming public. Vertical agreements are less likely to be suspect because they can be justified more readily on efficiency grounds. However, no agreement, horizontal or vertical, to fix prices is legal. Consequently, newspapers cannot fix the price that independent contractors may charge for their papers.

For competitors to agree to divide market territories is equally illegal. When newspaper distributors agreed to divide the market so that each had an exclusive area, the Supreme Court found it to be a classic example of per se illegal behavior. However, in 1977, the Supreme Court softened its earlier rulings regarding territorial restrictions imposed on a vertical level; a newspaper now may utilize exclusive dealerships in an area so long as a system of efficient distribution results and no substantial damage to competition is generated.[42] A newspaper may also assign dealers to areas of primary responsibility for full servicing and sales expansion; if they fail to meet newspaper expectations, they generally can be terminated without legal repercussions.

A concerted refusal to deal, often called a group boycott, exists when a horizontally aligned group refuses to sell to some other party. This behavior is always per se illegal. Thus, circulation managers from competing papers may not agree to refuse to sell to a particular distributor, nor may a group of distributors refuse to sell to another distributor if they traditionally sell in bulk to one another. While a circulation manager can lawfully refuse to deal with a distributor, this vertical refusal must not have monopolistic purposes; nor can it enforce an otherwise illegal restraint of trade such as price fixing.[43] A circulation manager almost always may lawfully refuse to deal for sound business reasons, however.

Restrictions against monopoly and attempts to monopolize fully apply to newspapers; but, unlike restraint of trade provisions, they affect circulation departments only in a limited way. When newspapers compete for subscribers in a specific geographical market, this activity will be closely scrutinized if it arguably can be interpreted as an attempt to garner a monopoly market. Two elements used by the courts to determine whether there was intent to monopolize are monopoly power (the ability to develop a monopoly) and the willful acquisition or maintenance of that power as distinguished from growth or development caused by superior goods, business acumen, or historic accident. For example, a daily metropolitan newspaper may experience natural circulation growth in a suburban market served by a smaller daily; but the larger newspaper may not take any overt action, such as a special discount for advertisers in that area, to drive the smaller paper out of business.

Monopoly power is the ability to control prices in a marketplace or exclude competition.[44] Ability to monopolize, even if never exercised, establishes monopoly power. Market is defined two ways, by product and geographical dimensions. The product market comprises relatively interchangeable items, or stated alternatively, items amenable to substitution (daily newspapers, for example). Newspapers as a medium generally are distinguished from other media. The appropriate geographical market constitutes the area in which the newspaper competes or can be purchased. No percentage per se is indicative of control, though no newspaper with less than a 70 percent share of the appropriate market has been found to be monopolistic.

Monopoly power in and of itself is not illegal—for example, if one newspaper has grown through superior business acumen, foresight, and industry, this is to be applauded. It is illegal, however, to maintain or extend one's monopoly by unfair practices such as predatory pricing.

Attempts to monopolize are likewise illegal if they take the form of exclusionary or predatory practices. Only a "reasonable probability" of success is required to establish illegality. A classic example of an attempt to monopolize was evidenced in one case in which a newspaper accused another paper of attempting to monopolize by blanketing homes in the plaintiff's hometown with free copies on numerous occasions.

The Clayton Act As a supplement to the Sherman Antitrust Act, the Clayton Act prohibits tie-in arrangements and exclusive dealing agreements, grants private cause of legal action to any person injured by antitrust violations, and forbids mergers and acquisitions that substantially lessen competition.

For newspapers, the law's impact falls most heavily on tying arrangements, agreements to sell one product only on the condition that another is purchased as well.[45] In 1953, the Supreme Court held that requiring advertisers to buy space in both a morning and afternoon newspaper did not amount to an antitrust violation because the advertising space was determined to be a singular product for advertisers. As a general rule, industry precedent and the particular situation will determine the legality of tying arrangements, particularly for combination sales. Sound business reasons, such as unjustifiably high single-sale costs, can serve to legitimize package arrangements.

The Federal Trade Commission Act The Federal Trade Commission Act of 1914 established the Federal Trade Commission as a watchdog agency with the power to identify and prosecute cases of "unfair methods of competition in commerce." Specifically, the FTC was empowered to curtail unfair practices that had not reached the seriousness of Sherman Antitrust Act violations.

Unfair methods of competition include the following two classes of action:

1. Practices regarded as antagonistic to ethical business conduct because they are characterized by deception, bad faith, fraud or oppression.
2. Practices regarded as contrary to public policy because they may unduly restrain competition or create a monopoly. Courts have wrangled over the precise scope of the FTC's power, and currently the FTC may legally proceed against methods of competition or acts that violate the letter of a federal antitrust law, the basic policies or spirit of those laws, or consumer interests independent of effects on competition.[46]

Circulation practices legal under the other antitrust laws are not immune from prosecution under this act if a competitor has or will be injured by the newspaper's conduct. Additionally, consumer interests are specifically protected by this law against misrepresentation, false advertising, and unfair practices.

FTC Franchise Disclosure Rule In 1979 the Federal Trade Commission (FTC) approved a rule entitled "Disclosure Requirements and Prohibitions Concerning Franchising and Business Opportunity Centures." The rule covers virtually all newspaper distribution arrangements unless the arrangement is structured to qualify for exempt status. FTC enforcement of the rule against a noncomplying newspaper can prove painful—violators expose themselves to FTC-instigated civil actions and fines of $10,000 per day.

The rule affects two types of so-called "franchise" arrangements common in the newspaper industry—the *product franchise* and the *business opportunity venture*. A product franchise exists if the publisher can exert a significant degree of control over the method of operation or provides significant operation assistance and requires the franchise to pay the publisher or affiliate as a condition of obtaining or opening the franchise. A business opportunity venture arises when the publisher, directly or indirectly, secures single copy retail outlets or vending machine locations for the franchisee and requires the franchisee to pay the publisher or affiliate as a condition for obtaining or starting the franchise. The FTC has concluded that a security deposit, escrow account, bond, or other method of satisfying the franchisee's performance obligation qualifies as a payment under the rule.

The FTC provides some guidance in interpreting the terms *significant control* and *significant assistance*. Controlling the franchisee's hours of operation or accounting practices, requiring the franchisee to participate in or contribute to promotional campaigns, or restricting the franchisee's customers or areas of operation are all significant controls. Establishing a formal sales training program or furnishing marketing advice, operating manuals, or promotional materials constitutes significant assistance. Furnishing route bags or poly bags or requiring newspapers to be delivered to specific locations on subscribers' property are other forms of assistance and control, respectively. An important condition, especially in working with youth carriers, is the extent to which the franchisee is inexperienced and looks to the publisher's experience for guidance.

The payment requirement extends to all financial obligations that a prospective franchisee must incur as part of the franchise. Accordingly, the FTC includes all payments required by contract or practical necessity, specifically including security and escrow deposits, equipment rental, and equipment or supplies. If the franchisee is free to refrain from purchasing or to purchase from another source, however, these payments will not be considered part of the franchise cost. Thus, if the franchisee must rent or purchase racks from the publisher or deposit funds to secure performance, the payment requirement has been met.

Both time and money enter into the definition of franchise: Franchise payments must total at least $500 within the first six months. However, payments for a reasonable starting inventory of goods for resale are excluded. Thus, billing for newspapers purchased in advance rather than in arrears avoids the need for a security deposit. Payments for poly bags and other supplies purchased by a franchisee but not resold are counted whether or not they are judged to be reasonable.

So long as the franchisee is not required to purchase supplies from a source that produces revenue for the publisher, such supplies or equipment do not count toward the $500 minimum. In addition, alternative methods can be used to assure that the franchisee pays for newspapers purchased. Thus, for example, a distribution contract may require a franchisee to post a performance and payment bond underwritten by an independent insurance or bonding company duly licensed to do business in the state, or the contract may require that the franchisee deposit a stated sum in an insured bank account against which the publisher has a lien. Under such circumstances, no payment is made to the publisher and the franchisee is exempt from the rule.

Other exemptions include a purely employer-employee relationship, oral arrangements, and so-called fractional franchises. Large distributors or single copy retailers who add a newspaper to their inventory are fractional franchisees if they have been selling comparable goods for more than two years and the newspaper accounts for no more than 20 percent of the distributors' gross sales.

The disclosure rule requires identifying the publisher and parent company; the trademarks and trade names that the newspapers bear; and the experience of the parent company, publisher, and key personnel. If any key personnel have been convicted of a felony involving fraud, violation of any franchise law, unfair or deceptive practices, embezzlement, misappropriation of property, or restraint of trade; have been held liable, settled, or are party to any civil litigation involving allegations of such conduct or brought by a present or former franchisee; are subject to any judicial or administrative restraining order or are party to any proceeding in which such an order is sought relating to such conduct; or have filed for bankruptcy, been adjudged bankrupt or reorganized due to insolvency, or been a principal, officer, or director of an entity that has, then the details of those matters must be disclosed. The publisher's balance sheet and financial statement must also be included.

The nature of the franchise must also be disclosed. The information must include a general description of the business, a detailed discussion of the product line, a description of the market, and a statement of the total initial funds that must be expended by the franchisee and of the franchisee's recurring expenses. The publisher must also identify the affiliates with whom the franchisee must deal, the goods and services that the franchisee is obliged to purchase or financing the franchisee must secure, and the revenues that the newspaper will derive from those outside purchases or financing.

There must also be significant disclosures concerning the substantive terms of the franchise arrangement, such as any customer or territorial sales restrictions or protection, and limitations on other products that the franchisee may distribute, requirements for personal participation by the franchisee, and any termination and renewal provisions. Prospective franchisees must be advised of any training programs available and must be given information concerning the number of franchises and publisher-owned outlets; the number of franchises terminated, refused renewal, or reacquired by the publisher; and the length of time between site selection and operation. The publisher must additionally furnish the names, addresses, and telephone numbers of at least 10 existing franchisees.

Any earnings claim must be reasonably supported and substantiated by facts in the publisher's possession at the time the claim is made, which will be made available to the prospect. The underlying data must be capable of independent verification and sufficiently broad based to assure representativeness. For example, the profitability of routes serving affluent suburban areas cannot be relied upon to secure a franchisee for a depressed inner-city area or remote country route.

Disclosure timing is also closely regulated by the rule. The Basic Disclosure Document must be furnished to a prospective franchisee at the first personal meeting held to discuss the sale or 10 business days prior to the franchisee's execution of a binding legal document or payment in connection with the sale, whichever is earlier. The Earnings Claims Document must be furnished at the first personal meeting at which an earnings claim is made or before that same 10 business-day period, whichever occurs first. The Basic Disclosure Document must be accompanied by the publisher's standard franchise agreement, and the completed agreement to be executed by the prospective franchisee must be given to him or her at least 5 days in advance of the time for execution.

The FTC Franchise Disclosure Rule has the potential for substantial impact upon newspaper distribution. No publisher should enter into, renew, or extend any distribution arrangement without soliciting the advice of expert counsel regarding the rule's applicability in a given situation.

STATE LAWS AFFECTING CIRCULATION

Many states responded to the federal laws regulating wages, hours, overtime, antitrust, child labor, and consumer fraud by passing their own legislation. Because of the separation of powers between the federal and state governments, the federal laws operate only where an interstate commerce issue or basic constitutional right is involved. Thus, many states have adopted legislation carrying over the various federal protections to intrastate commerce. These laws are enforced by state agencies through administrative hearings or by the state court system.

A knowledge of the precise state laws applicable to circulation is essential. Strong union states in the Midwest and Northeast, for example, have been successful in lobbying for legislation favorable to unions. Other states may prohibit lottery-style promotions or closely regulate pricing to distributors. Child labor laws vary widely from state to state. States can authorize sales taxes on newspapers, which the circulation department must collect and for which they are accountable.

Three areas of state law operate wholly apart from any federal legislation because of the preemptive jurisdiction of these state laws. These laws define and regulate: (1) legally binding contracts, (2) a distributor's proprietary interest in a route or subscriber list, and (3) a newspaper's liability for negligent or intentional acts of distributors.[47] Like the modified extensions of federal legislation discussed above, they vary among the 50 states.

Contract Law

A contract is an agreement that the law enforces and obligates the parties to perform. Four basic types of contracts exist: unilateral, bilateral, express, and implied.

A *unilateral contract* is one in which only one party promises something in exchange for another party's actual performance. An example is a district manager who offers $10 to the first carrier selling three new subscriptions. The carrier need only actually sell three subscriptions to receive the cash if he or she chooses to do so without formally agreeing to sell any. On the other hand, if both parties exchange promises of performance, this is considered a *bilateral contract*. An example is a district manager who offers a pizza party to five carriers on the condition that they agree to solicit subscriptions for two hours. Almost every contract between a newspaper and distributor is bilateral in nature.

An *express contract* can be either written or oral, but it always includes an actual agreement of intentions or ("meeting of the minds") between the parties. An *implied contract*, on the other hand, embodies obligations and promises that are inferred from the conduct of the parties without the aid of formal statements. If one distributor began covering the route of another distributor with the knowledge and tacit acceptance of the circulation manager, this is classified as constituting an implied contract. If the circulation manager agrees orally or in writing to the shift, it then becomes an express contract.

Contracts must contain several components in order to be enforceable by the courts:

1. The parties must mutually agree to enter into the contract.
2. The parties must exchange consideration (i.e., something of value) for their promises.
3. The terms of the contract must be certain and definite.
4. The parties must have the legal capacity to contract.
5. The contract must be lawful under state statutory and common laws.[48]

People can contractually agree to anything legal, but unless the terms are stated with reasonable clarity and definition, the contract is unenforceable. Price information is essential, and every circulation contract should carefully state the price, either in dollars and cents or in a precise percentage of profits, revenue, etc.

All parties to the contract must possess the legal capacity to enter into a contract, that is, both mental and age capacity. A minor (i.e., a person under 21 or 18, depending on the local law) may terminate a contract at will, although the adult party in such a contract can be held to it for its full duration by the minor. A newspaper can lawfully require that both the minor and his or her parents jointly contract in order to protect the newspaper's interests in enforcing the contract's terms. Moreover, a newspaper can, depending on state law, recover the value of benefits it has bestowed upon the minor under the contract, as well as subscriber lists in the minor's possession.

A contract generally may be assigned (i.e., transferred) to other parties as long as the assignment leaves the rights and duties unchanged. An assignment, however, is not effective if the contract expressly contemplates that a specific party alone is to perform the services (this would constitute a *personal services contract*). A contract generally is held to be in the nature of a personal services contract when the following circumstances arise:

1. Where, by reason of the nature, duration, or extent of the right, it is limited to exercise by the distributor alone
2. Where assignment of the right would materially change the newspaper's duty
3. Where assignment of the right would vary the risk assumed by the newspaper
4. Where the assignment would reduce the probability that the newspaper will receive the agreed upon service[49]

When a newspaper distributor seeks to assign his or her right to a particular territory to another person, he or she essentially is offering two distinct rights: a right to purchase goods (newspapers) and a right to perform personal services (delivery). On many occasions courts have distinguished the two, holding one to be in the nature of a personal contract and the other not. Thus, to safeguard against the assignability of distributorship rights and obligations, a circulation manager is always better off with a contract that expressly states that contract rights and duties are nonassignable or assignable only with the newspaper's written permission. These restrictive clauses should be made as clear as possible, specifying the rights that are to be nonassignable.

Legally, the relationship between a newspaper and independent contractor or distributor is governed by a bilateral contract, either express or implied, that most states classify as a principal-agent relationship. This means the newspaper, as principal, permits or directs another person to act for its benefit. The distributor, as agent, consequently attempts to advance the interests of the principal. This agency relationship creates certain legal rights and obligations.

A principal may always terminate an agency contract as long as the termination does not breach the contract itself. As an illustration, when the parties have entered into a fixed duration contract, the newspaper may lawfully terminate the distributor or agent only at the contract's expiration date or if the distributor breaches the contract. Terminable-at-will contracts may be dissolved with appropriate notice at any time. Thus, a terminated distributor has grounds for a damage suit against his or her former newspaper employer only when a contract of fixed duration is terminated prematurely and without the distributor's breach of its terms. The single exception to the rule arises when a distributor has an "agency coupled with an interest," that is, only when he or she buys the route directly from the newspaper and the contract expressly stipulates that the distributor cannot be terminated against his or her will. In one case, a court rejected the "agency coupled with an interest" suit of a distributor who purchased the route from another distributor, and a court in a subsequent case also rejected the suit of a distributor who purchased the route list from the newspaper pursuant to a terminable-at-will employment relationship.[50]

This does not mean a newspaper can terminate distributors without compensating them in some way. Legally, neither party in an agency relationship can receive something of value without paying for it. Conversely, when a distributor purchases a newspaper route or subscriber list, or devotes time and money to expanding or improving the route, or must purchase equipment, courts frequently require newspapers to reimburse the distributor if the latter has not had a reasonable opportunity to recoup the investment.

A newspaper distributor generally does not have a proprietary interest in a newspaper route or subscriber list unless the contract itself grants it. If granted a proprietary interest, the distributor has a right to compensation for its loss upon termination. The contract can grant a proprietary interest in an express provision or by implication, but an implied proprietary interest can be established in only two ways:

1. The terminated distributor must prove that the parties orally agreed but inadvertently failed to write ownership into the contract.
2. The distributor must prove that the contract was drawn up with the reference to established custom and usage, which recognized the distributor's ownership of the route or list. (Custom and usage means a practice

so common and long-standing that it is automatically assumed to be part of the negotiated contract.)[51]

In this latter respect, a distributor must demonstrate that the newspaper accepted the distributor's services with full knowledge of and acquiescence in the custom and usage and recognized the distributor's ownership interest in the route and the need to reimburse the distributor upon premature termination.

Laws Governing Newspaper Liability

Newspaper liability arises from two different areas of law: tort and agency.[52] The law of torts identifies the type of conduct that makes a newspaper liable for an injury; the law of agency governs the extent to which the newspaper is responsible for an employee's or agent's actions. For example, if an individual is run over by a newspaper distributor's vehicle, the law of torts controls the injured party's ability to recover damages; and the law of agency determines the extent to which the newspaper is liable for the distributor's act. Thus, if the accident occurs during nonworking time, the newspaper is not held liable.

Law of Torts   The two major types of torts of concern here are: intentional and negligent interference with the interests of another person. *Intentional interference* means that an individual does something that causes harm, injury, or damage to the property or person of another. The law posits three requirements for the successful prosecution of an intentional tort suit: an act (e.g., throwing a newspaper); intent (e.g., intent to throw the paper); and proximate causation (e.g., the paper shattering a plate glass window), that is, the damage or injury must be substantially attributable to the conduct in question.

The concept of *negligence* arises because society requires its members to exercise a duty of care with regard to the rights and interests of one another. Someone breaching that obligation is considered negligent and liable for injury inflicted on another. To establish a cause of action for negligence against a distributor, an injured party must establish four requirements: a duty recognized by law requiring the distributor to conform to a certain standard of behavior, a distributor's failure to conform to the duty, a reasonably close causal connection between the negligent conduct and damage suffered by another, and an actual loss or damage.

The duty requirement comprises an obligation to behave with a certain standard of care, such as making sure the brakes on one's vehicle are in good condition before driving it. A distributor's duty toward other persons remains constant, that is, the distributor is obligated to act as would "a reasonably prudent person" under the circumstances. Under the law, one must take precautions against events that are reasonably foreseeable. A child darting out from between parked cars is forseeable in a school zone in April but not so in a tavern parking lot at midnight.

For minors (e.g., newsboys), the duty measure reflects the "reasonably prudent" standard of minors of like age, education, intelligence, and experience; however, the standard is often made stricter for those minors participating in adult activities like driving. Since laws are assumed to be obeyed by "reasonably prudent" persons, breaking a law like the speed limit generally is considered proof of negligent behavior. Apart from this shorthand way of calculating negligence, a breach of duty is established ordinarily by showing that the individual acted unreasonably under the circumstances.

Agency Law   Agency law establishes whether or not and to what extent the newspaper is liable for its employees' or independent agents' actions. The newspaper is generally not liable for the actions of its independent contractors unless the newspaper shares in the negligence by failing to correct a hazardous situation. The newspaper is always responsible, however, for exercising reasonable care in hiring competent independent contractors.

A newspaper is liable only for employee actions falling within the scope of that employee's employment. Among several criteria considered by the courts, the most important appears to be whether the employee's intent in committing the action was in furtherance of the newspaper's business. An affirmative finding in this regard can override the fact, for example, that the driver acted contrary to express orders or that the accident occurred returning from his or her route. Equally as important, the newspaper is not liable for intentional acts that are not reasonably forseeable or have no substantial relation to the driver's function in the newspaper. Thus, a driver who injures another in a drag race collision on vacation creates no liability for the newspaper.

State Statutory Laws

State laws regulating business can create problems for an employer if their requirements differ from or even conflict with applicable federal requirements in the same statutory area. State law must yield, however, to federal law whenever it conflicts with, impedes, or burdens a federal law. This conclusion is mandated by the Supremacy Clause of the U.S.

Constitution. The Supreme Court has interpreted the doctrine of federal preemption to permit state regulation in three limited situations:

1. Where a federal law specifically provides for state jurisdiction
2. Where there is no federal law to preempt the area
3. Where the subject matter of the state regulation is beyond the scope of the federal regulatory power[53]

State Workmen's Compensation Laws

Whatever their idiosyncrasies, state workers' compensation laws generally operate on the principle that an employee is automatically entitled to benefits whenever suffering an accidental injury arising out of and in the course of employment. In order to collect benefits, the employee must usually show the following:

1. That the injury was caused by the accident
2. That the injury arose from employment
3. That the injury occurred in the course of employment[54]

Most states require that the injury be accidental in order to trigger eligibility for benefits, which generally means an unforeseen, chance, or unplanned action precipitates the injury. Definitions of accident vary from state to state. Any damage sustained to the body usually satisfies the injury requirement.

Street risks are the most common source of injury for circulation employees. The courts have even developed a *street risk doctrine* applicable to workers' compensation awards. Although originally concerned primarily with falls on icy streets and traffic hazards, the doctrine now has been more liberally interpreted and holds that if one's employment necessitates street travel, associated street risks are then considered compensable job hazards. The street risk doctrine evolved to provide protection for almost every injury that conceivably might occur on the street: For example, injuries sustained as a result of stray bullets, bombs, falling buildings or objects, thrown bricks, stabbings, and footballs and baseballs thrown into the street have all been treated as compensable.

MUNICIPAL ORDINANCES

Municipal ordinances most commonly affecting circulation include regulations on door-to-door solicitations and restrictions on newspaper racks and boxes.

Ordinances Governing Door-to-Door Solicitation

An ordinance restricting door-to-door solicitation (commonly called a *Green River ordinance* after the town in Wyoming that developed it) is constitutional as long as it does not discriminate against out-of-state businesses.[55] State courts often invalidate such laws on the grounds of state constitutions, however. Very often municipalities improperly exceed their police power as provided for in the state's constitution; and on other occasions the specific ordinance is found to be arbitrary, overly broad in wording, or classifies as a public wrong an act that is a private wrong and may not be punished as a crime.

Newspaper Rack Ordinances

Local ordinances restricting the placement of, design of, and litter from newspaper racks have sprung from local efforts to beautify public streets and increase safety. Ordinarily deemed to be valid exercises of a municipality's power when limited to "time, place and manner" regulations, these laws raise serious constitutional questions when they are used to unnecessarily or unjustifiably restrict the placement of newspaper racks on public streets.

As an illustration, a 1974 U.S. District Court decision struck down an

FIGURE 6.1   Denver ordinances brought competing newspapers into a common single-copy box as a means to keep streets neater. *USA Today* and other competing newspapers raise substantive questions about the practicality of such ordinances. Courtesy *Rocky Mountain News*, Denver.

ordinance making it unlawful to obstruct the free use of the streets or to conduct any commercial business on them. The ordinance also prohibited the display of merchandise on public sidewalks more than 3 feet from a business' premises. The ordinance was enforced against a newspaper by removing two of the newspaper's racks from public sidewalks. The court found the ordinance to have impermissibly abridged the newspaper's right of free access to the public streets for the dissemination of information. The court observed, however, that a more narrowly tailored ordinance might pass constitutional muster.

> In particular, if the feared evil is obstruction of the sidewalks that will interfere with the public's right to unhampered passage thereon, narrow regulations as to the size and location of newspaper boxes could be formulated which would certainly survive constitutional scrutiny.... If the feared evil is traffic congestion or illegal parking or stopping by motorists in order to purchase newspapers, narrow regulations with respect to the location of newspaper boxes in relation to the character of the roadway could also be formulated. If destruction or damage to municipal property ... is feared, suitable prohibitions could be enacted which could have only an incidental restrictive effect upon distribution by means of newspaper boxes.[56]

The legal dimensions of newspaper circulation touch every aspect of the system, from part-time driver and youth carrier to chief executive, and they affect everyone connected to the newspaper: employees, contractors, supervisors, readers, and competitors. No circulation manager can afford to be ignorant of the implications of the various federal, state, and municipal laws. While this chapter has provided an overview of the major points, intensive study of the *ICMA Legal Manual* is strongly recommended to anyone contemplating a change in any aspect of the system, facing labor organization or action, or planning a major competitive move in the marketplace.

The most important areas for circulation workers to understand are the following:

1. Federal laws regulating employee working conditions, wages, and labor rights

2. Federal laws regulating monopolistic and anticompetitive practices

3. Federal laws regulating discrimination

4. Federal laws regulating franchises and honesty in advertising

5. Law of torts, federal and state laws on liability for employees and agents of the newspaper

6. State laws regulating workmen's compensation and contracts

7. State laws regulating child labor and discrimination

8. Municipal ordinances on solicitation, noise, litter, and single copy box placement

In the United States, the legal dimensions of circulation can change rapidly from state to state and year to year. American courts decide guilt or innocence before the law on two major bases: the case facts and precedent. The basic laws are themselves changed by Congress, state legislatures, and municipal bodies. Rarely are two newspaper circulation cases exactly the same, no matter how similar they might appear. Moreover, court cases constantly set new precedents that can change what is permitted. For these reasons, it is important to work with a lawyer knowledgeable in circulation aspects of the law.

This chapter concludes Part I. Part II takes up the basic elements in each phase of the circulation system, beginning with the mailroom and transportation.

NOTES

1. Milton Konvitz, ed., "Bill of Rights in the United States Constitution," *Bill of Rights Reader* (Ithaca, N.Y.: Cornell University Press, 1968), 1.
2. Robert Ballow, *ICMA Legal Manual* (Reston, Va.: International Circulation Managers Association, 1978), 14. This handbook fully explains the federal, state, and local laws affecting newspaper circulation practices, and it is the basis for this chapter, which Robert Ballow has reviewed, revised, and helped polish.
3. Ibid., 16.
4. Ibid., 17.
5. Cited by Ballow, *ICMA Legal Manual*, 18.
6. 29 U.S.C. 201 Section 3(e)(1).
7. 29 U.S.C. 201 Section 3(g).
8. Ballow, *ICMA Legal Manual*, 20.
9. 29 U.S.C. 201 Section 14.
10. 29 U.S.C. 201 Section 13(a).
11. 29 U.S.C. 201 Section 13(d).
12. 29 U.S.C. 201 Section 13(b). For a fuller explanation of these exemptions and other nuances of this law, see: Ballow, *ICMA Legal Manual*, 63–89.
13. 29 U.S.C. 201 Section 13(a)(8).
14. 29 U.S.C. 201 Section 13(a)(1).
15. Ballow, *ICMA Legal Manual*, 72–73.
16. 29 U.S.C. 201 Section 13(a)(1).
17. 29 U.S.C. 201 Section 13(d).
18. Ballow, *ICMA Legal Manual*, 76–77.
19. 29 U.S.C. 201 Section 12.

20. 29 U.S.C. 151 Section 2 defines all terms used in the Act, and it is important for circulation managers to understand.
21. 29 U.S.C. 201 Section 2(11).
22. Ballow, *ICMA Legal Manual*, 32.
23. 29 U.S.C. 151 Section 7.
24. Ballow, *ICMA Legal Manual*, 37–38.
25. 29 U.S.C. 151 Section 8(a)(1).
26. The 1947 congressional amendment of Section 8(c) defines employers rights to express their opinion in keeping with their basic constitutional rights under the First Amendment of the U.S. Constitution.
27. 29 U.S.C. 151 Section 8(a)(1).
28. 29 U.S.C. 151 Section 8(a)(2).
29. 29 U.S.C. 151 Section 8(a)(3).
30. 29 U.S.C. 151 Section 7. Section 8(d) defines "bargain collectively": "to bargain collectively is the performance of the mutual obligation of the employer and the representative of the employees to meet at reasonable times and confer in good faith with respect to wages, hours, and other terms and conditions of employment...."
31. Section 7 guarantees the right in general: "Employees shall have the right to engage in other concerted activities for the purpose of collective bargaining or other mutual aid or protection...." Section 13 specifically provides the right to strike.
32. 29 U.S.C. 151 Section 7.
33. 29 U.S.C. 151 Section 10 defines the remedial powers of the National Labor Relations Board: Section 10(c) specifically addresses cease and desist orders.
34. 29 U.S.C. 201 Sections 6, 7, and 12. Section 6 covers minimum wage and wage calculation; Section 7 covers overtime hours and pay; and Section 12 addresses child labor.
35. 29 U.S.C. 201 Section 6.
36. *The Civil Rights Act of 1866* has been codified as 42 U.S.C. 1981, and it has become informally known as "1981."
37. Ballow, *ICMA Legal Manual*, 92.
38. Ibid., 93.
39. Ibid., 96.
40. 29 U.S.C. 201 Section 6(d).
41. 29 U.S.C. 621 Section 623.
42. Ballow, *ICMA Legal Manual*, 108–109 contains the precise wording of the decision and a useful analysis.
43. Ibid., 110. Ballow lists the basis for legally refusing to deal with distributors.
44. 29 U.S.C. 1 Section 2.
45. 29 U.S.C. 1 Section 3.
46. Ballow, *ICMA Legal Manual*, 132.
47. Ibid., 139.
48. Ibid., 142.
49. Ibid., 146.

50. Ibid., 150. Ballow covers the specific language of the court decision and its implications.
51. Ibid., 152.
52. Ibid., 13–15, 154–162. Ballow details the basis for tort laws and liability.
53. Ibid., 163.
54. Ibid., 166.
55. Ibid., 174.
56. Cited by Ballow, *ICMA Legal Manual*, 176–177.

PART II

Getting the Newspaper to the Customer

The sales, promotion, and marketing of newspapers discussed in the previous chapters are dependent not only on a good product but also on the efficient distribution of that product. Efficient distribution is the goal of circulation departments.

A good distribution system requires dependability, flexibility, economy, and control. *Dependability* is crucial both to continued readership and employee morale. Readers whose morning papers frequently are delivered too late to be read before leaving for work quickly lose the habit of newspaper reading. Subscribers have a right to expect that they will receive their newspapers in a readable condition and on time. Nonsubscribers wanting to purchase a newspaper on a particular day should find single copies easily accessible. Providing this type of dependable service is the responsibility of circulation managers, district managers, contractors, and carriers; but to provide such service, these circulation employees must rely on the newspaper's being produced and shipped on a dependable schedule. Erratic production and transportation schedules destroy carrier morale and result in dissatisfied customers. Dependability in circulation begins in the pressroom, mailroom, and loading dock, as discussed in Chapter 7.

Flexibility must be built into the distribution system to account for late-breaking news stories, press breakdowns, adverse weather conditions, changing circulation lists, and fluctuating number of insertions. Flexibility, which allows a newspaper to adjust circulation variables such as route size and number of carriers to offset other problems, may be achieved through mechanical means or by manpower realignment. On small newspapers a large number of inserts often necessitates the drafting of additional employees to stuff inserts on a particular day. On larger newspapers the bundling and insertion equipment must be flexible enough to make multiple insertions, separate zoned editions, and maintain the press pace. Flexibility in delivery patterns means the ability to adjust circulation routes daily to accommodate subscribers' requests and to add single copy outlets as the demand warrants.

The third requirement of a successful distribution system, *economy*, includes both economy of equipment and materials and economy of the labor force. Sophisticated bundling and insertion equipment and fully computerized circulation systems are not cost effective for all newspapers, especially in areas where labor costs are low. Decisions on the use of company-owned vehicles, as opposed to privately-owned or leased, are also affected by economic factors. Gasoline and diesel prices require a periodic review of transportation routes and systems and consideration of alternative fuels, such as propane.

The concept of *control* in delivery systems has significantly broadened in the past decade. Since 1912 the Audit Bureau of Circulation has verified the number of newspapers printed and returned as a means of determining actual copies sold. Internally, cost control has mandated reduction of returns, limited spoilage, and theft prevention. In recent years, with the increasing number of inserts, the concept of control has extended to the security of preprints. Coupon theft and fraud have become big business. Tightly controlling preprints with coupons has become necessary to maintain advertising revenues.

The next four chapters outline how these criteria of a good distribution system affect decisions made by circulation personnel in the preparation and transportation of newspapers from the plant to assorted distribution points, in the services provided to subscribers and single copy purchasers, and in the move toward computerization.

It is important to note here that the greatest difference between weeklies and dailies emerges in the distribution system. While a few weeklies rely on the system that Ben Franklin knew as an apprentice, most rely on the U.S. Postal Service for the majority of their circulation. There are some important variations requiring little explanation but meriting attention.

The 100 percent distribution systems employ door-to-door delivery by paid delivery agents who may be youths, unemployed adults, or homemakers. The two major systems are urban and rural. In the urban system, delivery is to the porch or yard by people in slowly moving vehicles or by carriers afoot. In rural areas, shoppers often place special newspaper tubes on every lot or next to every rural mailbox. Here, motor route drivers place the weekly newspaper.

Institutional newspapers also rely primarily on postal delivery. However, some religious newspapers ship bundles of newspapers to each church for free distribution or sale at the local level. While much less costly than second-class postage, this church distribution system limits readership to those who come to church or receive a copy from someone else.

The skyway system, which first interconnected the downtown buildings in Minneapolis in the early 1970s, spawned an ingenious distribution system for a weekly, *Skyway News*. A shopper, the *News* was simply left in open racks on the skyway system and led to a flurry of competitive shoppers obtainable from open stacks in restaurants, theaters, shops, and public places.

Daily newspaper systems dominate much of this section simply because they have more complex distribution systems and larger staffs.

CHAPTER
7

The Mailroom and Transportation

Timely delivery of the newspaper actually begins in the newsroom, as reporters and editors meet copy deadlines. This enables the presses to begin rolling on time, which, in turn, means transportation of the newspaper to various distribution points can occur on schedule.

The preparation of the newspaper for transportation—making the necessary inserts, bundling, and labeling for proper distribution—occurs in the mailroom.

THE MAILROOM

Deriving its name from the time when most newspapers were wrapped and labeled for postal delivery, the mailroom is the physical link between the production process and the circulation system. The mailroom workers take newspapers warm from the presses and prepare them for transportation. Thus, the mailroom is the last step in the production process or the first step in circulation. For weeklies, it is the first and last step in circulation, apart from delivery to a few stores or single copy racks.

Organizational Placement

The mailroom's organizational placement within the newspaper depends on the newspaper's size, its corporate philosophy, and its labor relations. Generally, circulation managers supervise the mailroom on smaller newspapers and production managers supervise it on larger newspapers. The latter organizational structure reflects the increased mechanization of large-circulation newspapers, with the direct mechanical links of the mail-room to the presses.

The small newspaper's circulation manager who runs the mailroom supervises an inserting machine or two; a counter-stacker-unit, which assembles newspapers into fixed-size bundles; a labeling machine; a bundle-tying machine; and hand preparation of papers for the Postal Service. The mailroom staff comprises three to five full-time employees and an equal number of part-timers. For instance, at the *Wisconsin Rapids Tribune*, having a circulation of about 10,000, the circulation manager handles all mailroom operations with the help of several high school students. On a medium-sized daily (50,000 to 100,000 circulation), the mailroom includes another 10 to 20 part-time employees and a second counter-stacker line.

Larger circulation newspapers require more mailroom machinery and staff. At the same time, circulation responsibilities—delivery, collection, sales, and service—are more complex. Thus, most large newspapers assign the sales, distribution, and service functions to the circulation department and the mailroom to the production department.

Labor and union jurisdictions sometimes play a role in the mailroom's organizational placement. Although most mailrooms are unionized, the work is semiskilled and unskilled and does not fit the craft unions representing other employees, such as pressmen, typesetters, and electricians. Mailrooms operate under unions as diverse as the Teamsters and The Newspaper Guild. Since production managers routinely work with union employees in the pressroom, publishers or circulation managers, especially those dealing with independent contractors for delivery, may prefer to have the mailroom under the production department.

Whatever the mailroom's organizational placement, it must facilitate the circulation department's work in two ways. First, mailroom workers must assemble and prepare newspapers for transportation in a timely fashion to insure on-time delivery to subscribers and single copy outlets. Second, mailroom supervisors must provide security for coupons and preprints.

Mailroom Tasks

Whether the mailroom is part of the production department or the circulation department, its staff is responsible for making most insertions and for bundling and labeling the newspapers after they leave the presses.

Insertions While many small and medium-sized newspapers still rely on hand insertions, often by youth carriers in the field, high-technology machinery has mechanized the insertion process on newspapers as diverse in size as the *Contra Costa Times* (88,382 Sunday) and the *St. Paul Pioneer Press* (244,218 Sunday).

In deciding whether to automate the insertion process, publishers must consider whether the equipment will meet future needs, if it will require plant expansion and/or skilled technicians, and if the initial capital expenditure will result in long-term savings. Such factors affect the distribution system's economy.

For many newspapers, such as the *Daily Journal* in Kankakee, Illinois, limited space; worker availability to do insertions, especially during periods of unemployment; and a need to produce several publications simultaneously operate against a decision to automate the insertion process.[1]

Newspapers that decide it is cost efficient to automate the insertion process must choose between on-line and off-line systems. An on-line system is directly connected to the presses, whereas an off-line system requires storing newspapers briefly between the presses and the insertion process.

The advantage of an on-line system is time savings. The disadvantage

FIGURE 7.1   Revolutionizing the mailroom, automated inserting machines like the Harris allows automatic insertion of multiple preprints into each newspaper as it moves from presses to machines which stack, count, and bundle papers.
Courtesy Harris Corporation.

FIGURE 7.2   Overhead newspaper conveyors like this Ferag system at the *Daily Oklahoman* carry newspapers from the presses to the on-line-inserters. The *Daily Oklahoman* was first newspaper to completely integrate components from different major manufacturers into a fully automated mailroom. Multiple press lines allow simultaneous production and insertion of different zoned editions. Storage for bundled preprints (foreground on skids) is one reason the paper devotes 1 acre to the mailroom. Courtesy *Daily Oklahoman*.

is lack of flexibility; tying insertion equipment to the presses means that a mechanical malfunction with an insertion machine can stop the entire press run. Thus, some newspapers use buffer or backup systems to eliminate press stoppage. For instance, in St. Paul large, round racks are used to store newspapers until insertion equipment is back on-line. At the *Milwaukee Sentinel* two Harris systems mean that if one insertion system goes down, papers from both presses can be tracked to the still-operable inserter without a production delay.

Even with the growth of mechanized insertion systems, the large number of preprints means that carriers for many large-circulation newspapers must still make at least one insertion or deliver two packages of material simultaneously.

Bundling and Labeling   The bundling and labeling tasks of the mailroom are closely linked. They encompass three types of distribution systems—bulk distribution, label distribution, and a hybrid system that uses both bulk bundles and a single, labeled bundle.

In *bulk distribution* all bundles contain the same number of newspapers; there is no label except, perhaps, one denoting edition or zone. The size of the bundles varies with the size of each day's newspaper. Daily bundles may include 25 to 50 copies, while the Sunday edition bundle may have only 5 copies. Weight is one means of determining bundle size, with 30 pounds the average weight. To provide carriers and dealers with the precise number of newspapers required, the truck driver or station manager opens a full bundle and counts out the odd number of papers.

The advantage of the bulk distribution system is its flexibility in relation to transportation. Since there is no precise truck sequence and trucks are loaded on a first come, first served basis, the loading is uncomplicated and rapid. A late truck does not disrupt the loading process.

The disadvantage of bulk distribution is the lack of control. Accountability for single copies within an opened bundle is difficult to maintain in a system based on full bundles. Yet both the cost of production and coupon security increase the pressure for accountability of each copy; newsprint has recycling value and coupons have cash value.

Some distribution systems, like that of the *Houston Chronicle*, almost mandate bulk distribution. The *Chronicle* moves its newspapers by semi-trailer from the mailroom to four warehouses, where contractors pick up their newspapers. This double handling makes label distribution too complex. Other newspapers using bulk distribution are the *Louisville Courier Journal* and *Times*, the *Minneapolis Tribune*, and the *Chicago Tribune*.

In *label distribution* most bundles contain the same number of copies, but the counter-stacker machine or a mailroom worker makes up an odd-sized bundle having the precise number needed for each dealer or carrier. Each bundle, whether the average size or odd sized, includes a label indicating the number of newspapers and the address of the drop point. Mail from the office, including stops and starts, can also be included with the odd-sized bundle.

Computerized circulation systems have made label distribution cost efficient, especially for medium-sized newspapers and for home delivery routes of 35 to 50 papers. In the mailroom, the label printer, connected to the computer, interacts with the counter-stacker and bundle-tying machines to provide the exact number of copies needed. Since each bundle is labeled, accountability is simplified. The system also provides carriers with updated route lists because the labels on each bundle include stops and starts. Newspapers using the complete labeled bundle system include the *Decatur* (Illinois) *Herald and Review*, the *Eau Claire* (Wisconsin) *Leader and Telegram*, and the *Cedar Rapids* (Iowa) *Gazette*.

The disadvantages of the label distribution system are the possibility of equipment breakdown and the size of the support staff needed to keep the computer current. Because computerized systems link counter-stackers to presses, a computer malfunction in the label delivery system can cause production delays, which, in turn, disrupt the distribution system's dependability. Thus, backup systems, like those discussed in the insertion section of this chapter, are necessary. The second difficulty with a computerized label system is that all circulation changes must move through the computer for accuracy in delivery; thus, the newspaper must educate both its carriers and customers to notify the office of stops and starts. This computerization, discussed in greater detail in Chapter 10, is costly in terms of both staff and equipment.

The third type of distribution system, the *lead bundle system*, utilizes features of both bulk and label distribution. While most bundles contain the same number of newspapers and go out unlabeled as in bulk distribution, a lead bundle, like the odd-sized bundle in label distribution, includes an odd number of newspapers and a label stating the drop point address or the route number and the number of newspapers to be delivered to that site.

The lead bundle system has the control advantages of the label distribution system without the concerns of mechanical/computer problems. In fact, most lead bundles are hand counted. The *Madison* (Wisconsin) *Capitol Times* and *State Journal*, the *Rockford* (Illinois) *Register Star*, the *Kenosha* (Wisconsin) *News*, and the *Waukegan* (Illinois) *New Sun* use lead bundle systems.

THE LOADING DOCK

Like the mailroom, the loading dock is a link between the production process and circulation. The loading dock's primary goal is the immediate transfer of the correct number of newspapers to the appropriate vehicles in a sequence designed to insure timely delivery and at a pace equal to that of the pressroom and mailroom.

Loading Dock Priorities

Dock operation priorities serve both the mailroom and the circulation distribution plan. The mailroom requirements are dominantly physical, that is, the space, location, and equipment define the rate at which newspapers reach the dock and the number of truck chutes served at one time. The press configuration determines which editions reach particular loading chutes. The rapid expansion of inserts has overburdened many mailrooms by requiring tremendous amounts of storage space. The development of zoned editions to serve advertisers has further complicated newspapers' movement through the mailroom, particularly when the newspaper has more than one press and each produces a different edition.

In determining a loading sequence, loading dock supervisors use three principles—time/distance, zone/edition, and simplicity. Provisions also must be made for schedule adjustments necessitated by weather conditions, particularly for newspapers serving a broad geographical area.

Time/Distance   The time/distance principle gives priority to trucks traveling farthest from the newspaper and the greatest amount of time. This priority takes into account the types of roads traveled, the number of drop points, and the average driving time required to complete the route as established by tests and adjusted for highway construction projects. The result is a fixed truck-by-truck loading sequence or a group loading sequence, with the truck sequence established on a first come, first served basis.

Zone/Edition   The zone/edition principle, which applies only to newspaper plants printing multiple newspapers or multiple-zoned editions of a single newspaper, establishes the loading sequence in accordance with the printing and insertion schedule of various editions. For newspapers with more than one press line, the zone/edition principle also assigns trucks to dock chutes fed by the appropriate press. Press stoppages and mailroom delays cause loading pattern shifts that must be immediately accommodated, perhaps causing half-loaded trucks to temporarily leave the dock so other editions can be loaded.

Simplicity   The simplicity principle encourages the least complicated system of identifying bundles for each zone or edition, of passing route information to drivers, and of adjusting the loading sequence as needed.

Among the bundle identification methods used are differently colored cover sheets, cover sheets from returned newspapers using the edition nameplate, cover sheets of different sections from returned Sunday newspapers, large numbers or letters written with colored marker pens, and computer or hand-produced labels. The goal is ready identification of the zone or edition from a distance. Routing information can be deposited in mailboxes for the drivers or handed out by dock supervisory personnel during loading, along with information for each drop in clearly marked envelopes.

While smaller newspapers with relatively few drivers can apprise drivers of loading adjustments face to face, larger loading docks require powerful public address or CB radio systems to keep drivers informed of their position in the line and changes in the sequence.

Loading Dock Procedures

Loading dock operations are directly tied to the bundling/labeling system used by a newspaper; therefore, dock procedures vary for bulk distribution, label distribution, and lead bundle distribution systems. In addition, fully automated circulation systems require other variations on the loading dock. For larger newspapers, loading schedules must also include provisions for the advance delivery of insert sections for Sunday newspapers and other special supplements.

Bulk Distribution The bulk bundle system offers the simplest, most flexible dock operation because all bundles are identical. A breakdown in one element of the mailroom can be overcome quickly by shunting newspapers to a different section and servicing the entire dock through it. Truck loading can be sequenced according to arrival time within the various time/distance and zone/edition groups without impairing efficiency. All route change and drop site information and all agent and carrier dispatches can be passed on in a single envelope or pouch.

FIGURE 7.3 A computerized loading dock system automatically routes bundles of zoned editions to waiting trucks. Bundles pass chutes at the top right and drop through computer controlled gates to the proper delivery truck. Courtesy *St. Paul Pioneer Press and Dispatch.*

FIGURE 7.4   The automated mailroom allows the *Sacramento Bee* controller to move zoned editions from press lines and inserters on the left to trucks at assigned chutes on the right. Courtesy *Sacramento Bee*.

Label Distribution   The label system requires a precise loading dock sequence because each bundle is produced for a particular route. The trucks must either load at the chute containing their bundles or the system, if computerized, must be able to deliver appropriate bundles to the chute where a truck is parked. Any problem in the bundle delivery for a particular truck ties up a chute and can create a backlog in the mailroom. Conversely, problems in the mailroom or with the presses can delay the entire distribution system by blocking the loading dock with partially filled trucks. On the other hand, a proven label system can expedite dock work and reduce the need for a special dock crew; and it provides absolute control over the newspapers loaded. All driver, agent, and carrier messages are printed on the bundle wrappers, insuring delivery.

Lead Bundle Distribution   Lead bundles must be produced according to the truck loading sequence and delivered to the appropriate trucks. As in the label system, either the truck must load at the chute containing the correct lead bundles or the system must deliver the lead bundle to the truck. An alternative to precise chute allocation is lead bundle storage, where the lead bundles are the first produced by the mailroom and are stored until trucks begin loading, when they are delivered to the driver.

FIGURE 7.5 Automated conveyors eliminate the loading dock. Control buttons allow the driver to extend conveyor as far as necessary into the delivery truck.
Courtesy *Sacramento Bee*.

Once the lead bundles have been prepared, the mailroom bundles the rest of the newspaper as in a bulk system; and a truck driver can load at any chute. Thus, the lead bundle system, especially with storage capabilities, provides flexibility in the event of mailroom or press slowdowns.

Automated Distribution Automated dock systems typically involve a computer-operated series of bins or trays that carry bundles on a circular route and drop them at designated chutes. The key to this system is that each bundle is identified for the computer as it leaves the mailroom. The drivers identify themselves to the computer after entering a chute; and the computer sends the precise number of bundles, whether bulk, label, or lead, to the truck. Automated dock systems reduce labor costs, increase security, and allow precise delivery of multiple-zoned editions with minimal confusion on the dock. The *Chicago Tribune, Houston Chronicle,* and *St. Paul Pioneer Press* use automated loading systems.

Advanced Distribution   Because the inner sections of Sunday newspapers and some supplements are printed days and even weeks in advance and because their weight precludes distribution with the main Sunday edition, most dock systems include a preloading operation on certain days. This means drivers load the insert sections before the pressrun begins then wait to load the regular newspaper. Security is critical for Sunday insert sections because of the valuable coupons they contain; moving the inserts from the printing plant to a variety of distribution points makes insert control more difficult and normally necessitates secured substations or contractor storage areas.

Another problem with advanced distribution is the long wait for drivers between the loading of inserts and the regular newspaper. For this reason, some newspapers prefer to load both inserts and Sunday main sections at the same time, using the printing plant as a warehouse through the week. However, the growth of preprints has increased the demand for storage space and forced advanced distribution for many newspapers.

Loading Dock Problems

Whatever priorities are set for the loading dock and whatever bundling system is used, security is a primary concern. Another problem involves labor relations with loading dock employees.

Security   Security on the loading dock, an element of control, involves the accountability for each newspaper and the prevention of theft. Since a bundle of 50 newspapers is worth $12 retail (at 25¢ per copy) or about $10 in return credit (at a wholesale rate of 20¢ per copy), the bundles have enough value to tempt drivers to steal them by overloading trucks. Even honest drivers can lose count of the number of bundles loaded, particularly with large vehicles.

Losing a bundle, by theft or honest error, both deprives the newspaper of income and reduces net paid circulation because sales are not verified. An 18-wheeled semitrailer can absorb a large number of unaccounted bundles on any given day, but even the daily disappearance of one bundle into each of five or six trucks produces a substantial loss. To prevent such loss, most newspapers have an employee count the number of bundles loaded on each truck, logging the total on a tally sheet. Unloaded bundles are placed in less accessible areas and closely watched. Once a truck has been inspected, it must leave the dock immediately.

Security also applies to returned newspapers if drivers or contractors receive credit for them. Some newspapers, such as the *Detroit Free Press*, immediately place returned newspapers in a secure area; others, like the *Sacramento Bee*, shred them and rebundle them for scrap. Some newspapers accept only complete nameplates from page one for return, leaving disposal of the remainder of the newspapers to the contractors; the *Dallas Times-Herald* uses this system.

Another element of security is safety. The dock area, with frequent, often rapid movement of vehicles, must be secured against children, pedestrians, cyclists, and inattentive drivers. Most newspapers restrict access to the dock area at presstime.

Employee Relations Loading docks can be the scene of conflicts among unions, between union and nonunion employees, and among workers in the same labor category. Because the dock is a gathering point for waiting drivers, it is a natural site for union organization activities and grievance exchanges. Waiting to load newspapers or to receive credit for returns also enables independent contractors and contract haulers to compare contract provisions that have been individually negotiated.

To minimize labor problems and facilitate efficient dock operations, many newspapers forbid truck drivers to arrive more than 10 or 15 minutes early and require drivers to remain in their trucks. Such a schedule limits the amount of parking space needed and eases the traffic patterns on the dock.

TRANSPORTATION SYSTEMS

Circulation necessitates getting the newspaper from the printing facility to the customer. The transportation systems discussed in this section involve the movement of newspapers from the loading dock to a substation, independent contractor, or wholesaler. Delivery to the subscriber, a retail outlet, or vending boxes is discussed in the next two chapters.

In determining the best methods for transporting newspapers, circulation personnel must consider whether to use newspaper employees or contract for transportation, whether to use company-owned or leased vehicles, and how best to supervise transportation workers.

Private vs. Contract Cartage

Private cartage is a distribution system fully controlled by the newspaper itself, either through owned or leased vehicles. Because the newspaper can determine the vehicles to be used on particular routes each day, private cartage increases both control and flexibility of the distribution system. However, private cartage also requires the newspaper to provide drivers, either through direct employment or as part of a contract arrangement, thus involving the company in employee supervision, the provision of fringe benefits, and, perhaps, union negotiations. Most metropolitan newspapers use private cartage for their city zones. Some newspapers, such as the *Toronto Star* and the *Janesville* (Wisconsin) *Gazette*, rely entirely on private cartage.

Contract cartage, normally less expensive than private cartage, is a transportation system in which the newspaper pays for hauling service. The newspaper receives a weekly cartage bill with no responsibility for either vehicles or personnel. Metropolitan newspapers typically use contract cartage for newspaper delivery to outlying areas.

There are two types of cartage contracts—exclusive or cooperative. An *exclusive contract* limits the hauler to newspaper delivery for one company; a *cooperative contract* allows the hauler to contract with anyone else, including other newspapers, for loads on the same trucks.

Newspapers using exclusive contracts, with either local or national firms, include the *St. Louis Post Dispatch* and the *Miami Herald.* Through its newspaper circulation program, one national company, Ryder, provides the vehicles and drivers to newspapers anywhere on any schedule a newspaper company sets.

Contract cartage is the dominant transportation system for Canadian newspapers, with 60 percent of the newspapers using contract haulers for city delivery and 6 percent using them for rural delivery.[2] Cooperative contracts are also more common in Canada and Europe than in the United States. In fact, some Canadian and many European papers have shared hauling in which several newspapers use the same trucks and drivers. A cooperative contract reduces the newspaper's cost, but it also reduces flexibility because newspapers must meet a predetermined truck schedule. This makes it nearly impossible to delay a pressrun, even for a major news story.

There are a number of variations of contract cartage. The *Oklahoma City Journal* and *Charlotte News and Observer* use wholly-owned subsidiaries to transport newspapers. This gives the newspapers, through the parent company, the absolute control available with private cartage, as well as maximum flexibility in dealing with labor relations and transportation scheduling.

Many newspapers, for at least part of their circulation, rely on common carriers such as trains, buses, and airplanes to provide point-to-point bulk delivery. Trains dominated long-distance newspaper distribution from the 1830s to the late 1950s; when the Post Office shifted to truck delivery, many newspapers shifted as well. Commercial bus companies provide economical, dependable service into smaller, out-of-the-way communities; but their load is limited by the baggage compartment's size. In addition, the timing of bus runs may not make bus delivery feasible for morning newspapers.

Newspapers with national delivery, such as the *New York Times* and *Wall Street Journal*, once relied on air transport for timely delivery. Today satellite relay of layouts to regional plants has reduced the need for air transport and made a national daily such as *USA Today* a reality. However, air transport is still the only realistic delivery system in some instances, such as the *New York Times'* Caribbean edition, and is occasionally used for quick delivery of special editions.

Many newspapers use a combination of private and contract cartage to cover their circulation areas. Contract cartage is the most common form of transportation outside the city and metropolitan area. A suburban newspaper or small-town daily may use contract cartage within the city as well and pay motor route drivers an extra fee to drop bundles for outlying carriers. A metropolitan newspaper may use both company-owned trucks to carry newspapers to substations and a contract hauling arrangement for dropping bundles at street corners or carriers' homes. The newspaper chooses the most economical transportation method that meets the criteria of flexibility and dependability.

Company-owned vs. Leased Vehicles

While contract cartage removes the newspaper from responsibility for transportation vehicles and employees, private cartage requires the newspaper to choose among company-owned vehicles, leased vehicles, and privately owned vehicles. The major considerations in selecting the type of fleet are capital, internal vs. external control, depreciation, taxes, and profit.

Capital Expenditures The transportation fleet size, and therefore the capital expenditure if company-owned, depends on the newspaper's circulation, the size of the geographical area served, and the distribution system. Most transportation fleets include trucks, vans, and cars. The newspaper either puts up the capital to purchase a fleet or spreads the cost over time with a lease. Subsidiary costs for a company-owned fleet can include the construction and operation of a garage or some maintenance contract. The federal Department of Transportation vehicle cost analysis, prepared annually, provides a guideline for comparing operating costs for newspapers considering the purchase of fleet vehicles. The Runzheimer Report, a commercial service, also evaluates costs of leasing and ownership. The *Toronto Star* and *Raleigh* (North Carolina) *Observer* operate company-owned fleets.

Some newspapers mix company-owned, leased, and private vehicles in their transportation fleet, allowing district managers to use their own cars for sales calls and, perhaps, redelivery. Company vehicles do the bulk of the hauling, but short-term leasing arrangements cover peak load periods and provide a backup if company vehicles are being repaired. A good example of this mix is leasing of large-capacity trucks to handle Sunday editions that cannot be carried in smaller, company-owned trucks or vans used for daily editions.

Control of Vehicles Control of vehicle maintenance and usage is internal in the case of company-owned vehicles and external with leased or employee-owned vehicles, unless the newspaper provides and requires company servicing and repair. Internal control allows the company to determine the replacement schedule for such components as brakes, oil, and tires or of the entire vehicle. The newspaper controls service level, the vehicle's appearance, and the disposal cost. Under a leasing agreement such decisions are part of the leasing contract and, thus, subject to negotiation. While the newspaper has input, it has no absolute control and little monitoring capability.

Actual control of fleet vehicle usage and drivers is possible with several devices on company-owned or leased vehicles. Hub meters tally actual mileage for comparison with projected mileage and allow for rapid checking of service intervals. A tackograph records mileage, speed, time, and duration of all stops on a continuous, 24-hour disc. Two-way radios provide a constant link with field employees. Some newspapers have their district managers and independent contractors maintain radio contact with the central office in order to handle service complaints. The radio not only ensures rapid redelivery of missed newspapers, it also permits supervisory control and effective communication during working hours.

Other Factors   Other factors in the selection of company-owned or leased vehicles are depreciation and taxes. With lease arrangements, the leasing company controls depreciation costs. Most leasing contracts require payment of the difference between accumulated depreciation payments and actual depreciation at the time of sale. Thus, if used car and truck prices fall, the newspaper pays an additional depreciation cost. If used car and truck prices rise, the leasing company may retain surplus depreciation payments as additional profit or share such payments with the newspaper if the contract requires such sharing. The newspaper controls the depreciation level of company-owned vehicles but has no involvement in depreciation costs of employee-owned vehicles.

State and federal taxes on the purchase or lease of employee and business vehicles vary, but they may tip the cost scale of company-owned vs. leased vehicles when other factors don't. Leasing costs include a built-in profit margin for the leasing company. Company ownership brings that profit and any extra fees that a leasing contract requires to the newspaper. On the other hand, company ownership necessitates provisions for vehicle parking and maintenance.

Thus, in choosing whether to own or lease transportation vehicles, a newspaper must weigh actual costs and the advantage of control over servicing and usage of company-owned vehicles against the actual costs and the advantage of flexibility of a leasing contract.

Transportation Personnel

The number and job responsibilities of transportation personnel partly depend on the type of distribution system a newspaper uses. Transportation personnel typically include district managers, drivers, and vehicle maintenance employees or contractors.

District Managers   District managers have a wide variety of circulation-related responsibilities, as discussed in the next two chapters. These include transporting and distributing the newspaper, working with carriers, making sales collections, and providing service to subscribers and single copy outlets.

Basically, depending on the newspaper's distribution pattern, the district manager will fit one of two roles—hauler or sales manager.

District managers in the hauler role are key transportation employees. They carry newspapers from the plant or distribution center to their carriers, whether at substations or at established drop points like the carriers' homes. Thus, district managers have not only the responsibility of primary distribution, newspaper delivery from the plant to various distribution points, but also responsibility for secondary distribution, or carrier delivery and service. The hauling role, most often used on small-circulation newspapers, influences the hiring of district managers because it necessitates assigning a van or small truck for each hauler/ manager to transport bundles; vans can also be used to take carriers to canvassing points for sales drives.

Some district managers play only an intermediate hauling role, with truck drivers loading bundles at the newspaper plant and hauling them to substations and the district managers picking them up there for further distribution to carriers, retail outlets, and/or vending machines. In this intermediate role, district managers have no direct contact with the loading dock.

District managers acting as sales managers do little physical labor themselves but supervise the distribution of newspaper bundles by a hauler—either an employee, an independent contractor, or contract hauler. The sales manager's primary responsibilities are to increase circulation in a specified geographical area, provide good service to carriers and/or retail and wholesale accounts, and make collections. This increased sales activity offsets the additional cost of the hauler to deliver bundles. Since the district manager in the sales manager role does not haul newspapers, the only transportation needed is a car, whether company owned, leased, or privately owned with the newspaper reimbursing the district manager for mileage. The district manager in the sales manager role is still responsible for carriers and, thus, for the newspaper's delivery to subscribers.

Drivers Drivers who transport the newspaper can be contract haulers, independent contractors, part-time employee truck drivers, or district managers. Many newspapers use a combination of these driver types.

The drivers' primary responsibilities are loading trucks or vans at the loading dock and distributing bundles to various sites. This distribution includes either delivery of large numbers of newspapers to substations or warehouses throughout the circulation area or delivery of exact numbers of copies to various outlets and carriers.

A major concern is driver safety. Many newspapers provide driver training as a means of reducing accidents, decreasing maintenance costs, lowering insurance rates, and, most importantly, reducing the risk of disabling injuries or death.

The American Newspaper Publishers Association and the International Circulation Managers Association began a safe driving campaign

FIGURE 7.6 Courtesy ICMA.

in 1940. The campaign now involves over 600 newspapers operating more than 12,000 vehicles over 280 million miles annually. The accident rate in 1983 was 1.39 per 100,000 vehicle miles, the second lowest rate in the campaign's history.[3]

The Safe Driving Campaign gives awards annually to the top three newspapers in each of seven categories; newspapers are divided into categories according to circulation and whether they use private or contract carriers. Awards are based on accident rates per 100,000 miles as reported by the newspapers and certified by their insurance carriers. ANPA/ICMA also provides quarterly reports on insurance ratings. Ratings are based on mileage and number of accidents, and the reports use key numbers rather than newspaper names to preserve confidentiality.

In addition to such industry efforts, driver safety can be enhanced by screening potential drivers in the hiring process and through driver education programs. Screening driver applicants requires the cooperation of the state motor vehicle department; by having applicants provide their driver's license numbers, the newspaper can obtain driving record abstracts listing violations. Insurance carriers can obtain out-of-state data and help evaluate the abstracts. Rejecting applicants with a pattern of speeding or minor accidents reduces the risk of accidents and higher insurance rates.

Many newspapers also use in-house driver safety campaigns. Ongoing educational programs, merit awards for safe driving, bumper sticker campaigns, and disciplinary measures for violations are among the techniques used. In-house campaigns can also promote concern for the appearance and maintenance of company-owned or leased vehicles. Assigning employees to the same cars, vans, or trucks on a daily basis enhances their sense of responsibility for the vehicle. Routine maintenance and safety checks both demonstrate the newspaper's concern for employee safety and provide control over vehicle use.

Vehicle Maintenance Employees Operating a company fleet often requires the newspaper to hire mechanics or sign maintenance agreements with area garages. The cost of vehicle maintenance forces some newspapers, especially those with statewide or widely scattered circulation areas, to lease rather than purchase transportation vehicles.

The number and skill level of vehicle maintenance employees depends upon the amount of service to be done in-house as opposed to the amount contracted out. There are three levels of service a company garage might offer. The first, light repair, includes the pumping of gas, cleaning, and replacing small parts such as light bulbs and screws. Such tasks can be accomplished with a few hand tools by a semiskilled person. The second level of service involves preventive maintenance, including tune-ups, oil and lube jobs, and diagnostic inspection. Such service requires an inventory of spare parts, more specialized tools, a grease rack, and some diagnostic equipment. The third level of service involves tire repair, engine overhaul, body repair, and transmission and brake repair. The cost effectiveness of each area of specialization will depend on the volume of work done in a typical month or year and the cost of contracting for the work elsewhere. Local costs and access to facilities will vary.

A company garage can be economically feasible for a newspaper with a large vehicle fleet. The garage's hours and location also influence the number of employees. Newspapers with multiple editions may require a 24-hour garage or at least a mechanic on duty at all times. A three-shift garage also assures immediate attention to breakdowns, reducing the possibility of delivery delays.

Many newspapers use a combination of maintenance methods, a garage for vehicles in the metropolitan area and maintenance contracts or other arrangements for vehicles operating in other areas.

The mechanical segment of the circulation system has slowly evolved with computerization because manual labor was the surest method and because union problems precluded an easy transition to mechanical solutions. Those realities have kept the mailroom and transportation units under the jurisdiction of the pressroom or mechanical department in many newspapers. Where circulation managers operate them, mailrooms and transportation are adjusted to the demands of home delivery and single copy sales, the circulation needs, rather than to the presses and other mechanical department needs. The next chapter picks up the first circulation step beyond transportation, home delivery.

NOTES

1. "A Look at Mechanics of Distribution," *presstime* 6, 7 (July 1984): 33.
2. Catherine Russell, *CDNPA/CCMA 1981 Survey of Newspaper Circulation Departments* (Toronto: Canadian Daily Newspaper Publishers Association & Canadian Circulation Managers Association, 1981), Appendix A–7.
3. "Safe Driving Campaign Names 21 Winners," *presstime* 6, 6 (June 1984): 65.

CHAPTER
8

Home Delivery

If the initial task of circulation delivery systems is to move newspapers from the printing plant to assorted distribution points, as discussed in the previous chapter, then the most visible task is the physical delivery of the newspaper to the customer. Physical delivery takes place in one of two ways—home delivery (by carrier or mail) or point-of-purchase delivery.

Point-of-purchase delivery, the subject of the next chapter, includes single copy sales from circulation boxes; at area stores; and such assorted distribution points as airports, office lobbies, and churches. The customer bears the responsibility for obtaining the newspaper.

In its most limited meaning, *home delivery* is the physical placement of a newspaper at a subscriber's home on a regular basis and at a predictable time. This simplistic definition does not, however, include such varied elements of the home delivery system as delivery of newspapers to carriers; carrier recruitment, training, and supervision; the provision of good service; redelivery of missed, wet, or torn newspapers; and collection. All these aspects of a home delivery system are discussed in this chapter.

The fundamental difference between a home delivery system and a point-of-purchase system is the commercial relationship between the customer and the newspaper. In home delivery, the customer agrees in a single decision to purchase each newspaper issue over a prolonged time, and the newspaper agrees to promptly deliver the newspaper to a stated address. Single copy sales, on the other hand, require customers to seek out the point of purchase and to make a separate purchase decision for each newspaper issue.

While many newspapers are experiencing a growth in single copy sales, 80 percent of all American daily newspapers are home delivered. The percentage varies only slightly based on circulation size.[1] In Japan, 98 percent of all daily newspapers are home delivered.

ADVANTAGES AND DISADVANTAGES OF HOME DELIVERY

The primary advantage of home delivery—affecting the editorial, advertising, and circulation departments of newspapers—is stability.

For the editorial department, home delivery provides a guaranteed circulation base that makes it easier for journalists to identify their audience and reduces the need for sensationalized news treatment designed to grab readers' attention at the newsstand. Home delivery also develops a newspaper reading habit in families, increasing the likelihood that children will become regular newspaper readers and, eventually, subscribers.

For the advertising department, home delivery provides guaranteed exposure for advertisers and a variety of advertising options. Advertisers look both to the home-delivered circulation and to the demographics of readership in allotting advertising dollars. The flexibility of most home delivery systems also makes it possible for newspapers to offer advertisers such options as zoned delivery (i.e., placing ads in newspaper editions going to particular neighborhoods) or total market coverage (i.e., assuring that even nonsubscribers get certain advertising inserts). In addition, home-delivered newspapers are likely to remain in the home for several days, increasing the likelihood that advertising and editorial copy will be read.

For the circulation department, home delivery means stability of income. Subscribers receive and pay for a newspaper no matter what the weather, day of week, major news story, or their personal mood may be. Home-delivered circulation is predictable and accounts for 20 percent of an average newspaper's total income.

The advantages of home delivery are not limited to the newspaper. The subscriber also benefits with the cost savings and convenience of home delivery. To attract subscribers, newspapers offer savings ranging from the single issue cost to as much as half of the weekly or monthly single copy rate.

However, home delivery is not without its disadvantages. Consider the following problems that a home delivery system must overcome:

Daily delivery of a highly perishable product within a two- to three-hour period to thousands or hundreds of thousands of homes, apartments, condominiums, and farms

A product that varies greatly in size from one day to the next, weighing as much as 7 pounds on Sunday

A product susceptible to wind, rain, or snow damage and often exposed to the elements for an hour or more between delivery and pickup

Delivery times between 3:00 a.m. and 6:00 a.m. or between 3:00 p.m. and 6:00 p.m., the former in hours of darkness, the latter in the midst of rush hour and after-school activities

Delivery over paved and unpaved roads in all weather conditions

Reliance on either youth carriers between the ages of 10 and 16, with the accompanying problems of turnover and reliability, or on adult carriers, who demand higher wages and can create labor problems

Effective home delivery systems are designed to overcome these problems.

TYPES OF HOME DELIVERY SYSTEMS

There is no typical home delivery system. Tradition, climate, population, demographics, the local labor situation, and a newspaper's corporate philosophy influence the type of home delivery system used. Many newspapers combine two or more systems, and what works well for one newspaper may not work well for another.

What home delivery systems have in common is their reliance on carriers. The carriers—either youth or adult, male or female—physically bring the newspaper to the subscriber's home. The typical American newspaper, with a circulation of about 25,000, uses 400 carriers. Most newspapers use a carrier force directly proportional to circulation, with the norm being approximately 1 carrier for every 100 newspapers.[2] The ratio is higher for newspapers using adult carriers and lower for newspapers using youth carriers.

The carriers responsible for home delivery fall into one of four categories: the independent contractor, the contract delivery agent, the employee carrier, or the postal service carriers. In examining each category, consider again the criteria of an effective delivery system—dependability, flexibility, economy, and control.

FIGURE 8.1   The concrete block substations of the *St. Petersburg Times and Evening Independent* contain an office for the district manager, tables for counting, assembling and folding newspapers, and large central area for truck delivery of bundles. District managers use these substations for meetings and daily business. Courtesy *St. Petersburg Times and Evening Independent*.

Independent Contractors

Most newspapers rely on independent contractors for all or part of their home delivery systems. Carriers acting as independent contractors contract with the newspaper to provide specific services; the level of service varies from simple newspaper delivery to a prescribed subscriber list to new sales territory development, including provisions not only for actual newspaper delivery but also for service, billing, and collection.

Independent contractors, whether adult or youth, buy newspapers wholesale and sell them at retail, gaining profit from the difference between what they pay the company and what they collect. Contractors receive the newspapers on credit and pay the bill weekly, on alternate weeks, or monthly according to the newspaper's billing procedures. As a high-cashflow business, newspapers constantly monitor the size of contractors' balances to avoid financial problems.

Independent contractors normally have a defined territory or route to service within the delivery times and delivery error standards established by the newspapers. The newspaper's obligation is to provide the established number of newspapers at the prescribed rate. Contractors are responsible for all incidental business expenses, such as forms, rubber bands, plastic wrappers, delivery bags, bicycle baskets, vehicle maintenance, and, if required by the newspaper, insurance and bonding against theft. They must also provide their own substitutes in case of illness or vacation.

The major variation in the independent contractor system is the use of youth carriers, often called "little merchants." Little merchants are legal minors, usually between the ages of 10 and 16, who contract to deliver newspapers on a route set by the newspaper. They differ from other independent contractors in that the territories they serve are very small (20 to 100 customers), and a minor cannot be held to the terms of a contract.

In theory little merchants have the same rights as adult contractors do to control over customers and newspaper pricing. However, when the status of little merchants has been questioned in court, they have generally been considered newspaper employees rather than independent contractors precisely because of the amount of control the newspaper retains.

More than 70 percent of the newspapers responding to a 1984 International Circulation Management Association survey reported that little merchants comprise over 60 percent of their carrier force.[3] Youth carriers are particularly popular in the eastern and northern parts of the United States.

Among the criteria newspapers consider in determining whether to use youth or adult carriers are the density of circulation routes, safety, and the local labor force makeup. In areas where 75 percent or more of the residents are newspaper subscribers, it is possible to construct routes that youth carriers can serve on foot in a reasonable time period. Where the coverage is less than one-third, as in New York or Los Angeles, the geographical size of even a small route makes it almost impossible to service on foot. In areas with high unemployment or many retirees, adults see newspaper routes as welcomed part-time employment, eliminating the need for youth carriers. The safety factor, especially for morning newspapers, which often necessitate delivery in hours of darkness, is also a consideration.

Since the late 1970s there has been a significant increase in the number of adult carriers, although youth carriers still predominate.[4] Adult carriers acting as independent contractors contract for a large route (200 to 600 customers) defined by the newspaper or contract to provide all circulation services in a particular geographical area (a suburb, town, or county) and define their own routes within that area. In either case, the adult contractor has the option of hiring others, including youth carriers, to sell and deliver the newspaper; in this case, the contractor acts as a district manager, finding, training, and supervising carriers. Adult contractors in the role of district managers sometimes rent facilities or use their garages as substations where newspapers are inserted, carriers pay their bills, sales meetings are held, and supplies are stored.

Advantages of Independent Contractors For a newspaper, independent contractors are the least expensive, least complex labor force for home delivery. Contractors receive no fringe benefits, except, perhaps, workmen's compensation; and there are no minimum wage provisions. Adult contractors require a modest employee supervisory force; while youth carriers require considerable supervision, a task that can be accomplished by using adult independent contractors (if the newspaper wants to limit the circulation staff's size).

The independent contractor system operates on entrepreneurial motivation, allowing contractors to make money in direct proportion to their efforts. To encourage independent contractors to develop their territories, the newspaper can adjust wholesale rates for increased volume. The rate can also be adjusted to benefit long-time contractors, to reflect increased fuel costs, or to compensate for subdividing a growing territory. The system is dependent on private negotiations between the newspaper and the contractor; the flexibility of the wholesale rate allows the newspaper to reward good service and punish mediocrity, thus, indirectly controlling service quality.

The primary advantage of the independent contractor system, therefore, is economic control, both in terms of maintaining low labor costs and in setting flexible wholesale rates.

Disadvantages of Independent Contractors The major disadvantage of the independent contractor system is the newspaper's lack of control in pricing and service. As the U.S. Supreme Court declared in the Albrecht decision,[5] the newspaper may recommend a retail price, but it may not regulate that price in dealing with independent contractors. Thus, the newspaper loses control of the pricing structure, particularly with adult carriers, who are more likely to exceed recommended prices in order to achieve greater profits.

The newspaper also has little control over independent contractors in the precise method of delivery and collection schedules. The paper's legal jurisdiction is limited to the timely delivery of a clean, dry newspaper and contract requirements to collect and sell subscriptions. The newspaper can recommend but NOT require that an independent contractor put a subscriber's newspaper in the mail slot, or collect at a certain time, or attend sales meetings. With youth carriers such recommendations usually have the effect of an order.

A third area where the newspaper lacks control over the independent contractor is subscriber information. Independent contractors, not the newspaper, service the territory; so the customers belong to the contractor, and the newspaper must negotiate access to subscriber information and records. In some contracts newspapers must refer all customer inquiries to the contractors without taking notes or keeping a record; such restrictions handicap a newspaper's efforts to resolve customer complaints.

Contract Delivery Agents

The second type of home delivery system is the contract delivery agent system. It began at the *Washington Post* in 1975 as a means of regulating the retail pricing of the newspaper after the Albrecht decision gave independent contractors the right to set their own prices. Within five years, 20 percent of American newspapers adopted some form of the contract delivery agent system.[6]

Contract delivery agents contract with the newspaper to provide specific services in exchange for a fee. The contract requires either delivery alone, as at the *Los Angeles Times*, or it includes subscription sales and collections, with additional fees granted for each. The contract may also require delivery agents to report all subscriber information to the newspaper; for instance, at the *Orlando Sentinel*, agents must process every start and stop through the newspaper's circulation department to ensure continuous updating of route lists.

Unlike the independent contractor, the contract delivery agent never actually owns the newspapers or subscriber lists. The newspaper sets the retail rate at which the papers are sold, retains ownership of the route lists, and controls service times and conditions. In most cases this includes a provision requiring delivery agents to deliver to every subscriber listed by the newspaper, including those in arrears; unlike independent contractors, delivery agents cannot drop customers without the newspaper's authorization.

Contract delivery agents are normally adults with routes of 300 or more newspapers. Their ability to hire others to help service the route can be limited by contract.

Advantages of Contract Delivery Agents The advantages of the contract delivery agent system for the newspaper are price and circulation control, ownership of subscriber lists, and increased cashflow.

The control factors are mandated by contract. As part of the contract, the circulation manager can stipulate the newspaper's retail price, the delivery and collection times and conditions, and sales requirements without incurring the employee carrier system's cost or the independent contractor system's legal problems. Circulation standards are set by contract, and violations can lead to fines or contract termination.

With legal control over the subscription list, the newspaper can develop a computerized subscriber information system and require contract delivery agents to provide accurate data on an ongoing basis. This allows the newspaper to monitor performance and study readership and penetration. In turn, the newspaper can expand its circulation and advertising services by offering zoned advertising or total market coverage.

Increased cashflow is a direct result of the difference in billing for independent contractors and contract delivery agents. Whereas independent contractors are billed at a wholesale rate and receive their newspapers on credit, contract delivery agents are billed at the retail rate less a collection fee of approximately 10 percent. The agent assumes the bad debt burden, although newspapers like the *Orlando Sentinel* normally cover any bad debt above 10 percent of the bill.

Disadvantages of Contract Delivery Agents The disadvantages of the contract delivery agent system include higher cost, reduced motivation for subscription sales, and minimal customer concern.

Contract delivery agents are more expensive than independent contractors. In order to make the system work, the newspaper must pay a substantial fee not only for delivery but also for any additional services required by the contract, such as billing and/or collection. In addition, the newspaper may give subsidies for preprint insertions, mileage, and low penetration routes.

Contract delivery agents, with existing routes of 300 to 1000 customers, have far less profit motivation for subscription sales than do independent contractors. Thus, new subscriber drives usually require hefty cash incentives, as well as reliance on telephone sales and door-to-door crews.

The size of the average agent's route limits the amount of personal attention a subscriber receives. Subscribers are unlikely to be able to request delivery in a back door or mail chute in a contract delivery agent system; thus, the system limits customer service flexibility.

Employee Carriers

Employee carriers dominated the home delivery of American newspapers through the Penny Press era because the editor/publishers relied on apprentices and part-time employees for distribution. With circulation of a few hundred to less than a thousand, this system worked well.

Today large newspapers such as the *Houston Post* and the *St. Petersburg Times* and *Evening Independent* use employee carriers, usually adults.

Advantages of Employee Carriers With employee carriers the newspaper retains tight control over price and circulation. The newspaper establishes all the rules, and the employee carrier must follow those rules or lose the job. Employee carriers can be directed to comply with each customer's delivery request; and the delivery times and methods, whether by car, bike, or wagon, can be strictly regulated.

Another advantage of the employee carrier system is its reliability. Because most employee carriers are adults, reliability is higher than with youth systems. Employee carrier systems are also stable, with less turnover than other systems, because the carriers receive full employee benefits: insurance, overtime pay, pension, and at least minimum wage.

Disadvantages of Employee Carriers The primary disadvantage of the employee carrier system is its cost. Employee wages and fringe benefits become newspaper operating costs, whereas independent contract or contract delivery agent systems incur few employee-related costs for home delivery. In addition to direct employee costs, the newspaper, rather than the individual carrier, bears the bad debt from uncollectible subscriptions because the customers belong to the newspaper and the carriers collect on the newspaper's behalf.

Other potential drawbacks of the employee carrier system are labor problems and the lack of a profit incentive to encourage subscription sales. As employees, carriers have the right to unionize, resulting in union negotiations and strike possibilities. While many circulation managers argue that a regular wage removes the profit incentive, executives at the St. Petersburg newspapers disagree. They report participation by more than 80 percent of the employee carriers in the 28 contests run each year;[7] thus, the incentive to sell subscriptions comes through special promotional and motivational techniques.

Postal Service Carriers

Almost every newspaper uses postal delivery in some form. Small weekly newspapers, dailies with rural subscribers, and national newspapers such as the *Wall Street Journal* use postal service as a regular home delivery system. Mail delivery of the newspaper is most frequent in nonmetropolitan areas and in the North Central states, where 12 percent of regular newspaper subscribers receive at least one paper by mail.[8]

Postal service newspaper delivery began in colonial times when Congress authorized special postal rates for newspapers on the premise that democracy operated only with a free flow of information and that an informed public was necessary. The low rates encouraged editors to rely on postal riders and, later, rural route drivers for delivery; exchange copies between newspapers were delivered free.

Today newspapers still apply for a special postal permit, called the *second-class permit*, to deliver their newspapers.

Advantages of Postal Service Delivery   The advantages of postal service delivery include accessibility and cost.

Almost all adults have a street address or postal box number where a newspaper can be delivered; and the U.S. Post Office provides delivery service to every part of the country, as do postal services in other countries. Most mail subscribers live on rural postal routes or at some distance from the city of publication, perhaps in other states or countries. For them, mail delivery is the only reasonable delivery service.

The accessibility of postal service delivery allows a newspaper to extend its subscriptions beyond the geographical boundaries of its carrier routes. This flexibility is particularly important for special interest and national newspapers. For instance, by coordinating the printing schedules of its satellite printing plants across the country with postal service schedules, the *Wall Street Journal* is able to provide day of publication delivery to subscribers in most large cities.

While the cost of mail subscriptions may be higher than other home delivery systems for most daily newspapers, mail delivery is often the least expensive delivery system for weekly newspapers, especially those in rural areas.

Disadvantages of Postal Service Delivery   The disadvantages of postal service delivery include steadily rising costs, unreliability, and changing postal regulations.

When the U.S. Postal Service became a federal agency concerned with financial self-sufficiency, the traditional subsidy for newspapers was abandoned. In the past decade mailing charges for newspapers have increased 400 percent. Newspapers passed the cost on to mail subscribers, many of whom refused to pay the high mailing charges and stopped their subscriptions.

Newspapers find it difficult to rely on the timeliness of postal delivery beyond their immediate community or county because they have neither control over it nor ready supervision of its efficiency. Moreover, there is no Sunday postal delivery. Since first-class mail receives delivery priority, mail subscribers regularly complain about unpredictable service.

Monitoring postal regulations for changing requirements, proposed rate increases, and rate restructuring is a necessity for circulation managers with large numbers of mail subscribers. Postal regulations have tightened the packaging, labeling, and sorting requirements for second-class service, increasing the burden on the mailroom and reducing the cost efficiency of postal service.

Although postal service remains a primary delivery system for some weekly newspapers and for national newspapers, its growing cost has made it economically unfeasible as a primary delivery system for most dailies. However, it is still used as a supplementary delivery system to provide delivery service to subscribers in widely scattered geographical areas.

WORKING WITH CARRIERS

Since home delivery remains the primary means of getting newspapers to subscribers in both the United States and Canada and since all home delivery systems rely on the personal services of a carrier, the circulation manager must be concerned with the recruitment, training, retention, and supervision of this large labor force. The level of management involvement varies with the type of home delivery system used; obviously newspapers with a large mail subscription list have little direct contact with the carrier, a postal employee. On the other hand, newspapers with employee carriers or those with extensive little merchant systems have daily contact with individual carriers.

Recruitment

Eighty-six percent of American newspapers rely on both adult and youth carriers;[9] thus, circulation managers and independent contractors must use recruiting practices to attract two diverse age groups.

Most adult carriers are hired to cover motorized routes; the average adult route includes a median of 259 customers.[10] In recruiting adult carriers, most newspapers use standard personnel advertising techniques, emphasizing the job's benefits. The most effective recruitment tool is in-paper advertising, particularly in the classified columns.

For part-time carrier vacancies, ads must emphasize the supplemental income and, especially for morning newspapers, hours outside the normal workday schedule. This will attract workers looking for a second job or homemakers who must fit work hours to their children's schedules.

Full-time positions as contract delivery agents or independent contractors for large routes can also emphasize income benefits in recruiting ads; ads for employee carriers may also include fringe benefits. However, screening for such applicants must be more intense because of their greater responsibilities.

Despite the fact that most newspapers employ adult carriers to some degree, the preponderance of home delivery carriers are youths between the ages of 12 and 16. Continued reliance on youth carriers will become more difficult in the next decade, however, as the number of 12- to 14-year-olds declines by 35 percent from 1980 to 1990. An increase in organized after-school activities and school busing has also limited the availability of adolescents for newspaper delivery. Both safety concerns and the rise in rural and suburban delivery, with its farther distances between stops, provide impetus for the hiring of adult carriers on motorized routes.

In many metropolitan areas, though, youth carriers remain the norm. Youths and their families are attracted by the supplemental income and business experience newspaper routes offer. The acceptance of girls as carriers has broadened the pool of available youth carriers.

The best recruiters are present youth carriers who enjoy their routes but may need encouragement to find other carriers. Finder's fees, whether in hamburgers or cash, have proven very effective. District managers and independent contractors acting in that role can also visit schools and scout groups, post flyers, insert flyers in newspapers on an open route (one without a carrier), and even knock on doors where they notice a basketball hoop or a lot of bikes in an effort to recruit carriers.

Getting young people interested in becoming a carrier is only the first step in the recruitment of youth carriers. Unlike adult carriers, youth carriers cannot be held to a contract; thus, many newspapers require a joint contract, with parents cosigning for the youth.

An explanation of what is expected of the youth carrier and the actual signing of the contract are the key points of the *parent call,* a formal visitation with parents and prospective carriers. The parent call allows the carrier supervisor to outline hours and bookkeeping responsibilities and to screen out applicants whose parents are not supportive.

Training

Most newspapers offer formal training sessions for carriers, both youth and adult, as a means of reducing turnover and assuring a common understanding of the job and its responsibilities.

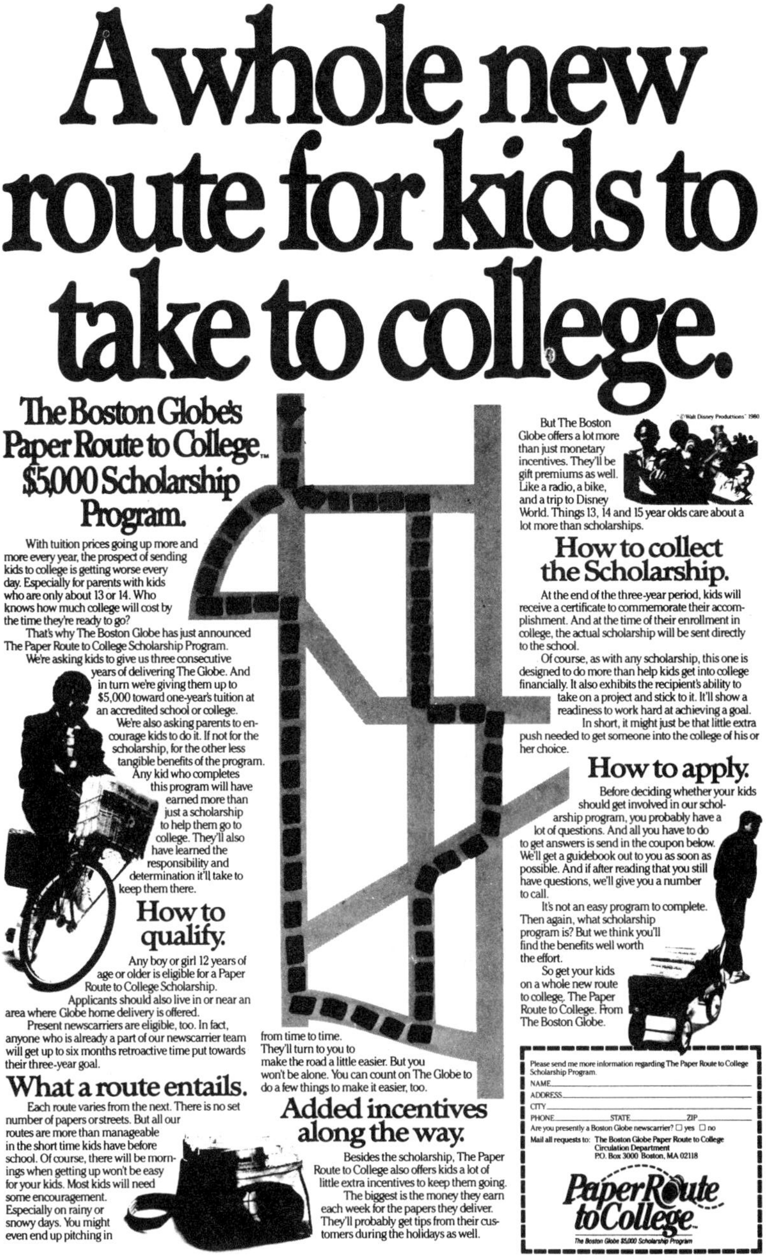

FIGURE 8.2   Making college education the focus of this carrier recruitment ad was part of a creative campaign mounted by the *Boston Globe*. Courtesy the *Boston Globe*.

Can a teen-age girl be a newsboy?

Let's make that newsperson. Newspaper carrier.

Sure, we're looking for girls as well as boys to deliver our paper, and make good money doing it.

What are the requirements?

A mature, responsible willingness to see the job through. Ability to handle money helps, too. You should like people, be cheerful and friendly. And be ready to "run your own show," create your own opportunities, and earn real cash.

If you're that kind of girl—or know that kind of girl—we'd like to know. Give our circulation department a call and let's talk about your future as a newsperson.

(Newspaper Logo)

 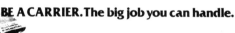 **BE A CARRIER. The big job you can handle.**

FIGURE 8.3 ICMA regularly provides several recruitment ads like the one shown. Newspapers then localize the copy. Courtesy ICMA.

The *St. Petersburg Times* and *Evening Independent* require carriers to attend three training sessions, with a test each time. The sessions use slides, tapes, and lectures to give carriers an overview of route work, the carrier's responsibility to sell as well as deliver, and the company's service standards.

Training for adult carriers often begins with independent contractors, who not only may be carriers but who also hire other adults and youths to assist in delivery. The *Dallas Morning News* requires its independent contractors to successfully complete a five-week course combining classroom instruction with field observation. The program exposes contractors to all newspaper departments. Students take a final exam based on the course's 120-page textbook, then two weeks of field training follow the instruction. The *Sacramento Bee* uses a three-day intensive orientation, beginning with an overview of the newspaper, including field observation with a district manager, and concluding with actual exercises using forms from the circulation department to test correct office procedures.

For youth carriers training actually begins before employment with the parent call, but youth training is both less intense and less common than adult carrier training. Carrier manuals explaining the basic forms and policies have become a popular supplement to the job training provided by the previous carrier and carrier supervisor. The *Toronto Star* issues a 41-page guide, "Get Off on the Right Foot," which explains subscriber options, basic job requirements (no missed deliveries, prompt bill payment), examples of sales slips, the insurance agreement, and the carrier contract. The manual for the *Sacramento Bee*, called "Carrier Guide to Good Route Management," includes tips on how to increase route profits and how to call on prospects.

Ongoing training is an important task of the circulation manager and district manager. As problems are pinpointed—a lag in sales, increases in customer complaints, or improperly filled out forms—retraining may be needed. For most carriers, this retraining comes in the form of explanatory sessions at the time of newspaper pickup or during bill payment, plus written explanations included with the bill or route changes.

Some newspapers place a high priority on training and retraining. At the *Tampa Times* a circulation training position is part of the managerial structure. The training manager organizes seminars, conferences, and the distribution of pertinent materials for both new and long-time circulation employees, including carriers. The programs range from a four-hour sales seminar to a nine-day classroom program for carrier supervisors to a 14-category form for evaluating field supervisors. Other newspapers, such as the *Orlando Sentinel*, include circulation employees in corporate management-level training programs.

Whatever the method used, newspapers have made initial and follow-up training an important part of working with carriers.

Supervision

More than 75 percent of U.S. and Canadian newspapers use district managers to oversee carrier operations; however, the district managers use more than 50 different job titles.[11] The average number of carrier supervisors, whatever their title, ranges from 3 for newspapers under 25,000 circulation to 94 for newspapers with 100,000 or more circulation.[12] Canadian newspapers operate with about 60 percent of the supervisory force of U.S. papers largely because the supervisors do not haul from the plant to their carriers.[13]

In the United States, carrier supervisors oversee an average of 50 carriers; but the number ranges from a low of 20 to a high of 81. The number of carriers varies according to the district's area, size, and difficulty of delivery. Canadian supervisors average 99 carriers in city circulation areas and 67 in rural areas.

A key variance in the supervisory load depends upon whether the carriers are youths or adults. Because adult routes are typically motorized and larger, a supervisor with 50 adult carriers is responsible for an average of 12,950 subscribers; while a supervisor of 50 youth carriers is responsible for 3050 customers. Thus, a newspaper with a predominantly youth carrier force requires four times the number of carrier supervisors that a newspaper with adult carriers employs.

Not only does the number of carriers being supervised vary from one newspaper to another, but also the level of supervision, in accordance with the type of home delivery system used. Supervision usually involves reviewing delivery errors, collections, and sales. The most direct type of supervision is through the employee carrier system, where the newspaper has absolute control over the carrier's hours and service level on a daily basis. For youth carriers, supervision usually occurs face to face. In contrast to the employee carrier system, the newspaper can exercise no supervision with postal delivery service.

Contractual agreements dictate the level of supervision a newspaper has over independent contractors and contract delivery agents. In general, the newspaper cannot supervise *how* the newspaper is delivered but only the fact that it *is* delivered on time and with an acceptable level of service errors. To determine service errors, the newspaper either fields complaints and records them or, if contractors handle complaints, the newspaper surveys subscribers. Such supervision is time consuming and costly, but it may be the only means of insuring that contractors meet service standards.

Youth carriers, including little merchants, and their parents tolerate and expect more direct supervision than their adult counterparts. This supervisory role can be a blend of *in loco parentis* authority, to keep youths out of trouble, and strict business accountability; but it almost always involves a touch of patient counseling as well. Youth supervisors must prepare themselves to listen to problems ranging from school to personal trauma. C. K. Jefferson, with 44 years in circulation at the *Des Moines Register* and *Tribune*, emphasized the need for even-handed and consistent discipline. Being too lenient, he observed, was as bad as being too severe.

Retention

Carrier turnover is an ongoing concern of newspapers. A 1984 survey indicated 65 percent of the responding newspapers had a turnover of more than 50 percent for their youth carriers each year; 18 percent of the morning newspapers and 14 percent of the afternoon newspapers reported more than 100 percent annual turnover among youth carriers. Adult carrier turnover was lower; 40 percent of the morning newspapers and 34 percent of the afternoon newspapers reported over 50 percent turnover.[14]

Turnover is not unhealthy and undesirable in itself; it produces a more enthusiastic sales force with the hiring of new carriers, and it eliminates those who are unwilling to work hard or who have become troublesome. However, high turnover among carriers can negatively affect home delivery dependability in two ways. First, it makes route lists less reliable; second, it overburdens district managers with open routes and new carrier recruitment and training. The reasons for turnover include job dissatisfaction, dislike of early morning hours, poor weather conditions, and other job possibilities (especially for youth carriers, who typically find other jobs upon turning 16). Adult carrier supervisors would probably add completed payment of bills or enough money saved to the list since many adult carriers take a route to earn extra money for a specific financial goal. Thus, a certain turnover rate, anywhere from 30 to 40 percent, is normal.

Newspapers combat excessive turnover with recognition programs such as the Carrier of the Week, in which a carrier's photo and biography appear in the newspaper, or with banquets and prizes for longevity. Rewards for error-free service, prompt bill payment, or special efforts similarly boost carrier morale. While adults prefer cash rewards, youths are more impressed by award ceremonies and other prizes. Special cash bonuses, such as a $50 savings bond for those who stay on a route from December through June, have greatly reduced winter turnover; and T-shirts proclaiming "I survived the winter" have turned suffering into a sense of accomplishment.

Training before and during carrier work has an important bearing on turnover by reminding carriers that they perform valuable work. Carriers become easily discouraged by fat newspapers, poor collections, and hostile customers. Youth carriers, in particular, need regular encouragement and tips on problem solving. Adult and youth carriers alike need retraining to overcome sloppy habits and faulty understanding.

Turnover can be a problem for carrier supervisors as well. Annual supervisor turnover averages 32 percent among American newspapers, ranging from a low of 18 percent among midsize newspapers (50,000 to 99,999 circulation) to a high of 50 percent for newspapers with a circulation under 25,000.[15] Like carrier turnover, some supervisor turnover is desirable because it brings in fresh energy and weeds out the unproductive. Circulation departments have traditionally accepted supervisor turnover as a normal reflection of the difficult work and modest pay, particularly during times of full employment. The median salary for a district manager was $12,451 in 1980, ranging from $8900 on the smallest dailies to $17,400 on the large metropolitan dailies.[16]

Newspapers adapt to supervisor turnover in a number of ways. Screening tests can identify promising applicants. Management training programs, seminars, and conferences help not only to improve performance but to reduce tensions that often lead to turnover. Papers like the *Contra Costa Times* use a system that anticipates high turnover by organizing carrier supervisors in groups of four; each group has a lead manager, and supervisors are required to submit written records to the newspaper.

Routes

Home delivery routes are less the product of reason and long-term planning than the children of necessity and historical accident. With population growth, the number of newspaper subscribers rose. As the number of subscribers became too much for one carrier to handle, a route was split, with one section becoming an independent route or being combined with sections of adjacent routes.

Route size varies widely because a route must be large enough to be profitable to carrier and supervisor yet small enough to be manageable on days when thick newspapers must be carried. A carrier makes approximately 28 percent of the subscriber cost of the newspaper or about 28¢ to 29¢ per week for each daily newspaper.[17] With a median route size of 61 newspapers, youth carriers make about $17 per week for daily delivery or

$22 per week for daily plus Sunday delivery. Adult carriers, with an average 259 customers, earn more than $75 per week for daily and more than $93 per week for daily/Sunday delivery.

Carrier routes require periodic review, with consideration given to route profit, carrier ability, and timely delivery. Based on the average route profit, district managers must calculate how big a route must be to insure a profit that will attract and hold carriers. Experience, turnover rates, and circulation department guidelines are the main criteria for route profit assessment. Newspapers may subsidize routes in some areas where carrier recruitment or retention is a problem.

Carrier ability is another factor in route size. While routes covered by adults in vehicles are obviously larger than routes handled by youth carriers on foot, route conditions and carrier motivation are also important. An energetic carrier, whether youth or adult, can deliver twice or even three times the number of newspapers that another, less enthusiastic carrier can deliver.

Delivery time can cause a route structure revision. A route regularly yielding complaints about late delivery is a candidate for restructuring if the carrier supervisor is certain the carrier is reliable and picks up the papers on time. Geographical territory alone is an inadequate means of determining route size; a route of 30 customers may require as much time as a route of 90 customers simply because the distance between customers varies.

Thus, circulation managers must consider route profit and size, carrier ability, and the distance between customers in establishing or revising routes.

PROVIDING HOME DELIVERY SERVICE

The type of home delivery system, tradition, geographical region, newspaper policy, and individual carriers all affect the level of service a subscriber receives. Service generally encompasses the gathering and maintenance of subscriber information, the actual newspaper delivery, the handling of complaints, and billing/collection procedures.

Subscriber Information

The flexibility inherent in most home delivery systems—that is, the subscriber's ability to request the newspaper's placement in a particular spot, to stop the newspaper for varying amounts of time, or to opt for various payment plans—demands the maintenance of up-to-date records.

Accurate subscriber information facilitates delivery, redelivery, sales, billing, and collection.

Data gathered from the subscribers are used in the mailroom to insure correct bundle sizes, on the loading docks for matching bundles with route size, by the carrier to keep track of stops and starts, and by the district manager to provide timely redelivery and organize sales drives for new subscriptions. Subscriber information is also valuable to a newspaper's advertising department; only with detailed subscriber records can newspapers move to total market coverage and zoned advertising.

Information Gathering The information gathered on subscribers varies from one newspaper to another. Basic information includes the name, address, circulation district, carrier route, specific delivery instructions, and collection and billing data. These basic records are routinely updated to reflect service errors, vacation holds, and stops and starts.

The growth of computerized circulation systems, which will be discussed in Chapter 10, has made it possible to add other information to the basic record; this information includes collection and billing history; service complaint history; telephone number; postal carrier route; name and phone number of the district manager or independent contractor responsible for that subscriber; and carrier's name, address, and telephone number.

Basic subscriber information is usually gathered the first time a customer calls the newspaper to begin service or a sales call is made to the customer's home. Records are then kept in such simple fashion as a carrier's route book or, with more complex systems, in a computerized data base.

Newspapers with employee carrier or contract delivery agent systems are likely to have centralized recordkeeping, with the newspapers responsible for gathering, maintaining, and updating the records.

Information Processing Once subscriber information is available, either through manual records or a computerized system, it must be used. Processing begins with a request regarding a subscriber and ends with successful execution of the request. Accuracy and speed of response are important to customer satisfaction.

Speed, however, is relative. What takes an hour to execute at a newspaper with 10,000 circulation may take two days at a newspaper with 300,000 circulation. Nonetheless, a newspaper incapable of assuring that a customer's new subscription will start within two or three issues or that a vacation hold will take effect within a day or two has a sluggish subscriber information system, which adversely affects customer relations.

Newspaper Delivery

Once the basic subscriber information is available, the carrier provides the next step in home delivery service—the actual newspaper delivery to the subscriber's home or office. A subscriber has the right to expect the timely delivery of a newspaper that is in good condition, easily accessible, and conveniently paid for.

Timely Delivery   Most newspapers establish guidelines for home delivery times. Typically morning newspapers are delivered between 6 and 7 a.m. Earlier delivery limits production deadlines and increases safety concerns, particularly for youth carriers; while later delivery lessens the usefulness of a morning newspaper for working subscribers.

Presstimes have a greater influence over afternoon delivery hours, with late-breaking stories occasionally causing a delay. However, most evening newspapers try to insure home delivery between 4 and 6 p.m., making the newspaper available when a subscriber returns home from work and during dinner hour.

Newspaper Accessibility and Condition   Geographical region and tradition are major factors influencing subscribers' expectations of *how* their newspapers should be delivered. In most northern states, where weather conditions are often unpredictable, subscribers usually have the opportunity to indicate a point-of-delivery preference, the front door, the back door, or the mailbox. In most southern states, where adult carriers typically handle much larger routes, property line delivery is common; in other words, the carrier tosses the paper into the yard from a vehicle. Of course, on rural and some motorized routes in cities, home delivery means placement in a newspaper box adjacent to the mailbox along the roadside.

Improper safeguarding against weather conditions is a common cause of service complaints. Wet, windblown, or ripped newspapers make reading difficult. Circulation managers, district managers, and carriers use a variety of techniques to insure the newspaper's delivery in good condition. This may mean placing it in the door or mailbox for all subscribers, or it may mean wrapping newspapers in a plastic sleeve during adverse weather conditions. Most wrapping is done by the carrier, although there are mechanical plastic wrap machines that can be used in the mailroom or at substations.

Complaint Handling

Most subscribers are very satisfied with their home delivery service; in fact, only 5 percent of those surveyed in a 1980 readership study expressed dissatisfaction.[18] On the other hand, 22 percent of nonsubscribers cited service problems as the primary reason for not having subscribed to a daily newspaper;[19] in addition, 20 percent of both subscribers and nonsubscribers cancelled a subscription at some time because of delivery problems.[20]

As in all consumer-oriented business, the list of complaints in newspaper home delivery is long: The paper never arrived; the paper was late; the paper landed in a puddle; the paper broke a window. All complaints have one thing in common—negative feeling. Service problems may result in a loss of subscribers, while good service will help to maintain steady customers.

Complaints are usually handled in one of two ways—by the carrier or through direct notice to the newspaper's circulation department or customer service office.

Complaints to the Carrier Most newspapers expect carriers to handle service complaints directly. This is especially true for independent contractors, including little merchants, and employee carriers.

Under this method, the customer calls the carrier. This may require a preliminary call to the newspaper to obtain the carrier's name and telephone number, although the newspaper will usually try to contact the carrier and will advise the subscriber to keep the information for future reference. It is then the carrier's responsibility to get a newspaper in good condition to the customer, either by getting an extra copy from the substation or by buying one from a nearby vending box. In the case of a missed newspaper, the carrier is responsible for crediting the customer's account.

The advantage of this method is its low cost; the newspaper incurs no additional personnel or overhead costs for staffing and operating a telephone room to handle complaints. On the other hand, the newspaper loses its control over service levels, sometimes remaining unaware of service problems until circulation totals are affected. In addition, carrier handling of complaints minimizes the newspaper's direct contact with the subscriber, thus making it more difficult to maintain up-to-date subscriber information.

Complaints to the Newspaper Concern over service levels has prompted many newspapers to handle complaints directly, making internal phone rooms the published telephone number for complaints. This method enables the newspaper to monitor service levels of each carrier and also facilitates billing, the maintenance of subscriber records, and redelivery.

Most newspapers offer redelivery service, although the methods of redelivery vary widely. Some newspapers have a radio dispatch operation that maintains contact with district managers or contract delivery agents, notifying them of redeliveries. Others have carrier supervisors telephone for complaints on a regular basis. Carriers are charged for each redelivery.

Swift redelivery minimizes a subscriber's dissatisfaction, although the most important part of the complaint process is not redelivery per se but correcting the service problem. District managers and circulation managers need to locate the problem, especially if it is persistent, to insure dependable delivery in the future.

Newspapers with no redelivery system usually pass the complaint on to the district manager and carrier through regular forms. In one way or another, the customer expects credit for undelivered or unreadable newspapers. This credit may be in the form of a coupon from the newspaper, through direct negotiation with the carrier, or, in the case of computerized billing, deduction of the day's value or an extra day added onto the subscription period.

One problem with complaints handled through the newspaper is business hours. Most newspaper business offices operate with traditional 9 to 5 hours, but daily newspaper delivery often occurs outside these hours; thus, some newspapers, such as the *Denver Post*, have extended their hours. While this may increase the service error rate, it provides a more accurate assessment of service problems since all complaints are heard.

Billing/Collection Procedures

Circulation revenue flow (that is, how money moves from the customer to the newspaper) varies according to the type of home delivery system, billing periods, local market conditions, and the newspaper's business office practices. In general, billing/collection procedures can be broken into two categories: those handled by carriers (called carrier collection) and those handled by the newspaper's circulation department and/or business office (called office payment).

Carrier Billing/Collection The type of home delivery system used by a newspaper partly determines whether or not carriers bill and collect.

With the independent contractor system, the contractors are theoretically responsible for all billing and collection. They buy newspapers from the publisher at a wholesale rate, establish a retail price, market the newspaper, and determine the best collection system. Independent contractors, including little merchants, must keep accurate delivery records to insure proper billing, crediting subscribers for missed papers and vacation time, and accurate payment records.

As indicated earlier in this chapter, the disadvantage of this system is the lack of control newspapers have over pricing and collection procedures. Independent contractors have the freedom to cut off slow payers or do whatever is necessary to maintain a profit. The advantages are economic since carriers personally assume most of the bad debt burden and newspapers have low personnel and overhead costs for billing and collection.

With the contract delivery agent system, the newspaper usually bills customers; and the agent may either collect or push for office payment. Agents responsible for collections receive a flat fee and commission; the fee is typically 10 percent of the total collections. However, because the delivery agent is normally billed for 90 percent of delivered newspapers, the agent must collect 100 percent in order to earn the 10 percent collection fee. Employee carriers may or may not receive extra payment for billing and collections.

No matter what delivery system is used, most carriers share some billing and collection responsibility. The level of involvement varies. In a 1980 study, 78 percent of the responding newspapers reported that their youth carriers collected from subscribers, but less than 50 percent delivered bills. The exact opposite was true for adult carriers, who were more likely to deliver bills but less likely to make collections.[21] Route size and newspaper size both influenced billing/collection procedures. On large, motorized routes, typically served by adult carriers, the carriers made few collections. Newspapers with circulations of 100,000 or more had a higher percentage of both youth and adult carriers delivering bills.

Collection is time consuming, with carriers sometimes forced to return to a home three or four times before payment is received; thus, some carriers prefer to have subscribers opt for office payment options, as discussed in the next section. On the other hand, in-person collections may increase a carrier's profit since subscribers often tip carriers, particularly youth carriers. More importantly, in-person collection maintains the carrier/customer contact; this contact improves understanding of customer needs and usually results in better service.

Office Billing/Collection   Computerization is likely to increase the number of subscribers who receive bills from and pay a newspaper's central office. While on many newspapers only mail subscribers are billed directly, 14 percent of the newspapers in a 1980 readership study said they billed 40 percent or more of their subscribers directly.[22]

Billing and collection either follow a subscription period (billing in arrears), precede a subscription period (billing in advance), or cover a period half in advance and half in arrears. While carriers typically bill in arrears, most office billing involves paid-in-advance subscriptions. This reduces the newspaper's bad debt total, since subscribers must pay for newspapers before receiving them. Although perhaps a circulation trend of the future, paid-in-advance (PIA) subscriptions account for less than 20 percent of the total subscribers on most newspapers.

A full office payment system involves computerized recordkeeping, increased clerical help, mailing costs for bills, and some provisions to accommodate subscribers who resist office payment. All of these factors add up to a high initial cost, the chief disadvantage of office billing and collection. Yet newspapers, particularly those with computer systems in circulation, increasingly push the office payment option. It is a means of retaining complete control over billing and collection and, less directly, service levels. Circulation managers also see it as a means of maintaining accurate route and subscriber lists and reducing carrier turnover by freeing carriers from collection problems.

Another disadvantage of office billing and collection, in addition to its cost, is less personalized service. Newspapers trying to force subscribers to shift to office billing and collection, including the *Minneapolis Star and Tribune* and the *Atlanta Constitution and Journal*, experienced a 10 percent circulation decline. The *Waukegan* (Illinois) *News-Sun*, which pioneered mandatory office payment in the 1960s, reverted to a carrier collection system 20 years later to encourage better carrier/subscriber relations and, therefore, better service.

A new development in office billing and collection is the use of credit cards. A 1982 ICMA survey showed 59 Canadian and U.S. newspapers allowed credit card payments. The advantages of credit card payment are convenience for the customer and a reduction in bad debt.[23] Credit card collection usually includes a handling fee of 7 to 15 percent charged to a newspaper; therefore, if a newspaper's bad debt ratio is less than it would take to pay the handling fee, credit card collection has no economic advantage for the newspaper.

Billing Periods Billing periods are affected by the newspaper's cash cycle, the type of area served, payment schedules for workers in a particular area, and time constraints of carriers responsible for collection.

Weekly payments allow subscribers to pay for their newspaper in small allotments; monthly payments may move the newspaper from a small change item to a monthly budget item that may seem nonessential. On the other hand, monthly collections reduce collection time and record-keeping for carriers and, therefore, district managers. Some subscribers also prefer less frequent collections.

Billing periods for office payments are even longer. While, theoretically, computerized billing systems can handle any cycle, mailing bills weekly is simply too costly. Most office billing systems use monthly or quarterly bills.

MAKING HOME DELIVERY WORK

Home delivery has been the primary means of distributing newspapers in the United States and Canada. It is an expensive, labor intensive, complex system that must operate under all weather conditions with timeliness and dependability.

Home delivery is encouraged with subscription prices below the single copy rate, even though actual distribution costs are higher. Publishers know that advertisers and customers favor home delivery with its personalized service and guaranteed circulation. The complex home delivery systems and their subscriber records today allow newspapers to offer such options as total market coverage and zoned editions.

While habit and tradition play a major role in the type of home delivery system a newspaper uses, concern over cost may lead a publisher to consider an independent contractor system. Newspapers seeking more route list, newspaper pricing, and service standard control may consider contract delivery agents or employee carriers. For newspapers having subscribers in broad geographical areas, postal service delivery may be the only feasible method.

The type of home delivery system used will influence the newspaper's carrier recruitment and training policies, subscriber information systems, and billing and collection procedures.

NOTES

1. Newspaper Readership Project, *The Home Delivery Population* (Washington, D.C.: American Newspaper Publishers Association, 1978).
2. Newspaper Readership Project, *Circulation Department Practices* (New York: Newspaper Readership Project, 1980), 4.
3. "Newspapers Still Utilize Youth Carriers," *ICMA Update* 80, 12 (July 1984): 8.
4. "Youth Carriers Still Predominate," *presstime* 6, 8 (August 1984): 46.
5. Albrecht v. Herald Co., 367 F.2d 517 (8th Cir. 1966).
6. Won Chang and Joseph B. Forsee, *A Study of Circulation Distribution and Collection Systems* (Columbia, Mo.: University of Missouri, 1979), 3.
7. David Fluker of the *St. Petersburg Times and Evening Independent*, interview with author, 15 April 1982.
8. Newspaper Readership Project, *Circulation and Home Delivery Patterns* (New York: Newspaper Advertising Bureau, November 1983), 15.
9. Catherine Russell, *CDNPA/CCMA 1981 Survey of Newspaper Circulation Departments* (Toronto: Canadian Daily Newspaper Publishers Association & Canadian Circulation Managers Association, 1981), Appendix A–2.
10. *Circulation Department Practices*, 12.
11. Chang and Forsee, *Study of Circulation Distribution*, 4.
12. *Circulation Department Practices*, 14.
13. Russell, *CDNPA/CCMA 1981 Survey*, Appendix A–13.
14. "Interest Is High in Carrier Turnover and Total Market," *ICMA Update* (July 1984): 9.
15. *Circulation Department Practices*, 18.
16. Ibid., 25.
17. Ibid., 13.
18. *Circulation and Home Delivery Patterns*, 16.
19. Ibid., 20.
20. Ibid., 22.
21. *Circulation Department Practices*, 31–32.
22. Ibid., 33.
23. Margaret Genovese, "Use of Credit Cards for Classifieds, Subscriptions Offers Many Advantages," *presstime* 6, 8 (August 1984): 22–23.

CHAPTER
9

Single Copy Sales

For hundreds of thousands of newspaper customers, the home delivery discussed in the previous chapter is unavailable or does not offer the flexibility they desire. They may live outside the home delivery area. Because they travel frequently, they may not want the paper delivered daily to their homes, piling up and signaling their absence. Because they do not read the newspaper daily or, if they do, read different newspapers, home delivery may not be cost efficient. Because they read the newspaper while commuting, it may be easier to buy the newspaper at the subway station. Point-of-purchase delivery, commonly referred to as single copy sales, best fits the needs of these nonsubscribers.

Point-of-purchase delivery includes sales from newsstands, retail outlets, a few remaining hawkers, and vending boxes. It comprises about 20 percent of the overall circulation of American newspapers, with much higher percentages for morning metropolitan newspapers but a relatively small percentage for small city and most afternoon newspapers. Some newspapers, such as the *New York Daily News* and *Toronto Sun*, rely on single copy sales for the majority of their circulation.

Interest in single copy sales as a means of increasing circulation is growing. One of every three newspapers that gained circulation in the past decade attributed most of the gain to single copy sales. The emergence of *USA Today*, with its heavy reliance on single copy sales and the competition it generated, has forced competing newspapers to pay greater attention to the nonsubscriber.

Growth through single copy sales requires different marketing and sales techniques and different distribution systems. While generally simpler than home delivery, single copy sales demand more aggressive sales and advertising tactics and a large number of sales outlets. Other factors to consider in planning an effective single copy sales system are the selection of an appropriate delivery system, identification of potential customers and outlets, selection of distribution methods, and the provision of nonsubscriber service. This chapter examines these factors in light of the criteria of an effective delivery system—dependability, flexibility, economy, and control.

TYPES OF SINGLE COPY DELIVERY SYSTEMS

The single copy delivery system can be part of the home delivery system, run by the same supervisory employees, or it can be an entirely separate system. For example, the *Milwaukee Journal* and many small-town dailies integrate single copy sales with their home delivery systems. The *Houston Chronicle*, which uses contract delivery agents for home delivery, uses employees for single copy sales. The *Louisville Courier Journal* and *Times* has a separate single copy department, with a manager and three division chiefs—for racks, corner sales, and stores.

Newspapers relying on youth carriers for home delivery often use district managers for single copy delivery and collection, especially in the primary market area or city zone; beyond the PMA, newspapers tend to rely on contractors for single copy delivery. Even within the PMA, newspapers sometimes mix single copy systems; district managers deliver to newsstands and other dealers, while a separate force stocks vending boxes. The key point is that a dealer operates like a carrier, with the same need for supervisory attention to problems, billing, and collection; vending boxes, on the other hand, are mechanical and require less attention.

The mix of single copy systems means that the same types of delivery systems used for home delivery—independent contractors, contract delivery agents, and employees—can be used for single copy sales as well; or separate systems can be established. While the structure of each system was discussed more fully in the previous chapter, the following sections outline the advantages and disadvantages of each system as related to single copy sales.

Independent Contractors

With an independent contractor system, the newspaper, by written agreement, gives the responsibility for and profits of single copy sales to the contractor. As in the home delivery system, the contractor buys the

FIGURE 9.1

FIGURES 9.1, 9.2, 9.3, & 9.4   Single-copy box designs reflect adaptation to
market conditions. The *Toronto Star* designed a special box (right) which is built
into the lobby wall of new apartments. Subscribers have the key to their own box,
thereby preventing theft. Berkely Small, a major manufacturer, produced a line of
wood cabinet racks (p. 268) for use with customers who object to the look of
conventional metal machines. The deep box displays the full front page as a
promotional device, and it holds up to 50 copies of a large Sunday newspaper.
The distinctive *USA Today* box (above) emulates a television set and focuses
attention on it colorful page-one design. Courtesy *The Toronto Star*, Berkely Small
Inc., Mobile, AL and *USA Today*.

FIGURE 9.2

FIGURE 9.3

FIGURE 9.4

newspapers at a wholesale rate, then sets the retail price at which they will be sold. The contractor is a retail store manager, a newsstand owner, or an individual with circulation rights to a particular community or geographical territory.

By law, the newspaper can contract for timely delivery to outlets and sufficient redelivery to make the newspaper readily available to customers. Beyond this, the newspaper can seek circulation increases by encouraging—but not requiring—contractors to advertise, add more vending boxes, or experiment with different locations.

The newspaper can offer contractors several options regarding ownership of equipment. The newspaper lends or leases equipment to the contractor, often at low cost; or it requires the contractor to purchase the equipment, using a favorable rate to encourage use of a particular brand. The newspaper and contractor also work out an agreement on maintenance, repair, and replacement of vending boxes, particularly if the newspaper wants to maintain a consistent image. These arrangements have significant implications for financial disclosure, as explained in Chapter 6.

Among the newspapers using independent contractors for single copy delivery are the Raleigh (North Carolina) News and Observer and Times and the Bakersfield Californian. The News and Observer, a morning newspaper, is totally distributed by adult carriers, each of whom has his or her own vending boxes and stores that he or she supplies. The afternoon Times has two salaried employees to service boxes in the downtown area, but the rest of the circulation area is served by independent contractors. The contractors pay one price for newspapers, whether home delivered or sold through single copy outlets. At the Californian contractors are billed a wholesale rate for papers and allowed a fixed return percentage of 10 percent. The company owns the racks and leases them to the contractor.

The advantages and disadvantages of independent contractors for single copy sales are similar to those of independent contractors used for home delivery. On the positive side, independent contractors provide services to nonsubscribers at relatively low cost to the newspaper. On the other hand, the newspaper does not have control over the paper's price, location of single copy outlets, or recordkeeping.

Contract Delivery Agents

Contract delivery agent systems give the newspaper full control over price and sales methods by hiring people for limited services, such as filling the newspaper's vending boxes or selling at a particular location. The newspaper retains ownership of each copy and all equipment, thus maintaining control over the number, location, and redelivery schedule for single copy sales.

The control advantage is particularly important with vending boxes because the newspaper, with its ownership, is responsible for their appearance, operation, and usage. For retail outlets, there is little difference between the independent contractor and contract delivery agent systems, unless the delivery and collection fee in the contract delivery agreement is larger than the profit from the wholesale-retail arrangement.

Employee Carriers

Employee carriers offer complete control over single copy sales outlets, ranging from outlet numbers and locations to newspaper numbers and prices to redelivery and collection frequencies. Because the newspaper controls the outlet, whether vending box or newsstand, it can freely experiment with advertising devices and different locations, adding an element of flexibility to the single copy system.

While the newspaper bears the full burden of theft, vandalism, and labor costs in an employee carrier system, it also retains all profits from single copy sales. Even so, the employee system is more expensive than the other systems.

Where used, this system is usually limited to circulation zones where employees perform other work, for instance, routes traveled by employee drivers.

Employee carriers are more common for single copy systems than for home delivery systems, but variations in both employee functions and reimbursement methods make the single copy system difficult to categorize. While some newspapers, such as the *Rockford* (Illinois) *Register Star*, the *Santa Barbara* (California) *News-Press*, and *Kenosha* (Wisconsin) *News*, pay their single copy employees a straight salary, others, such as the *Chicago Tribune, Detroit Free Press*, and *Detroit News*, pay salary plus commission. The *Chicago Tribune* uses salaried Teamster drivers to deliver, pick up returns, and collect from single copy outlets and boxes; the drivers also receive a commission, the difference between the wholesale and retail rate for papers sold. At the *Free Press* salaried Teamster district managers are responsible for all classes of circulation—carriers, racks, and stores. In the downtown area three managers handle single copy sales exclusively; in other areas managers supervise both single copy and home delivery. As at the *Tribune*, the managers keep the difference between the wholesale and retail rates for copies sold.

Another variation in the employee carrier system is used at the *Tampa Tribune*, an all-day newspaper. Distributor employees buy newspapers at a wholesale rate, receive full returns, and get the difference between the wholesale and retail rates. While they receive no salary, as employees they do have a benefit package. The *Tribune* uses three different wholesale rates—for the sunrise, a.m., and p.m. editions—based on the sales potential of each; the a.m. edition has the highest rate and greatest sale.

IDENTIFYING POTENTIAL CUSTOMERS

Single copy purchasers can be divided into two categories—those for whom a newspaper purchase is an impulse buy and those for whom it is a planned expenditure.

Impulse purchasers buy a newspaper because they are attracted by a particular picture or headline, they respond to TV or radio advertisements promoting a particular feature, or they find themselves with additional leisure time and pick up a newspaper for perusal. Supermarket newspapers such as the *National Star* and the *National Enquirer* rely on impulse purchasers and, as a result, use sensationalized headlines to attract attention.

On the other hand, nonsubscribers for whom the newspaper is a planned expenditure buy the paper on a regular, though not a daily, basis. Only one-fifth of single copy buyers buy a newspaper every day, although the percentage is higher in metropolitan areas; however, most single copy buyers purchase a newspaper more than once a week.[1] Weekday single copy sales are highest on Wednesdays, when the papers usually include a food section, and Fridays, when they contain news of weekend entertainment; and they are lowest on Mondays.[2] Despite their higher cost, Sunday editions outsell the dailies.

In addition to the day of the week, other factors that influence single copy sales are travel schedules, budget, use of free time, and residence. The difficulty of home delivery in many multiple-unit dwellings encourages residents to rely on single copy sales; only 21 percent of residents in apartment buildings with five or less stories and only 2 percent of those in buildings with six or more stories have daily home delivery.[3]

Cost affects the single copy purchaser in one of two ways. For some, an occasional newspaper purchase, averaging 25 cents per daily issue, best meets their budgetary constraints. For others, cost is not a factor in their purchase decision; cheaper subscriber rates do not offset the flexibility of choosing when to buy a newspaper and which newspaper to buy.

Nearly 20 percent of single copy purchasers are also subscribers.[4] They leave their home-delivered paper at home and buy another copy for work or to read while commuting; or a subscriber may purchase a single copy to replace an undelivered or late paper. Two-thirds of the single copy purchasers living in areas with more than one newspaper and 50 percent of those in single paper areas have been solicited for subscriptions[5] but choose to rely on single copy purchases.

The key factor in single copy purchases is the flexibility available to customers. They decide daily on whether or not they have the time to read a newspaper and the money to buy it, and they decide on what newspaper to buy.

IDENTIFYING POTENTIAL OUTLETS

A newspaper's ready availability, a factor of dependability, also influences single copy purchases. Customers must know where to buy the paper with minimal effort.

Easy customer access begins with the identification of likely sales sites, ideally in areas of high pedestrian traffic with a known concentration of potential readers. High traffic areas include bus stops, mass transit entrances, factory gates, restaurants, and mailboxes. Areas with a concentration of potential readers normally include hotel and motel lobbies; airport boarding areas; and the lobbies or entranceways of large, multiple-unit dwellings, where restricted access makes home delivery difficult. Such areas are common locations for vending boxes.

Locating retail outlets follows the same principles—high traffic area and concentration of readers. In Denver a research study identified 1400 potential new outlets for the *Rocky Mountain News*; more than half of the untapped sales locations became outlets, increasing single copy sales.[6] In its comprehensive manual for single copy sales, the *Toronto Globe and Mail* lists 47 types of retail outlets to consider and provides guidelines for box location.[7] The manual estimates that it takes four to six weeks for a new outlet to establish sales. But, a *Globe and Mail* box at the end of a jogging trail proved to be an instant success among young singles.

SELECTING DISTRIBUTION METHODS

Once it has identified potential sales sites, the newspaper must determine how best to serve the single copy purchaser in a particular area. The distribution methods fall into three categories: active hawkers and newsstands, neighborhood dealers, and vending boxes and racks. Most newspapers use a combination of these methods to provide service for nonsubscribers.

A 1983 readership study indicated that while nearly a third of single copy purchasers did not care where they got their newspaper, nearly

FIGURE 9.5   In newsstands and drug stores, newspapers vie with magazines for buyers' attention, putting an emphasis on color and page-1 design. Courtesy *Newsday*, Long Island, NY.

one-half of the nonsubscribers preferred to buy their newspapers at retail outlets. Only 19 percent, given other options, chose to buy a newspaper from a rack or machine.[8]

Hawkers and Newsstands

The Norman Rockwell image of a newsboy standing on the street corner shouting "Extra, extra, read all about it" is a thing of the past in most American cities, although still a part of a tradition in some Northeast cities. While a few newspapers, such as the *Boston Globe*, the *New York Post*, and the Los Angeles Times, continue to use hawkers both to increase single copy sales and to improve the newspaper's visibility, they have replaced most corner newsboys with vending boxes.

Some hawkers go door to door in a few cities. In an effort to reach weak circulation areas in Muskegon, Michigan, the *Muskegon Chronicle* hired young adults to sell the newspaper in low-income neighborhoods. In the first test run, the hawkers sold their bundles of 50 newspapers each within a half hour.[9]

Little merchants and even adult carriers may act as hawkers on holidays, ordering single copies to service nonsubscribers on their routes.

Although nearly 30 percent of single copy purchasers buy their newspapers at a newsstand,[10] the newsstand is also a diminishing source of newspaper sales. It remains popular in the Northeast, especially in New York City, and is particularly valuable in serving subway and other mass transportation locations. However, the U.S. Census Bureau has reported a dramatic decline in newsstands with employees.[11]

Advantages of Hawkers and Newsstands   The primary advantage of hawkers and newsstands as a means of increasing single copy sales is the active sales effort they involve. Nonsubscribers are *encouraged* to buy a newspaper. Hawkers and newsstand employees can attract attention from busy passers-by who can too easily ignore vending machines. For instance, in some cities hawkers move among cars stopped at toll booths or bridge/freeway access ramps (although this is strictly prohibited in other areas). Hawkers make it possible for customers to buy a newspaper without leaving their car or porch.

Frequent customers also enjoy the regular interaction with a hawker or newsstand employee. The more personalized service becomes part of a customer's daily routine.

Disadvantages of Hawkers and Newsstands   With newsstands, the newspaper's primary disadvantage is lack of control. Site location, newspaper placement, and sales effort are vendor decisions. Because of the higher profit margin for magazine sales, newsstand operators tend to showcase and push magazines rather than newspapers. The decreasing number of newsstands makes reliance on them for single copy sales almost impossible.

The disadvantages of hawkers are similar to those of working with carriers in a home delivery system. Recruiting, training, supervising and paying for hawkers, particularly youth, is not the most economically feasible means of increasing single copy sales. Dependability is also a factor; it is important that hawkers be in the same location at approximately the same time each day to provide consistent service for nonsubscribers. For the hawker the job is hard work, with long hours, and a low income level.

Bad weather affects both hawker and newsstand operations. Hawkers do not want to be on the street in rain or snow or even severely cold or hot weather. Bad weather also decreases the traffic for newsstands.

Another concern is safety, especially in high-crime locales and high-traffic areas. Newspapers using hawkers provide training on basic traffic regulations and on anticipating and avoiding trouble.

Neighborhood Dealers

Dealers include gas station, pharmacy, motel, or any other business owners who purchase newspapers at a wholesale rate and sell them at a retail rate for profit (independent contractors) or who receive a collection fee for stocking and selling the newspaper (contract delivery agent). Few dealers consider the newspaper a major money-making item. They usually carry the newspaper to encourage traffic into the store or to provide a service to customers.

A district manager, contractor, or driver delivers the requested number of copies, called the *draw*, to a dealer and picks up unsold copies. The dealer receives credit for the unsold copies. The district manager or contractor also works with the dealer to find easily accessible display space for the newspaper.

Advantages of Neighborhood Dealers Because most dealers display news- papers on open racks, they encourage impulse sales; it's easy for a customer to pick up a newspaper, glance at it, and, if interested, make the purchase. In addition, the customer does not have to worry about having the exact change that's necessary for a vending box; and the newspaper is in good condition.

Disadvantages of Neighborhood Dealers The restricted hours of most retail outlets limits the flexibility of single copy purchases. Although home delivery of a morning newspaper is usually between the hours of 6 and 7 a.m., few businesses are open at that hour to sell single copies. Many stores are also closed Sundays, a key time for single copy sales. However, convenience stores, with their longer hours and seven-day-a-week schedules, are ideal retail outlets.

Another disadvantage is the lack of control newspapers have over returns. Returns are a major factor in the cost of a single copy delivery system. While newspapers try to maintain returns at 10 percent or less, the return ratio is often much higher.

There are several difficulties related to returns. Sometimes dealers try to return papers that have been read. Daily return bundles padded with old newspapers or Sunday edition sections may also be a problem. Constant vigilance is required to detect returns fraud. Most district managers or single copy service personnel are adept at detecting attempts to falsify returns. Since single copy supplies are based on actual sales, the dealer may end up with too few newspapers for customers, resulting in a loss of business for the store and unhappy customers.

Some returns are essential, but there is no universally accepted figure. The low end (other than zero) is 1 percent, the high about 18 percent. Some newspapers do not accept returns. Others anticipate high returns; for instance, the *Toronto Sun* uses a marketing formula that calls for 15 to 20 percent more newspapers on the shelf than will be sold. For many newspapers such a return rate is too high, based on newsprint costs and limited reliance on single copy sales.

Vending Boxes and Racks

More than three-fourths of the nonsubscribers who buy newspapers purchase them from vending boxes and racks.[12] Three basic types of circulation racks—the honor rack, the semiautomatic box, and the automatic box—provide more than 633,000 outlets for single copy newspaper sales.[13]

The *honor rack* is an open wire basket or carrier that holds newspapers and perhaps a small box for coins. Usually placed inside a building, it is used primarily in small towns. Its advantage is the easy customer access, the disadvantage is the possibility of theft.

The most frequently used vending equipment is the *semiautomatic box*. The customer inserts a coin, which unlocks the mechanism, allowing the customer to remove a newspaper. Unfortunately, the unscrupulous customer can remove more than one newspaper. At a cost of $300 to $500 apiece, semiautomatic boxes are a cost-efficient means of distributing single copies. The average box holds 25 to 35 average-sized daily editions and 10 to 12 Sunday edition copies. Special deep-loading boxes and new racks that display the full front page hold more newspapers; however, they cost more, require more space, and cannot be hung from telephone and light poles, common sites for vending boxes.

The third type of circulation rack is the *automatic box*. The automatic box allows a customer to take only one newspaper, eliminating the possibility of theft that exists with an honor rack and even a semiautomatic box. However, the automatic box is almost twice as expensive as the semiautomatic box and is difficult to adjust for daily variation in newspaper size.

Semiautomatic and automatic vending boxes that are located outside should be easily accessible, well functioning, and clean to attract single copy customers. Ideally such boxes should face the flow of traffic, allowing drivers to see whether or not the box is full and what the headlines are.

For any type of circulation rack, the district manager's or contractor's goal is to have a single copy left at the end of the day. This means not only minimum returns but also that every nonsubscriber wanting to buy a newspaper had the chance to do so. Because of the limited size of most boxes, this may mean redelivery several times a day in high traffic areas or the installation of several boxes within a short distance of each other. As discussed in the next chapter, some newspapers use computer programs to determine the draws for individual boxes and dealers. Such factors as the day of the week, news values, weather forecasts, and past sales patterns are fed into the computer to assess the draw for a particular day.

Advantages of Vending Boxes and Racks   From the customer's viewpoint, the chief advantages of vending boxes and racks are convenience and speed. Vending boxes are accessible at all hours at a wide variety of locations; and they do not require, as dealers do, any wait for service.

For the newspaper, the primary advantage of vending boxes and racks is the flexibility their use gives the newspaper in selecting sites for single copy sales. Small vending boxes can be placed unobtrusively in almost every neighborhood, on almost every street corner.

However, this location flexibility is being limited by the advent of municipal license fees and an increasing number of new or restricted newsrack ordinances regulating the number, location, and appearance of vending boxes. Such ordinances are a result of increased competition among newspapers. As newspapers extend their circulation areas and weeklies and free shoppers begin to use racks and boxes, the proliferation of boxes can be confusing and unattractive. In Washington, D.C., for example, one can find over 20 boxes of different newspapers chained together in a row.

In Denver, newspapers share a city-owned, four-box frame mounted on a steel pole and anchored in the pavement. While city newspapers usually get first choice of vending box space, other newspapers, such as the *Wall Street Journal, New York Times, Los Angeles Times*, and *USA Today*, must fight for space in each frame. In Appleton, Wisconsin, all newspaper vending boxes must be painted a standard brown to match the street decor. Some motel and restaurant chains require that boxes be a certain color to harmonize with their decor.

Disadvantages of Vending Boxes and Racks   For the customer, the primary disadvantages of vending boxes are the need for exact change and, if driving, the need to leave the car to purchase a newspaper. Thus, single copy sales are affected by weather conditions.

For the newspaper, the disadvantages of vending boxes are maintenance and theft. Vandalism, theft, and simple wear and tear mandate periodic vending box maintenance. The *Dallas Morning News*, with more than 5000 semiautomatic boxes in use, employs three people full time in its box repair facility. Boxes are brought in every four to five years for removing rust and dents, repainting, and, if needed, updating lock mechanisms. Some newspapers, in an effort to hold down overhead costs, contract out box maintenance and repair. In some climates the periodic maintenance schedule used in Dallas is inadequate; particularly in northern cities with heavy snowfalls and street salting, annual maintenance is necessary to keep boxes attractive and in good working order.

Theft is a key factor in the newspaper's lack of control over single copy sales. Because vending machines contain money, they naturally attract thieves; such thefts, which necessitate breaking into the money box, not only cause an income loss but also significantly increase repair costs. A new generation of protective covers made of thick steel housings for the padlocks has reduced on-site theft; however, entire boxes are sometimes carried to an isolated spot and broken into. Employee theft, using master keys, is also a problem and may be difficult to detect if only portions of the cash receipts are taken.

A frequent target of thieves is the coupon sections of newspapers. Individual and groups of newspapers may be stolen as well. Newspaper theft makes it impossible for newspapers to accurately determine single copy sales and, thus, overall circulation; it also raises questions about coupon security and results in dissatisfied customers if they continually find a vending box empty or newspapers missing valuable coupon sections.

To determine if thefts are occurring, newspapers must calculate the cash received per newspaper in each box and on each route. The theft rate is the cash received divided by the number of papers in the box; for instance, if a box with 19 papers takes in $4.00, that's 21.05¢ per copy. With the price of the newspaper set at 25¢ a copy, that's a 3.95¢ loss per copy, or a 16 percent theft rate. An alternative method calculates the numbers of newspapers stolen. Since $4.00 pays for 16 newspapers, the theft rate is three newspapers. This method is more difficult to use in route comparisons because of the differences in sales volumes between routes.

The Audit Bureau of Circulation accepts a newspaper's calculation of single copies sold, provided that adequate return records are maintained and that the net revenue on sales equals 75 percent of the retail value of the papers placed in boxes. For example, a box with 20 copies at a 25¢ retail price should net $5.00 in revenue if all customers pay the full price.

If the box produced less than $3.75 (75 percent of $5.00), ABC could cut the net paid sales. Of course, ABC works on total single copies sold, not individual box figures.

Newspapers use a number of techniques to reduce vending box theft. Putting boxes in the lobbies of buildings significantly reduces both vandalism and theft. Rotating padlocks on boxes deters theft by those with access to keys. Using marked coins or counting receipts ahead of time may help detect employee theft. Most important is the day-to-day calculation of the theft rate; however, this is time-consuming and therefore costly in terms of man-hours. Most drivers simply empty the cash boxes and load the boxes as quickly as possible, without keeping per box figures; thus, the newspaper has only route totals. A route with consistently high theft rates can be monitored on a per box basis. Computerization has made such recordkeeping easier, not only for vending boxes but also for dealer outlets.

Billing for Single Copy Sales

Billing for single copy sales reflects the type of distribution system used. District managers bill and collect directly from dealers. Newspapers bill dealers acting as contract delivery agents or independent contractors by using house or bulk accounts.

Those having house accounts, usually dealers, hawkers, and newsstand operators working directly with the newspaper, receive and pay their bills directly through the newspaper's business office on a weekly, monthly, or quarterly basis. The contract delivery agent or employee servicing the account has no billing or collection responsibility. The newspaper maintains a record of the draws, returns, and wholesale rate.

Those having bulk accounts buy single copies in bulk, with no pickup of unused newspapers. Thus, contractors are encouraged to have exact draws and sell all newspapers or to establish a retail rate high enough to cover any anticipated loss. Independent contractors then set up their own collection system with individual distributors.

IMPROVING SINGLE COPY SALES

As a delivery system, point-of-purchase delivery involves a network of outlets that must be supplied, machines that must be replaced and serviced, attention to changing market patterns, collection, integration of single copy and home delivery systems, and unique sales techniques.

The day-to-day responsibility of the person serving single copy outlets—whether newsstands, hawkers, dealers, or vending boxes—is the dropoff of newspapers and pickup of unsold newspapers. The most important function, however, is the calculation of the daily draw.

With home delivery, sales are constant. With single copies, sales vary according to the day of the week; the weather; major news stories; outlet locations; promotional campaigns; and market pattern changes caused by new bus routes and buildings, economic conditions in a particular area, or neighborhood decline. District managers and contractors must consider all these factors in determining the number of copies an outlet receives each day. They can also offer sales tools—posters and displays—and advice to dealers and newsstand operators.

Dealers can be helpful in informing a district manager or contractor of the need for additional papers on a regular basis or, by phoning in, on a particular day. On the other hand, vending boxes at key locations ideally should be monitored once or twice a day to add papers if needed or shift papers from one location to another until a firm sales pattern is established.

Adjusting the draw is a complex procedure involving the pressroom, mailroom, loading dock, and data processing department (if bundle sizes are computerized). Multisectioned newspapers, often including numerous preprints, make it difficult to adjust draw size on a daily basis because the newspaper is likely to have fewer preprinted sections than it may need. Once the pressrun is locked in, for whatever section, adjusting the draw is a major concern lest the newspaper have too many copies left or too few copies to serve all customers and dealers.

Dependability in terms of timeliness is just as important in single copy sales as in home delivery. Customers expect to buy a paper at a particular time of day; therefore, late deliveries result in missed sales. Monitoring timely delivery involves recording truck departure times and route driving times; spot-checking boxes at random; and comparing route sales with presstimes, weather, and other factors affecting sales. Computer programs used at some newspapers calculate the draw based on such factors. Redelivery is important at high sales locations, whether newsstands, dealers, or vending boxes.

The return rate of single copies is a measure of wastage, a barometer of sales, and a guide to possible theft and future sales. Because newsprint costs run high, the number of unsold newspapers has a cash value in addition to the coupon value of special sections.

Increasing point-of-purchase circulation requires using some of the innovative sales and promotional techniques discussed in Chapter 5, making copies of the newspaper readily available at a wide variety of outlets, and providing dependable service to both readers and dealers.

In competing markets, circulation workers may keep track of their competitor's single copy sales in order to compare sales rates. The information can be used to evaluate the impact of promotions and news treatment, but its primary purpose is knowing the competitor.

Profit stability and advertiser questions caused newspapers to adopt home delivery as the major circulation mode in the United States, despite the high costs and complex systems required to place the paper at the front door of hundreds of thousands of readers each day, whatever the weather. In today's audience, however, single copy sales have become increasingly important for reaching the affluent, single, and other highly mobile segments of the readership, This shift has caused a minor revolution in the philosophy of some circulation departments. The other revolution was caused by computers, the next topic.

NOTES

1. Newspaper Readership Project, *Circulation and Home Delivery Patterns* (New York: Newspaper Advertising Bureau, November 1983), 31.
2. Ibid., 27.
3. Ibid., 8.
4. Ibid., 30.
5. Leo Bogart, "Circulation: The Key to Successful Newspaper Marketing," address to the International Circulation Managers Association convention, New York City, 21 June 1982.
6. *Circulation and Home Delivery Patterns*, 8.
7. *Single Copy Circulation Practices Manual* (Toronto: Toronto Globe and Herald, 1982), 19–21.
8. *Circulation and Home Delivery Patterns*, 37.
9. C. David Rambo, "Single Copy Sales," *presstime* 6, 7 (July 1984): 8.
10. *Circulation and Home Delivery Patterns*, 25.
11. Bogart, "Circulation: Key to Successful Marketing."
12. Ibid.
13. Rambo, "Single Copy Sales," 7.

CHAPTER

10

Computerized Circulation Systems

The computer has revolutionized the newspaper business—in the composing room with electronic typesetting, in the editorial department with the use of video display terminals for writing and editing copy, in the advertising and art departments with computer-assisted design, and in the business office with electronic images replacing triplicate business forms.

Only gradually has the computer moved into various parts of the circulation department because of the difficulty of writing programs capable of handling complex circulation functions. In 1979 the International Circulation Managers Association, the American Newspaper Publishers Association, and the Institute of Newspaper Controllers and Finance Officers sponsored the first circulation computer symposium in order to acquaint newspaper executives with the problems, costs, and prospects of computerized circulation systems. At the time, only 57 newspapers in the country had computers in their circulation departments,[1] although other newspapers were using computers for such circulation-related functions as customer billing and recordkeeping for mail and paid-in-advance subscribers. However, these uses were really extensions of accounting programs and were not easily expandable to other circulation functions.

The use of the computer in circulation functions began to expand in the late 1970s, as many newspapers experimented with computer-prepared carrier invoices, drivers' schedules and stops, and reports for the Audit Bureau of Circulations. By 1984 an ICMA survey indicated that

93 percent of the responding newspapers had a computerized circulation system.[2]

Previous chapters have cited the use of computers in such activities as calculating single copy draws, preparing subscriber lists for carrier routes, and labeling bundles in the mailroom. This chapter examines the different uses of computerization in circulation departments, the data requirements for various subsystems, and the advantages and disadvantages of computerization.

VARIATIONS OF COMPUTERIZED SYSTEMS

Circulation managers need not be computer programmers, but they must understand the general structure of computerized data processing in order to take full advantage of an existing system or to understand the variations among systems being considered for adoption. In other words, managers must know what they want to accomplish with a computer, as well as the computer's capabilities and limitations.

Computerization is not the same for every circulation department not only because the departments differ but also because a newspaper may not find full computerization cost beneficial.

At its simplest level circulation department computerization involves using the computer for normal bookkeeping and accounting transactions. Such programs are usually developed in cooperation with the accounting or billing office and have little usefulness in terms of employee supervision, marketing, or even the transmittal of information to all affected parties. This level of computerization is sufficient for small newspapers that dominate their market or for newspapers with independent contractors who control subscriber lists.

The second, and most common, level of computerization in circulation departments includes not only accounting functions but also such circulation functions as subscriber information, transportation data, and customer service. Such systems are more difficult to implement because they require the development of an extensive data base; however, once operational, the system is easily maintained. For many newspapers this level of computerization, in combination with manual records, is sufficient; this is particularly true for newspapers having proprietary interest in their subscriber lists and handling all customer complaints internally.

The most sophisticated level of computerization is based on an address list involving both subscribers and nonsubscribers. With this addition, the computer can perform a wide range of supporting tasks, from automatically assigning subscribers to carrier routes to printing labels for all nonsubscribers. This level of computerization, discussed more fully later in this chapter, is particularly useful for large newspapers in highly competitive markets. However, the sheer volume of data needed to initiate the address file and the laborious task of maintaining its accuracy make this level of computerization difficult to achieve.

At whatever level it exists, computerization is a combination of information (called the *data base* or *file*) and of information processing (called a *routine*). The following sections describe the most common processing methods and data bases.

Types of Information Processing

Computerized systems use either batch or on-line processing. In batch processing, the terminal is not connected directly to the main computer unit but to an intermediate memory storage system, which holds the data until the main processing unit has time and space for the full transaction. The operator has no access to stored records. In on-line processing, each terminal is connected directly to the computer's central processing unit; thus, each transaction is handled as soon as it is entered, and the operator can access all stored information.

Batch Processing Batch processing is less expensive than on-line processing because it allows use of a smaller mainframe computer, thus making the expansion of an existing computerized system more feasible. Batch processing was more common before the development of relatively inexpensive high-speed computers with enough capacity to serve an entire department though not necessarily all departments within a business. Today it is typical of a system with only one large, central computer for all departments.

Batch processing limits the use of computerized data because the terminal cannot interact with other units. For instance, a service representative on the phone with a customer cannot review the customer's full payment and service history and instantly process a request because the information required is stored elsewhere in the computer and cannot be readily accessed. The transaction must be handled later, with others, in the batch.

On-line Processing An on-line system requires a larger, more sophisticated computer system than batch processing does because each terminal has access to the main computer unit, and an operator can instantly trigger a transaction. This enables an operator to build and correct a customer file, notify the carrier or contractor of changes, and adjust the pressrun or draw automatically. On-line processing also facilitates file maintenance because the operator can verify existing data each time a customer contact is made. In addition, an on-line system, if connected to a monitor, allows supervisors to review the activity level and performance of individual operators. Many circulation departments have their own computers on-line linked by batch systems to other computers within the newspaper.

Types of Routines

Most computerized circulation systems begin with office billing and collection, then interface customer service, transportation, carrier and contractor, and subscriber data. Building such data files can take from one to three years.

Some of the routines, such as subscriber billing, may be operated in batch processing, while others can be used on-line. A review of each subsystem illustrates the range of possible functions.

Subscriber Billing Basically an accounting program, this subsystem generally handles all billing and payments for paid-in-advance and office payment customers. The subsystem can be adjusted to any billing cycle or combination of advance-arrears billing when used to produce subscriber bills. It automatically calculates different rates for standard, mail, and discount subscriptions.

The subscriber file forms the data base for this subsystem; it includes up-to-date information on each subscriber's address, delivery requirements, and billing data. Another file includes information on subscriber complaints, starts, stops, and so on; this file is commonly referred to as the *subscriber history file.*

Customer Service The customer service subsystem enables a circulation department to rapidly process starts, stops, complaints, and holds and then produce memos for anyone affected by such transactions. In addition, because the terminal operator in an on-line system has access to complete customer histories, the subsystem allows updating and verifying customer information.

For circulation workers in the field, the most significant file in this subsystem, commonly referred to as a *dispatch file*, records all complaints and memos; these are sent to district managers or carriers with the newspapers or are radioed to the field. For circulation managers, the subsystem's summary file provides a breakdown of all complaints by type and route.

Transportation This subsystem usually includes files detailing the truck routes; drivers; dropoff points; and carriers, contractors, or dealers serviced by each route. Each element generates its own file; for instance, a drop/route file lists the routes served by each drop point.

Linked to the subscriber subsystem, the transportation subsystem can produce truck manifests, loading sequences, bundle labels, and messages for those picking up bundles. For instance, a subscriber's stop notice is automatically transmitted to the carrier serving that route. The subsystem's flexibility permits mixing labeled bundles of different newspapers and key labeling for lead bundles.

Carrier/Contractor A draw/accounting subsystem records and tracks all data related to draw; routes; and carrier and contractor employment, accounting, and bonding. Data generated include the number of newspapers per carrier, contractor, or dealer and corresponding bills.

Coupled with customer service files, the subsystem can generate a service record for individual carriers and for district managers. Linked with subscriber billing, it automatically credits carriers and contractors for office payments.

Such incidental carrier/contractor charges as mileage, supplies, and insurance and such bill adjustments as returns and sales bonuses are entered into this subsystem and, thus, figured in carrier/contractor bills. The subsystem is particularly useful in generating data needed for Audit Bureau of Circulations reports.

The file includes the rates, payment records, and addresses of each carrier/contractor.

Types of Data Bases

Subscriber Data Base Newspapers typically maintain an address base of subscribers. Entries are organized by address because address is the point of entry, a unique element, and the information factor least likely to change rapidly. Addresses are also the key element in developing route lists.

Address bases are generally cross-referenced by name and telephone number; this enables a supervisor or customer service representative to access and verify information more easily. In the most sophisticated systems, addresses are listed by street and divided into data groups according to newspaper carrier route, postal route, ZIP code, or route identification number.

An accurate data base allows production of mailing labels for subscribers by ZIP code, street, route, or even telephone exchange. The address base requires constant maintenance for accuracy. Errors, once in the system, can be difficult to eliminate. In addition, new subdivisions, apartment buildings, demolished buildings, and restructured postal routes necessitate frequent file revision.

The *router* is a set of cross-indexing routines using the address base. Router files often include a street name file, a ZIP code file, a street code file, an alternate name file, and an apartment file.

The router interacts with the address file in most routines to provide one of the following several services:

1. Identify new subscriptions

2. Assign new customers to a carrier

3. Identify all addresses on a particular route

4. Separate multiple-unit dwellings from single-family homes

5. Provide current route lists for carriers and supervisors

Subscriber/Nonsubscriber Data Base The most sophisticated—and most difficult—step in a computerized circulation system is establishing a subscriber/nonsubscriber file. Such a file is an expansion of the subscriber address base.

The development of a subscriber/nonsubscriber data base is particularly important in areas where shoppers or direct mail operations are cutting into newspaper advertising revenues because of their higher market penetration. By maintaining a nonsubscriber data base, newspapers can offer advertisers a total market coverage product, delivering advertising supplements to nonsubscribers as well as subscribers. The subscriber/nonsubscriber data base also offers other sales and marketing capabilities, which will be discussed more fully in the section on advantages.

A Newspaper Readership Project manual, *Building a Subscriber-Nonsubscriber File*, cites the following 11 potential applications for the file:[3]

1. Delivery of advertising material to nonsubscribers by third-class mail presorted by postal carrier route and even delivery sequence. (This is another way of describing the total market coverage product offered by many newspapers.)

2. Penetration studies by route or ZIP code or geographical territory.

3. Direct mail solicitation of nonsubscribers.

4. Door-to-door sales efforts targeted at nonsubscribers.

5. Telephone sales targeted at nonsubscribers.

6. Verification, accounting, and retention studies of new subscriptions.

7. Automatic cross-matching of starts and stops against office payment and reader service plans.

8. Emergency route lists.

9. Immediate production of a complete customer listing for each carrier.

10. Studies matching subscriber lists with census and demographic data.

11. Matching of subscriber lists with advertiser charge card lists.

Of course, some of these tasks can be accomplished without a computer, although in a more time-consuming fashion.

The development of such a file is not only costly but also difficult and time-consuming. The use of the file requires continuous maintenance, both updating the address base and verifying the subscription status of each household. Routine verification is the only way to purge errors that might accidentally be entered into the file. For this reason, newspapers with a subscriber/nonsubscriber system build in correction steps for every customer contact. The labor involved in such maintenance activities varies with the number of entries, the complexity of the community, and the type of circulation system used. The frequent household changes in high-transiency and low-income areas have made file maintenance for nonsubscribers so difficult that most newspapers simply avoid building address files for such areas.

The first step in building a subscriber/nonsubscriber system is accumulating and inputting the data. The data must include information about the household, any newspaper subscription, solicitation history, complaint history, and file maintenance records.[4]

Household data should include

House number
Directional (North, South)
Street type (Avenue, Blvd., etc.)
Apartment number
ZIP code
City (perhaps taken from ZIP code)
State (perhaps taken from ZIP code)
Type of housing unit (single/multiple/business/vacant)

VIP code
Census tract
Demographic group codes
Advertising zone
Newspaper carrier number(s)
Newspaper carrier delivery sequence number(s)
Off-route delivery carrier(s) code
Postal carrier number
Postal carrier delivery sequence
Alternate delivery carrier number
Alternate delivery carrier sequence
Subscriber information:
 Last name
 First name
 Middle initial
 Telephone area code
 Telephone number

Subscription information should include

Subscription status (with allowance for multiple copies)
Temporary stop with/without restart date
Original start/stop dates
Latest start/stop date(s) and type(s)
Delivery/collection instructions
Office payment, PIA, or cross-reference code to billing file
Reader service data/charges

Solicitation history should include

Dates, types of latest solicitations
Objections given to subscribing
Objection to any telephone solicitation
Sales credit data

File maintenance information should include

Date information was last verified
Date subscription status last verified
Date and type of last transaction for this address

The complaint history file should include

Dates, types of latest complaints
Number of complaints, year to date (perhaps by type)

The Newspaper Readership Project study identified seven steps, schematically portrayed in Figure 10.1, that should be used in building a subscriber/nonsubscriber file. Each entry should be validated before becoming part of the permanent file.

The seven steps are as follows:

1.   Obtain a list of the addresses of all households in the target area. A few sources such as the utility companies or local governmental offices have highly accurate and nearly complete lists, but the files are kept secret or are expensive to purchase. Lists can also be purchased from several direct mail houses or publishers' mailing houses. However, the accuracy of such lists should be carefully checked.

2.   Produce a summary street listing from the household list in order to verify addresses and identify inconsistencies in spelling, directional and abbreviation patterns.

3.   Match the housing file against the newspaper's router file to insure that each address can be routed. Create an exception file for addresses that will need manual routing.

4.   Resolve exceptions and problems in the router with a standard procedure, including the decision to handle them on-line or manually. Some locations, particularly rural ones, will have multiple valid addresses (by highway number and rural postal route, for example).

5.   Print a housing unit list sequenced by address for the newspaper carrier and have the carrier validate every address, whether subscriber or nonsubscriber. This is a critical check for accuracy, and it must be verified by a supervisor since carrier input may be based on "guesses" rather than actual checking. Such checking is usually done once or twice a year.

6.   Process carrier corrections and identification of subscriber status, including those on vacation.

7.   Audit carrier lists and input data, with particular attention to the route draw.

Once an address file is 95 percent accurate, the Postal Service will review it and correct the remaining errors by paying postal carriers to correct the route lists. However, less accurate lists can be rejected by local postal officials. The Canadian Postal Service, which updates its routes and postal codes annually, sells its master tapes to allow all businesses to update and maintain their address files.

To build its address file, the *Fayetteville* (North Carolina) *News and*

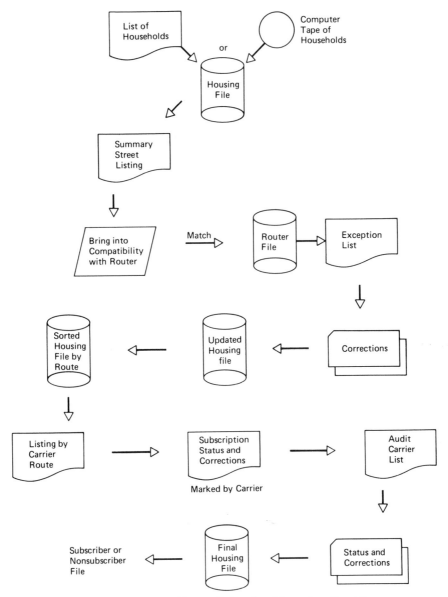

FIGURE 10.1   Building a Subscriber/Nonsubscriber File

(Adapted, by permission, from Todd. *Building a Subscriber/Nonsubscriber File*, new source new copy)

Observer began by hiring students to type in addresses from the telephone directory, having them walk the streets to verify addresses, and purchasing lists from direct mailers. Local utility companies charged an unacceptably high fee for access to their computer lists, as did the city clerk, whose property lists are precise and highly desirable. Advo, a major national competitor of newspapers for advertisers, refused to sell its Fayetteville list because of its direct mail operation there.

The following chapter includes a case study of the *Sacramento Bee* and its fully computerized circulation system, including a subscriber/nonsubscriber data base. However, such extensive computerization is neither necessary, economically feasible nor advantageous for all newspapers.

SELECTION CRITERIA FOR COMPUTERIZED CIRCULATION SYSTEMS

Like all computerized systems, computerized circulation systems are dependent upon good systems design, accurate base data, and the inputting of error-free data. Circulation managers who decide to computerize their operations have the option of designing their own, individualized system or purchasing a standardized circulation system.

A 1982 study indicated 11 major suppliers offer tested computerized circulation systems at prices ranging from $75,000 for a 5000 subscriber system to more than $1 million for a newspaper with circulation of 100,000 or more.[5] Some commercial systems can handle 250,000 to 1 million subscribers. Knight-Ridder jointly developed a system with Collier-Jackson for newspapers in the 100,000 to 200,000 range. Groups like Ottaway, Gannett, and McClatchey, owners of small and medium-sized dailies, hired computer firms to design circulation systems for their newspapers, which are now marketed to other newspapers. The Stauffer Group developed a circulation system for small dailies and now sells it to other papers. The majority of packages on the market are aimed at newspapers with under 100,000 circulation.

One of the major differences among packages is the computer systems on which they will run. Some are built for computers typically used by accounting departments, such as IBM and Burroughs; while others are designed for different brands and dedicated to circulation functions. The 1984 ICMA computer study indicated that more newspaper circulation systems (35 percent) operated on IBM computers than any other brand; the runnerup was Digital Equipment Corporation (DEC) with 27 percent.[6]

In designing a computerized circulation system—or choosing a packaged system—consideration should be given to the system's security, expandability, and backup procedures. Security is crucial for maintaining the accuracy and confidentiality of subscriber and employee records; the system must have safeguards to limit access and to prevent unauthorized tampering with circulation data, either maliciously or accidentally. Expandability applies both to a system's technological capabilities and to the newspaper's growth rate. A computerized circulation system should be able to accommodate normal anticipated growths in circulation and also be sophisticated enough so it is not obsolete within a few years. Backup procedures are essential, since computer systems are subject to electrical blackouts, equipment malfunctions, and accidental erasure of data files. Backup procedures may include emergency generator power, duplicate discs, and hard copies of computer data.

In deciding whether or not to computerize the circulation department, each newspaper must review its desired computer capability, its market, and its data needs. Initial cost is obviously a factor; only the largest newspapers have problems unique enough to justify the expense of an individually tailored circulation system. Newspapers contemplating computerization should undertake a thorough study to answer such questions as: What will computerization accomplish that we aren't already doing? What will be the cost? How will it affect the staff? Are there other ways of accomplishing our objectives? A newspaper with a good recordkeeping system, good market coverage, and low costs may not need extensive computerization.

ADVANTAGES OF COMPUTERIZATION

This section examines the major reasons for computerization of circulation departments—management control, preparation of reports, customer service, and sales and marketing capabilities—and how these uses help circulation departments meet the criteria of economy, control, dependability, and flexibility.

Management Control

Computerization makes data about all aspects of the circulation operation readily available to both district managers and department managers.

Most computerized circulation systems maintain lists of independent contractors and contract delivery agents with billing and draw history for both home delivery and single copy sales, route lists, sales per single copy outlet, and return records. The statistical basis of such data provides a more dependable means of making subjective decisions about changes in route sizes, increases in single copy outlets, or the need for further investigation of certain sites showing high return rates.

Basic home delivery and single copy records, coupled with computerized collection and payment data and customer complaint records, can help management assess contractor, carrier, and/or district manager performance. The computer can also track hours worked, part-time wages, and supervisory costs.

Over the long term, computerization assists the planning process as data are examined in a historical context to identify trends and patterns. For instance, in considering a price increase, newspaper management can track the effect a price increase had on circulation in the past—and the duration. Did the subscriber loss offset the revenue generated by the price increase?

Report Preparation

Computerization requires the design of special video forms that appear on the terminal screens, limiting the amount of operator input and, therefore, the possibility of error. As a visible data processing system, the video display terminal reduces entry error by 20 percent.[7] The computer also reduces error by rejecting inappropriate entries or asking for verification before filing the data.

Reducing human error increases computer-generated data dependability. The computer also speeds the processing of such data, which can result in cost savings because circulation departments must compile daily and weekly circulation reports to comply with Audit Bureau of Circulations requirements.

Customer Service

While carrier service quality remains the primary criterion of good customer service, the computer, with its storage capability and ability to link all circulation system components, can enhance customer service with rapid information processing. As a sophisticated bookkeeper, a computer can maintain a constantly updated circulation list that is both more detailed and more readily accessible to all employees than manual records are. At the push of a few buttons, a customer service representative can call up the entire circulation history of any customers; this means most service problems or changes can be handled with a single phone call. During the call, the newspaper employee can start or cancel a subscription, explain a bill, provide a carrier's or district manager's phone

FIGURE 10.2   Data entry clerks have taken over the task of keeping subscriber records current in computerized circulation systems. In an online system, this operator reviews a customer file while discussing the status over the telephone. Courtesy the *Orlando Sentinel*, Orlando, Fl.

number, or deal with complaints in the context of the customer's past billing and service history.

Pertinent information is then automatically transmitted to all necessary parties. Quick handling of customer needs and complaints enhances the customer's image of the newspaper as being dependable. Rapid information processing also allows follow-up within 24 to 48 hours, usually in the form of a phone call to the customer, to insure service has been properly adjusted.

The most visible use of the computer for customer service is through subscriber billing. Ninety percent of the newspapers with computerized circulation systems have provisions for computerized office payment; 60 percent of these interface their customer service and billing systems.[8] Computerized billing increases the collection system's flexibility by allowing subscribers to opt for payment by mail rather than carrier collection. Computers are also widely used to generate carrier bills, with usage ranging from 69 percent on newspapers with over 250,000 circulation to 98 percent on newspapers with 50,000 to 100,000 circulation.[9]

Sales and Marketing

While many widespread uses of the computer in circulation can also be accomplished manually, although in a more time-consuming and perhaps less dependable fashion, computerized data used for sales and marketing purposes are more difficult to duplicate manually.

Computerized circulation data enable a newspaper to target its sales efforts. Lists of ex-subscribers, generated from the subscriber data base, become contact lists for telephone sales and door-to-door crews. Comparisons of household penetrations in districts with identical demographics can pinpoint areas in need of intensive sales efforts. Since many national advertisers want to reach a high percentage of households with above-average annual incomes, a newspaper may use census data in combination with its subscriber data base to identify neighborhoods possibly having a high penetration of such households. Of course, all such efforts are aimed at increasing revenue.

Computerized circulation data also give a newspaper increased flexibility in its marketing efforts. The existence of a subscriber/nonsubscriber data base enables a newspaper to offer direct mail, total market coverage, and target market advertising options. Such options appeal to advertisers interested in high penetration or particular segments of the circulation area.

Another advantage to advertisers is the extensive market analysis developed by some newspapers based on computerized data. For instance, the advertising department of the *Minneapolis Tribune* provides individual advertisers with an extensive analysis based on the newspaper's research of shopping habits, shopper demographics, metropolitan demographics, and consumer behavior. Built into the presentation is an analysis, based on summaries of circulation data, of the *Tribune*'s research into targeted customer segments.

DISADVANTAGES OF COMPUTERIZATION

The primary disadvantages of computerization for newspaper circulation departments are similar to those encountered not only in other newspaper departments but also in other industries—cost and the need for organizational change.

Cost Factors

The immediate disadvantage of computerized circulation systems is high initial cost. While initial outlay can be reduced by purchasing a software package, such packages are not easily adaptable to a specific newspaper and often are insufficient to handle the data processing needs of newspapers with circulations of 100,000 or more.

Initial costs include not only software but also hardware (mainframe and terminals). Some newspapers reduce their hardware costs through shared usage arrangements for the mainframe computer.

A newspaper with under 10,000 circulation may be able to purchase a software package for $75,000 to handle its circulation data requirements. At the other end of the spectrum, large newspapers may require several years and millions of dollars to develop their own computerized circulation systems. The *Toronto Star* began its move toward computerization in the 1970s with a team of employees representing the circulation, advertising, accounting, data processing, and other business departments. By 1983, after a decade of false starts, problems, and millions of dollars expended, the *Star* had a fully computerized system tailored to its individualized needs and large subscriber base. The *Star*'s large subscriber base, the city's rapid growth, and high transiency created particularly acute programming and capacity problems.

In addition to the initial costs, other economic considerations include the costs of hiring data processing professionals and/or training existing staff and the costs of maintaining the system. Responses to a 1984 ICMA survey indicated that most newspapers with under 100,000 circulation had either no programmers assigned to their circulation departments or had a person working only part-time. However, 86 percent of the circulation departments at newspapers with more than 100,000 circulation had a systems coordinator and several programmers.[10] The technical expertise of data processing professionals often carries with it a high wage scale. In addition, whether or not a newspaper has a professional data processing staff, circulation employees and customer service representatives must be trained to input data and retrieve information stored in the computer.

One of the most expensive elements in a computerized circulation system is the development of the subscriber/nonsubscriber data base. The sheer volume of data makes its collection and input both expensive and time-consuming. Thousands of subscribers must be listed, many of them regularly changing subscription patterns as they go on vacation, stop daily delivery, add Sunday delivery, and so on. Verification is an expensive though crucial step because many newspapers rely on youth carriers for the raw data. If the youth carrier doesn't report every change correctly, the record is automatically incorrect. Even more difficult is the gathering and verification of nonsubscriber data.

Thus, while computerization may result in some cost savings by reducing staff time required for recordkeeping, billing, and report preparation, its high initial costs and ongoing maintenance and operating costs may offset any economic advantage. The decision to computerize is not fundamentally made to save money.

Organizational Change

Computerization of circulation department records and functions necessitates changes in the organizational structure and procedures of a newspaper. The effects of computerization on each circulation task must be reviewed. It is easy to underestimate the problems involved in revising manual records, transferring the data to the computer, and verifying both existing and new data.

For instance, in considering vacation start/stop orders, the following questions must be answered: From where does the order originate—the carrier, the subscriber, by phone? Who enters the order? Is it coded for billing, bundling, etc., at the same time? Who is affected by the order—mailroom, loading dock, contractor, carrier? How is each notified? All of these questions must be addressed in the systems design; but the answers also affect internal procedures, especially at newspapers using a combination of computerized and manual systems in their circulation departments.

While not all organizational change is troublesome, a negative side effect of computerization has been the reallocation of district managers' time. Some newspapers have doubled their district manager staff to feed the computer; others find district managers spending so much time on computer work that sales efforts suffer.

Organizational change necessitated by computerization also includes the revision of forms; the retraining or reassignment of staff; the development of new procedures for processing subscriber information, billing data and supervisory information; and the physical arrangement of office space to accommodate data processing equipment.

SUMMARY

The amount of computerization within a circulation department depends on the newspaper's marketing needs and staff and budget limitations. Computerization can increase a newspaper's knowledge about itself and its customers, improve efficiency and control, and facilitate the offering of such services as total market coverage and zoned advertising. At the same time, computerization requires huge financial outlays, the centralization of some circulation operations, and the hiring of new staff and/or retraining of existing staff. Traditional circulation tasks, such as carrier recruitment and development and sales, may be sidetracked. Thus, a newspaper must assess the cost effectiveness and advantages of each level of computerization prior to implementation.

Use of the computer in normal business office functions, such as billing, carrier invoices, recordkeeping, preparation of drivers' manifests, and development of press orders, is widespread within the newspaper industry. Such systems, when installed, are generally quite effective, dependable, and cost efficient.

More questions surround the development of a computerized subscriber and subscriber/nonsubscriber data base. While there is substantial movement in this direction, there have been few complete success stories. Certainly the development and implementation of this subsystem requires more staff and substantial expense. The benefits are better customer tracking, a better sales base, and the ability to deliver a total market coverage product to nonsubscribers.

NOTES

1. John Neighbors, "How to Select the Best Circulation System," *Editor and Publisher* 115:26 (June 26, 1982): 13.
2. "Computer Survey Results Published," *ICMA Update* 80, 9 (April 1984): 1.
3. *Building a Subscriber/Nonsubscriber File* (New York: Newspaper Advertising Bureau, Inc., undated), p. 1.
4. Ibid., 7.
5. Neighbors, "How to Select Best System," 13.
6. "Computer Survey Results Published," 16.
7. Benjamin Compaine, *The Newspaper Industry in the 1980s* (New York: Knowledge Industry Publications, Inc., 1980).
8. "Computer Survey Results Published," 16.
9. Ibid.
10. Ibid.

CHAPTER
── *11* ──

Case Studies of
Circulation Departments

The structure of every circulation department evolves in response to such traditional factors as ownership and corporate organization, marketing and revenue concerns, and such practical considerations as the delivery system type, circulation size, and customer demands.

While previous chapters have referred to circulation practices at specific newspapers, this chapter deals in greater depth with the organizational structure of circulation departments at 11 newspapers and how such structures evolved in response to corporate, marketing, and technical factors. Organizational charts for the circulation department at each newspaper are also included.

CONTRA COSTA TIMES

The *Contra Costa Times*, in San Francisco's East Bay area, began as a voluntary pay shopper with total market delivery published from a centralized plant that produced similar products for other communities in the area. When the *Oakland Tribune* eliminated home delivery in the area, the *Times'* publisher wanted a circulation system that required little managerial staff, low overhead, a large sales and service field force, and continued 100 percent morning circulation by youth carriers. The result was a "den-mother" district manager system employing homemakers to work part-time from their homes and easily adapting to the high turnover rate among carriers and district managers.

The district managers, paid for 20 hours work each week, work in groups of four headed by a lead district manager, who recruits and trains

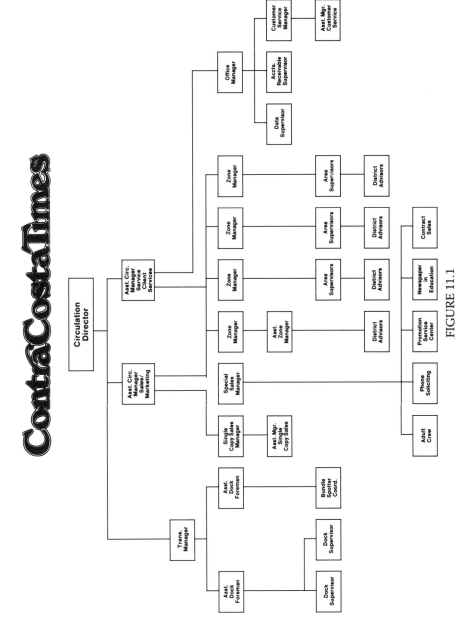

FIGURE 11.1

other district managers. She is paid for 30 hours' work each week. A full-time employee supervisor oversees 32 district managers (eight groups of four), thereby greatly reducing the need for office space and commuting while simultaneously keeping the effort closely tied to the neighborhoods. District manager turnover is rapid; the average term is 18 months. The working groups of four slow turnover by developing personal bonds and ease recruitment and training of replacements by providing group support, close local supervision, and a large recruiting staff.

As part of its corporate culture, the *Times* insists on precise delivery. The paper must be delivered with the paper folded in quarters and the upper right-hand quarter of the front page facing whoever opens the door to pick it up. District managers, who recruit and train carriers, are expected to spot-check delivery each morning by 6:30 a.m., covering each route at least once every two weeks. Twice each morning they call in for misdelivery complaints, which they redeliver. As required by carrier turnover, district managers recruit in the afternoon or evening and meet with carriers and their parents. Once each month the district managers meet with their carriers to adjust collections and bills. Separation from the office requires substantial paperwork and heavy reliance on printed material to maintain consistency across the system.

The *Times* has found the den-mother system particularly effective for its dominantly suburban circulation system. Enthusiasm runs high among the district managers, almost all of whom are college graduates reentering the labor market because their children have entered school. They develop close ties to carriers, know their districts intimately, bring a great deal of creative energy to problems, and closely monitor carriers. Their supervisors are enthusiastic about the system, emphasizing the strong local presence of home-based district managers, their ability to recruit carriers, and their attention to service.

The den-mother system suited the *Times* when it was a voluntary pay newspaper in the 1970s and early 1980s, but whether it provides the sales support required of a pay newspaper through the 1980s, while maintaining supervision, carrier recruitment, and collection, remains to be seen.

DALLAS TIMES-HERALD

The *Dallas Times-Herald*, an all-day newspaper owned by the Times-Mirror Company, has morning and evening home delivery. It broke away from traditional circulation department structure when it converted from afternoon publication in 1980, as the organizational chart shows (Figure 10.2).

Locked in competition with the *Dallas Morning News* in one of the fastest growing markets in the country, the *Times-Herald* chose conversion over continued circulation decline in the afternoon. As a complex market with strong white-collar and blue-collar components, Dallas has been attracting headquarters of national corporations because of its geography and climate.

The circulation department's reorganization was rooted in a belief that metropolitan market dynamics require specialization in delivery, sales, service, and collections rather than the traditional, multiple-task approach. Multiple-task circulation workers, the *Times-Herald* believes, concentrate on their strength to the detriment of the other areas; and the number of exceptions to the basic system eventually overloads circulation managers. The *Times-Herald* has no circulation department divided by delivery zones; instead, the marketing vice-president oversees two advertising units, consumer marketing and consumer services, that include all circulation functions. The restructuring seeks to organize people around clearly defined tasks: to sell newspapers, to maintain present customers and obtain new ones, and to provide delivery and collection service. The mailroom and transportation tasks are the responsibility of another department.

Working within the consumer services division, carriers deliver and collect within a structure resembling the traditional divisions: home delivery, state, and apartment groups under the supervision of the consumer services manager. Adult contractors deliver the morning edition; youth carriers, working under independent contractors, deliver the afternoon edition. Separate managers supervise the two delivery cycles and the collections. The afternoon home delivery manager maintains a training office near the *Times-Herald* office, where new district managers learn the work routines and corporate culture under the supervision of a seasoned district manager and company trainer.

All sales and customer service tasks fall to the consumer services division, which includes Newspaper in Education, a newcomer program, and a training program, in addition to telephone sales, youth crews, and all single copy sales. There are no overlapping responsibilities from unit to unit or across the circulation department. The consumer services people sell subscriptions and develop promotional campaigns for both newspapers, working with the overall marketing plan developed within their department. While far from the only newspaper to emphasize marketing, the *Dallas Times-Herald* is one of a very few to divide the traditional circulation tasks according to a marketing framework.

An all-out sales effort will be required to stay abreast of the Dallas market and compete with the privately owned *Morning News*, whose

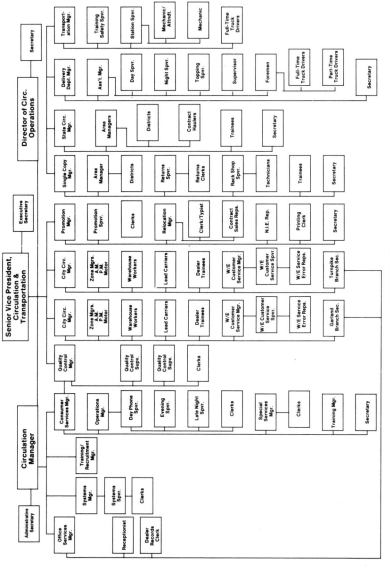

FIGURE 11.2

traditional circulation department has long experience as a morning newspaper. The *Morning News* emphasizes district manager training with a lengthy course combining classroom work and field study, and it relishes the competitive nature and potential for growth. In some ways the competition is between a seasoned and highly successful traditional circulation department and an innovative, marketing-oriented newspaper that has radically redefined circulation.

GOLDSBORO NEWS-ARGUS

One of seven newspapers in the Bucheit Group, the *New-Argus* is partially owned by its publisher, Hal Tanner, and firmly rooted in this rural North Carolina county seat. Daily circulation averages 21,000, Sunday circulation 24,000; and both are growing.

The *News-Argus* exudes stability because the publisher is a major owner and because the basically agricultural market changes little apart from fluctuations in the local air force base or one of the few local industries. The military base is a major circulation problem because the personnel, while transient, are counted among the residents of the NDMA. In addition, the high transient rate of this training facility creates special delivery, sales, and collection problems; and no single copy box can be placed on the military base without special permission. Despite this overall stability, the *News-Argus* faces the same competition for readers' time and advertisers' attention as its big-city counterparts. Consequently, the newspaper has developed a special sales staff, a total market coverage product, and a computerized circulation information system.

Like all newspapers its size, the *News-Argus* operates with minimal administrative staff (Figure 11.3). The circulation manager doubles as business manager, and the assistant circulation manager runs the mailroom whenever the regular supervisor is on vacation or ill. City circulation operates with one district manager, who supervises carriers and spots bundles. A second driver also spots bundles. The state zone is supervised by the assistant circulation manager, who negotiates contracts with the independent motor route drivers. Computerization has streamlined all of the record keeping for the *News-Argus*. Prior to computerization, carriers received handwritten bills each month. Stability runs through the carrier force, some of whom have delivered the *News-Argus* for more than 25 years. To ensure longevity, particularly among motor route contractors, the *News-Argus* offers a substantial income for good service.

N Goldsboro News-Argus

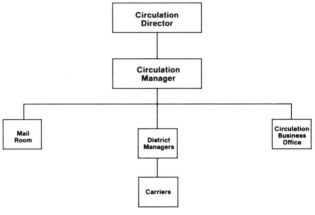

FIGURE 11.3

Faced with flat sales response to the usual carrier contests, the circulation manager experimented with an external telephone salesperson who had recently retired from real estate sales. Working on a commission basis, the salesperson produced a surprisingly large number of new subscriptions. The *News-Argus* converted the experiment to a formal contract, adding the telephone numbers of previous subscribers to the random-number dialing system.

Linked by freeway to distant corners of the county, Goldsboro is a regional shopping center that hosts national discount department stores and chain outlets that use sales materials, particularly preprints, in conjunction with the regional and national campaigns of their chains. To serve these advertisers with 100 percent distribution, the *News-Argus* has a TMC product that it developed in the 1970s to counter the competition from a series of short-lived shoppers. The *News-Argus* TMC goes by postal delivery to all nonsubscribers in the PMA, whether rural or city.

The limitations of hand accounting led to a computerized circulation system, which the *News-Argus* purchased from the Stouffer Group. As a small newspaper in a small group, the *News-Argus* could not afford to develop its own computer system or employ a computer specialist; so the Stouffer package included a service contract and 24-hour access to a specialist by telephone or in person. However, computerization forced a revision of circulation staff tasks and consideration of the addition of a staff member whose responsibilities would include the computer.

Despite its size and rural market, the *Goldsboro News-Argus* faces the same readership problems as other newspapers; and it has worked hard to increase circulation. Its advantages include intimate personal understanding of the market and willingness to adapt. Like every other newspaper, this county seat daily must adjust to its customers and meet its competition in order to survive.

GREEN BAY PRESS-GAZETTE

A member of the Gannett Newspapers, the *Press-Gazette* is responsible for local *USA Today* circulation as well as its own net paid average 62,000 Monday through Friday afternoons. Saturday and Sunday (net paid 72,000) circulation does not include *USA Today*. Youth carriers deliver both newspapers in the primary market area, and the single copy operation integrates both newspapers in the NDMA and state zones. The regional circulation territory, including a heavy tourist resort area and a portion of Michigan, mandates distinctly different circulation systems in the NDMA and state. Competitors include daily and Sunday newspapers from Detroit, Madison, and Milwaukee.

The circulation manager has three subordinate managers, one responsible for the state and single copy circulation, one for home delivery in the city zone, and one responsible for integrating *USA Today* in the established system. In the Gannett system, the circulation manager works under the publisher, who makes decisions in consultation with his superior in Gannett, but also under the supervision of a regional Gannett circulation executive, who evaluates the circulation department regularly.

The 110 youth carriers who deliver the newspaper in the city zone purchased their routes from previous carriers, subject to approval by the district manager and circulation manager. The newspaper endorses this system in which the price is based on the number of subscribers and averages $300 per route because it produces high reliability and unusually low service and collection problems; but the negotiations are strictly between the carriers. Carrier sales are a problem in this system because youths typically hold their routes for two years or more and require highly creative motivation; many are content with their 50+ customers, working only to replace cancellations.

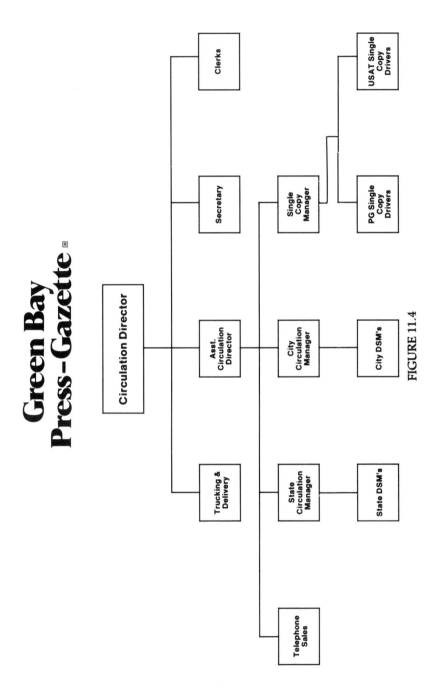

**Green Bay
Press-Gazette**

FIGURE 11.4

The youth carriers delivering newspapers in the state zone work under local employee managers or contract agents in the community. With a large tourist industry in the region, the *Press-Gazette* uses agencies in smaller towns and resorts. These agents develop their own carrier system. From the opening day of fishing season (mid-May) to the last day of deer hunting season (late November), the state circulation expansion includes paying agents for unsold daily and Sunday newspapers to encourage full use of single copy outlets. Out of season, when daily single copy sales are predictable, agents are paid only for unsold Sunday papers to reduce waste.

The *Press-Gazette* has a daily household penetration of over 70 percent, but it is declining. A series of price increases from 1979 to 1983 sent subscriptions from $1.35 per week to $2.25 per week following Gannett's purchase. A successful shopper in a nearby community is reducing sales in that county. Carrier sales form the basic marketing technique, but to reach nonsubscribers the newspaper uses radio sales spots and outdoor advertising with special appeals keyed to circulation sales campaigns. A Cincinnati telephone sales solicitation firm provides contract solicitation.

The *Press-Gazette* is an afternoon newspaper because the local industrial base includes paper manufacturing plants where workers begin at 6:30 a.m. To serve these readers, a morning newspaper would have to be on the porches before 5 a.m., an impossible delivery situation for youth carriers, particularly in the winter. The local businesspeople, university employees, and professionals who start work later do not comprise a sufficiently large readership for morning and afternoon publication. The *USA Today* cycle, which is early morning in large cities, cannot be so in Green Bay because the newspapers arrive from the Chicago printing plant in midmorning.

USA Today circulation is integrated in both home delivery and single copy sales. Carriers add *USA Today* subscribers to their routes and sell subscriptions to both newspapers, although all *USA Today* subscriptions are paid in advance to simplify accounting. For single copy sales, a *USA Today* box is placed next to each *Press-Gazette* box; and each single copy outlet receives both newspapers. The *USA Today* manager works with the city and state managers to fully integrate *USA Today* circulation with that of the *Press-Gazette*.

Press-Gazette circulation managers say circulation did not drop with the introduction of *USA Today*. Instead, *USA Today* appears to have found a unique audience among nonsubscribers and to have become a second newspaper for *Press-Gazette* customers. Controlling circulation for two afternoon newspapers required minimal adjustment to the circulation system, partly because promotion of *USA Today* was a portion of a national campaign.

HOUSTON CHRONICLE

Privately owned, the independent *Chronicle* finds itself in a booming, bustling economic market complicated by chaotic urban sprawl and total lack of zoning laws. Jammed, inadequate freeways complicate distribution with rush hours beginning at 5:30 a.m. and 3 p.m. and lasting nearly four hours. Houston's rapid development as a major oil capital attracts white- and blue-collar workers and high-rise construction at a pace almost unmatched elsewhere. The *Chronicle* competed so fiercely with the morning *Houston Post* (also privately owned and independent) in the 1960s that a full-time ABC auditor was assigned permanently to Houston simply to monitor sales. Each newspaper finally agreed to end cut-rate offers and promotional prizes and compete on other terms.

The fierce self-determination of Texans, who resist unionization, allows the independent contractor system to flourish. To serve the market and avoid the rush hours, the *Chronicle* converted from afternoon to all-day publication with home delivery in the morning or afternoon in the metropolitan zone, which covers five counties. In the state zone, the newspaper offers only morning delivery. Traffic congestion and explosive suburban development made distribution so difficult that the *Chronicle* built four large distribution centers around the metropolitan area; here independent contractors receive their newspapers, which arrive from the main plant on 18-wheel semitrailer trucks. Circulation responsibility begins in the distribution centers.

The independent contractors purchase their newspapers at the wholesale rate for resale in their assigned geographical territory. They employ youth carriers to deliver the afternoon editions, as a rule, although they are free to use whatever system meets *Chronicle* standards. Adult motor routes dominate morning delivery. The exception to independent contractors is the metropolitan single copy system. Following a protracted lawsuit with the American Independent Newspaper Distributors Association (AINDA) in the late 1960s, the *Chronicle* brought in contract delivery agents, whose employee supervisors locate the boxes, determine the draw, and collect the money. The single copy system also has a little merchant system for newsboys and girls, who hawk about 7000 copies of the afternoon and Sunday bulldog editions along jammed freeway onramps and downtown city streets. To encourage new subscriptions and independent contractor longevity, the *Chronicle* reduces the wholesale rate for those who have built circulation in their territory or whose territory has been subdivided due to massive growth. Also built into the annually negotiated wholesale rate are confidential factors to offset contractor vehicle cost, compensate for route distance, and subsidize low penetration areas.

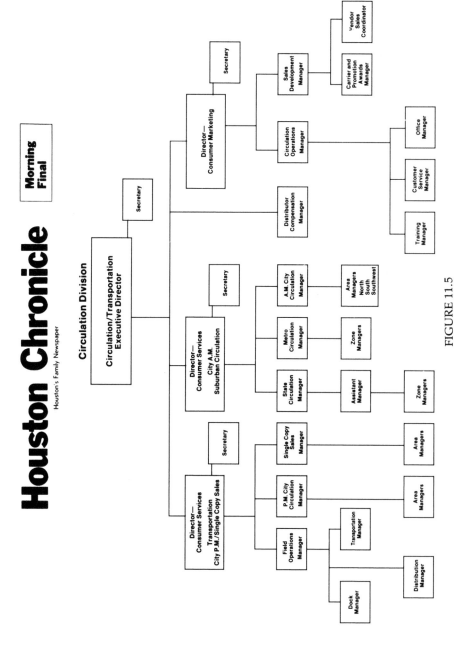

FIGURE 11.5

Independent contractors using youth carriers differ from employee district managers only in their autonomy and income, which will rise and fall with their success. A competent independent contractor can earn $40,000 per year and more by mastering the art of recruiting and motivating carriers. Contractors, not the newspaper, handle the front-line circulation tasks; the newspaper receives a predictable wholesale rate income. Contractors must work out of their homes or a rented office; the newspaper provides nothing. In the metropolitan area, only 332 employees supervise a circulation of 377,000, because each independent contractor handles an average of 1200 newspapers. In the state zone 40 contractors handle 16,000 circulation.

Youth carriers have proven inadequate to the physical requirements of high-rise delivery, particularly with the Sunday *Chronicle*, which weighs about six pounds, so many contractors have shifted to adult carriers or subdivided their territory and assigned high-rise delivery to adults. The size of the Sunday paper complicates single copy sales because only 35 of them will fit in a vending box, and the boxes must be refilled hourly, even when two boxes are used in prime locations.

In a booming market of highly transient professionals and laborers, the *Chronicle* mounts its own promotional efforts. A separate managerial division supervises a special multiple-unit circulation effort designed to accommodate the unusual problems of a market where 30 percent of apartment dwellers move each month. Like other newspapers, the *Chronicle* seeks a computerized circulation system capable of identifying nonsubscribers by address and telephone number for direct mail and telephone solicitation. However, in an independent contractor system, the route lists are the contractor's property and the newspaper would have to purchase them.

Independent contractors are not the rule for Houston; the morning *Post* converted from independent contractors to adult employee carriers in 1976 in order to gain full control of circulation, embracing the high labor costs involved. To compete for workers willing to deliver 200 newspapers each morning in a market with a 4 percent unemployment rate, the *Post* pays $6.50 per hour for delivery alone; collection and sales are handled by other *Post* employees. Even at that wage, adult carriers turn over steadily. A large proportion of them are college students; many are marginally employable immigrants. Although market conditions favor an independent contractor system, corporate goals can mandate another one.

LA CROSSE TRIBUNE

Sitting astride the Mississippi River where Minnesota and Iowa meet Wisconsin, this newspaper's territory includes a regional, multistate readership with a net paid average 35,000 circulation. Home delivery is available in nearby Iowa and Minnesota communities. The *Tribune*, part of the 19-member Lee Newspapers group, has limited competition in its circulation zone, but the organizational structure (Figure 11.6) reflects heavy circulation responsibility for zoned editions, preprints, and the mailroom. Nonunion since 1980, the *Tribune* relies on a youth carrier system with adult motor route drivers in the rural area. Reflecting the sales emphasis at the *Tribune*, the six district managers report to a sales manager. Geography sets the managers' district boundaries: three in the city (north, central, south) and three beyond the city limits.

The three-state market creates special content and delivery problems because several communities have distinctly different political interests that are integral to community identity. Several special products have been developed to serve these areas, including a weekly TMC product mailed to nonsubscribers in the primary market area and a special zoned supplement for Iowa subscribers. In 1983 the *Tribune* added a weekly supplement for a nearby Wisconsin community when it revived a defunct weekly as an insert.

Despite this growth, household penetration has slipped gradually to 70 percent, while population has increased. New construction has brought multiple-unit dwellings to serve the young singles, empty nest elderly, and mobile professionals. With an expanding economy and a mix of blue- and white-collar employees, the market may demand further adaptations, including a revision of the *Tribune* itself.

Sales efforts fall to district managers and carriers in big spring and fall campaigns and in a few small summer and winter campaigns. Youth crews of top carrier salespeople canvass between carrier campaigns. Random number telephone solicitation continues throughout the year; but the high household penetration in La Crosse makes calling from lists of exsubscribers and nonsubscribers, which the computer system can generate, a more effective system.

Lee Newspapers developed the computer information system used by the *Tribune*, and it offers sales promotions in which member newspapers can compete for expensive prizes. Another group benefit is a design expert who helped remodel a limited mailroom into a facility capable of handling the multiple zoned supplements and advertising preprints. Increased use of supplements created special scheduling problems for the mailroom and loading dock and the need for additional space to warehouse supplements and preprints.

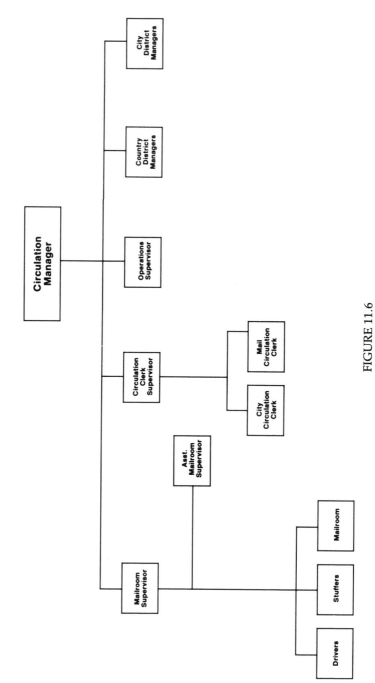

FIGURE 11.6

MILWAUKEE JOURNAL AND MILWAUKEE SENTINEL

Employee owned, the Journal Company's success with the morning *Sentinel* and evening and Sunday *Journal* rides on the bicycle tires and sneakers of 9600 little merchants between 12 and 18 years old. With over a century of experience with youth carriers, the Journal Company successfully recruits, guides, and motivates an impressive carrier force. The traditional, family-oriented market provides a large pool of children raised in the work ethic of their Polish, German, Irish, and Italian ancestors. In many ways unchanged from the 1950s, the circulation system has evolved slowly by retaining what works and modifying what doesn't. *Journal* executives prefer proven systems to fashionable but untested change, reflecting the conservative atmosphere of a market based in craftsmanship. Employee ownership contributes to a corporate culture emphasizing careful stewardship of resources and inhibiting hasty changes.

The far-flung circulation system of this regional newspaper includes most of the major cities in the state and Michigan's Upper Peninsula. While youth carriers dominate the entire circulation system, adult carriers cover motor routes. To meet rising energy prices and retain regional distribution, a special predated issue of the afternoon *Journal* goes to press just before the outstate edition of the *Sentinel*. Both are trucked to the state zone in a single run, halving the transportation costs. Outstate carriers deliver both newspapers.

The circulation department includes the fleet and garage operations, with its responsibility beginning on the loading dock. As the organizational chart shows (Figure 11.7), the youth carrier system for two separate newspapers requires a large employee force headed by the vice-president/circulation director, the circulation manager, and the circulation marketing manager. Together with seven area supervisors, they make up the executive staff. Division of the city zone by newspaper and the state zones by geography grew from the heavy sales of both papers in the city, the unique suburban problems in the metropolitan zone, and the different character of circulation beyond the retail trading zone. The 200 part-time circulation drivers, by company policy, must be full-time students, a boon to two generations of college students and an effective method for gaining flexibility and operational cost effectiveness in a highly unionized industrial city.

In the city, the *Journal* and *Sentinel* use different distribution systems. The *Journal* uses a substation system in which carriers are given their newspapers in special buildings scattered strategically around the city. Under the supervision of a part-time station captain, youth carriers count

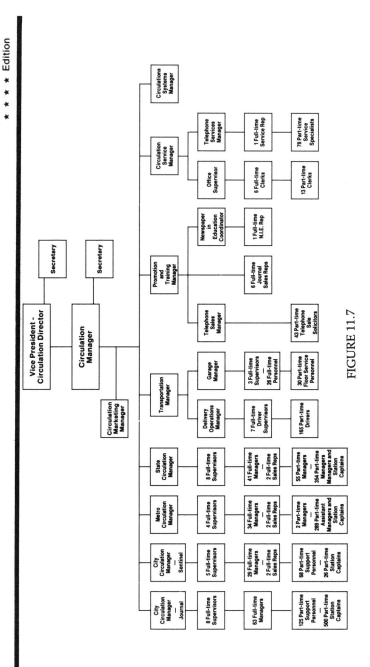

THE MILWAUKEE JOURNAL
MILWAUKEE SENTINEL
★ ★ ★ ★ Edition

FIGURE 11.7

out their newspapers and insert sections. The *Sentinel*, to speed morning delivery, is delivered to the carrier's home. *Sentinel* carriers do no inserting. In some suburban areas, *Journal* carriers receive their newspapers at home as well. In addition to hauling newspapers from the plant to substations and carriers' homes, *Journal* and *Sentinel* district managers supply dealers and single copy outlets. While the *Sentinel* has more than 1200 boxes around the city, the *Journal* has fewer than 150. Thus, the *Journal* has few vending box drivers, and the *Sentinel* has a single copy supervisor and large driver force.

Outside the city zone, district managers supervise circulation of both newspapers with an increased emphasis on sales. Because they do not haul newspapers to carriers or substations, state district managers are expected to dress in suits and ties and to devote more time and energy to sales. Once outside the city, the newspapers become competition for a local newspaper and therefore require greater sales efforts.

Managing a large little merchant force requires 169 full-time and 92 part-time district managers plus 485 station captains. The need for so large a force lies in recruitment and training more than in day-to-day supervision of delivery. Mounting the biannual sales campaigns also requires a large employee force because, while youth carriers provide a cost-efficient delivery and collection system, they offer an even more effective sales force. The *Journal* is committed to youth sales because 9600 young carriers can knock on hundreds of thousands of doors in each campaign, and they have a sales appeal of their own.

To bolster sagging daily *Journal* sales, the circulation department added five sales representatives who plan and direct short-term sales efforts in the metropolitan area. A part-time employee telephone sales force works throughout the year to supplement the door-to-door efforts. Experiments in sales techniques using television, direct mail, and other methods are conducted by sales specialists and the research unit.

To meet the demands of the market, the Journal Company is moving toward a computerized circulation system. The first step was development of a TMC product mailed to all nonsubscribers. Careful planning and cautious development continue to adapt the capabilities of the classic little merchant system.

ORLANDO SENTINEL

The *Sentinel*, a member of the eight-member *Chicago Tribune* group, delivers an all-day newspaper with one of the most successful contract delivery agent systems in the country. Its success rests on two factors: First, it was designed following thorough study of contract and wholesale

The Orlando Sentinel

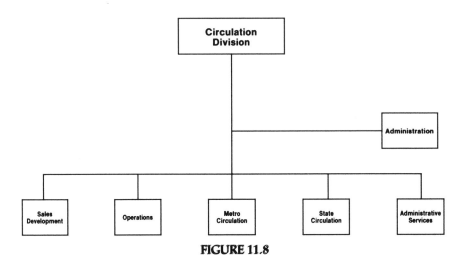

FIGURE 11.8

problems in Kansas City, Houston, and Chicago; and, second, it is willing to allow contractors to earn large incomes in return for high-quality service. Indeed, with a circulation just under 200,000, the *Sentinel* had only one open route in 1981; and that remained open for a single day. Its state-of-the-art computer information system supports an alternate delivery system, in addition to keeping track of all households and subscribers in the primary market area.

In the *Sentinel* system, the agents contract with the newspaper to provide specific services: delivery, insertion, and collection. In return, they have earned as much as $200,000 a year in delivery, insert, and collection fees. The newspaper retains full legal control over the customers, the price, and the routes, requiring all subscription changes to go through the central office computer. Failure to perform satisfactorily gives the newspaper the right to terminate the contract immediately. To build carrier commitment to contract compliance, the *Sentinel* allows agents to sell their routes, subject to approval by the newspaper. An average route of 600 customers costs about $18,000 to $20,000 and yields about $35,000 yearly income. A carrier terminated for nonperformance automatically loses the right to sell the route because it reverts to the company. In other words, the circulation system works efficiently because each carrier has thousands of dollars riding on it. The newspaper can also terminate the contract without cause upon 30 days notice, an approach used for chronic problems short of nonperformance and one which enables the agent to sell the route.

In return for high income, agents agree to deliver the newspaper each day to every customer on the company route list within the prescribed times and with an error rate below the prescribed minimum. They also agree to process the names and addresses of all starts and stops through the computer, to sell subscriptions, to collect in advance from all subscribers, and to pay their bills on time. The newspaper will not extend credit or carry unpaid balances. The newspaper can mandate sampling and door-to-door canvassing on any route at any time.

Agents are billed weekly at the retail price minus a 10 percent collection fee; subscribers pay either four, eight, or twelve weeks in advance. Advance payment substantially reduces bad debt, but the carrier absorbs all bad debt up to 10 percent of the bill; the company absorbs any loss over 10 percent, but only after a full audit of the route. Retail rate billing provides the *Sentinel* with a large cashflow and minimal loss.

As the organizational chart (Figure 11.8) demonstrates, a contract delivery system requires few supervisory employees. The 20 substation supervisors monitor newspaper allocation in the PMA, where eight zone managers control 134,000 net paid daily circulation. The separation of single copy from home delivery in the PMA allows greater specialization and simplifies the structure of motor routes. Single copy routes operate on the same contractual basis as home delivery; because of their large circulations, they are the most lucrative. And, because collections and sales are simple, they are the highest priced. State circulation operates on the agency system, with all the agents supervised by one manager and two assistants.

The character of Orange County, Florida, the primary market area, requires special sales attention because it has a strong tourist industry, is growing rapidly, and has high transiency. The sales development staff includes an artist, three special sales representatives, the Newspaper in Education coordinator, and an internal telephone sales room with 12 part-time solicitors. While carriers are obliged to sell subscriptions, sample, and canvass door to door, the *Sentinel* more greatly emphasizes sales through this special division because of the diversity of its home market. The *Sentinel* also wants carriers devoting less time to sales than to efficient delivery and collection. Nonetheless, it mounts regular carrier sales campaigns in which about two-thirds of the carriers participate beyond their requirements.

The computer system and customer service areas include 26 full-time and 14 part-time employees, befitting the circulation department's reliance on its circulation information system. The computer has every household in the NDMA listed by carrier route and postal carrier route in preparation for a direct mail effort. The operations group comprises 39 full-time and five part-time employees. The company's size allows special training and development programs to be offered to all employees. As one of the *Tribune* newspapers, it is a farm club for the flagship; for instance, the circulation manager who designed the contract delivery system in Orlando was subsequently transferred to a higher position in Chicago.

SACRAMENTO BEE

The flagship of the privately owned McClatchey Group, the *Sacramento Bee* boasts successful conversion from afternoon to morning publication, a sophisticated computerized circulation information system, a TMC product, and a new generation of district managers. Based in the capital of the state, the *Bee* serves customers in a circulation territory extending east to Nevada and north to Oregon. Its circulation department reflects the dynamics of its California market and the corporate commitment to developing employees in a sales and marketing mentality.

When a strike led to union decertification, the *Bee* revised every phase of its circulation system from the mailroom to carrier supervision, restructuring work loads and responsibilities without the complications of union negotiations. The circulation department includes the mailroom, transportation, and marketing manager in addition to the multiple divisions of a traditional circulation unit. As a youth carrier system with heavy regional single copy sales, the *Bee* employs a large number of district managers. The city single copy operation employs adults; state circulation has youth carriers working for agents and employee supervisors in larger communities.

After circulation losses struck the evening McClatchey newspapers, the corporation decided to experiment with conversion to morning publication beginning with the smallest, the *Modesto Bee* (net paid 60,000). Successful conversion of the *Fresno Bee* led to conversion of the Sacramento paper as well. After market studies and extensive planning, the conversion went smoothly. Within a year, the *Sacramento Bee* gained more circulation than it had lost in the state zone over the preceding decade. Along with the conversion, the role of the district manager was changed.

For the new generation district manager, sales obligations became foremost, but without sacrificing concern for delivery, service, and collections. A part-time force of drivers was hired to drop bundles at carriers' homes. District managers are assigned to one of three office-style sub-

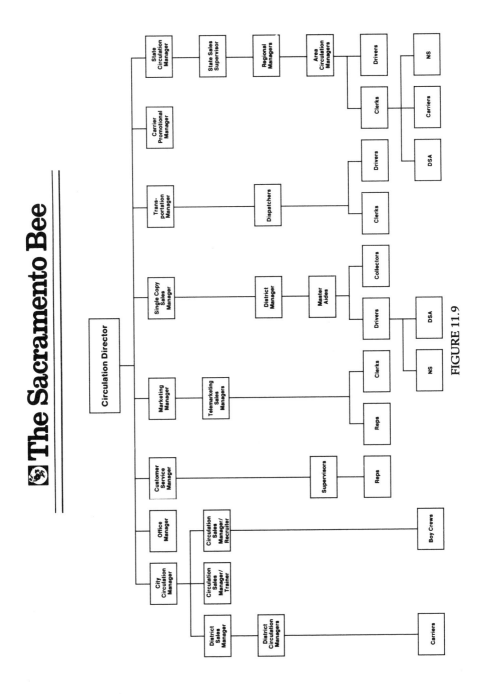

FIGURE 11.9

stations where they have their own work carrels and operate as teams of nine under the supervision of a sales manager and senior manager. The offices include a receptionist/secretary and a relief district manager. Situated close to the center of their territories, the substations operate independently of the main circulation office for maximum local control and supervision.

The *Bee* provides extensive training in time and resource management for its district managers to prevent burnout. Each district manager has a small budget for part-time carriers who deliver open routes; district managers are strongly discouraged from being so poorly organized that they deliver newspapers themselves. Carrier recruitment through a pool of prospective candidates is encouraged.

In the *Bee*'s management by objectives (MBO) system, district managers and sales managers negotiate quarterly goals in sales, service, and collections. If approved by the circulation manager, the goals become the determining factor in allocating quarterly performance bonuses. Sales managers similarly negotiate their MBO goals with supervisors, who, in turn, negotiate goals with the circulation manager. In the heat of a California market, constant sales activities are a necessity.

Because it produces three different zoned editions, the *Bee* equipped its mailroom with inserting machines linked by computer to bundle counters and the presses. Together they produce precounted bundles labeled for each route, and they selectively insert preprints for each route or district. To eliminate dock injuries, the *Bee* eliminated the loading dock, replacing it with hydraulically controlled roller tracks that extend into the trucks.

The *Bee* has a complete computerized information system. All complaint and subscription calls come through the telephone room, where 14 stations have computer terminals. Complaints, stops, starts, and requests for special service are entered directly into the system. The computer tracks the number of callers, the average time for each call, and the average wait for service. The supervisor can obtain transaction summaries for each operator, and daily transaction summaries are printed for each district manager and zone manager as a record of operation. A telephone transactions list organized by carrier route includes the time of the call, address, customer name, telephone number, operator's number, and special comments. When not handling telephone calls, the operators switch to batch processing routines, such as updating office payment files, or on-line file maintenance using carrier corrections.

While the *Bee* has every address in its primary market area on the computer, it uses a commercial mailing service to generate nonsubscriber labels for its TMC product because routine file maintenance of the subscriber-nonsubscriber data is too costly. The *Bee* sends its subscriber tape to the mailer, where it is run against a daily maintained address file. The mailer then provides nonsubscriber labels for the newspaper.

The computerized system provides up-to-date information for both carriers and district managers. Carriers receive computer-generated notices of stops, starts, complaints, and payment changes, as well as complete route lists, organized by address and delivery sequence, whenever needed. The carrier must periodically verify the route list, submitting a correction sheet used for file maintenance.

The computer also prints monthly subscriber bills on perforated cards. The carrier gives the card to the customer, who keeps one part as a receipt and also notes any address or spelling inaccuracies. The carrier provides all stubs to the district manager.

The district manager not only submits all carrier corrections but also is responsible for providing new street names and obtaining new lot addresses. The computer generates summary reports on each circulation district, as well as reports on individual carriers.

The computer system also monitors single copy sales by route and box, keeping records of theft and delivery variations. The system has a transportation data base that handles truck routes, drop points, bundle labels, and related tasks for the NDMA and state zones. Overall, the computer provides maximum control over the newspaper flow, precise single copy sales records, subscriber and carrier records, and staff performance evaluations.

ST. PETERSBURG TIMES AND EVENING INDEPENDENT

The corporate culture of these two newspapers emphasizes high-quality performance, and the circulation department translates that into employee carriers who are well paid and consistently able to meet company standards. The high cost of an employee circulation force reflects the commitment to standards and the financial advantages of a newspaper owned by a not-for-profit institution. The culture also encourages interdepartmental communication and cooperative efforts, so the circulation manager chairs a committee on the ethics of news content in the paper, and an editor chairs the market development committee. Ownership by the Modern Media Institute provides impetus for experimentation with modern management practices.

Taking advantage of local demographics, the *St. Petersburg Times* and *Evening Independent* developed an adult carrier force responsible for sales, delivery, service, and collections. College students, homemakers, and retirees form the carrier corps, but only after successfully passing courses in carrier school, where they study the newspaper and learn the

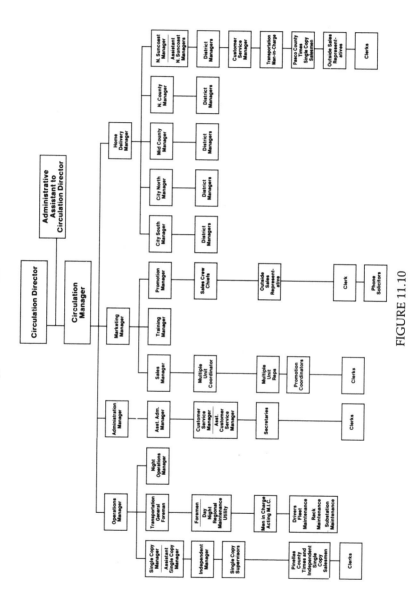

FIGURE 11.10

standards set for their performance. Those who don't believe they can meet the standards are encouraged to drop out. Each class session is followed by a written examination. The result is a stable carrier force well versed in the corporate culture. In return, the carriers enjoy nine benefits (life insurance, pension, unemployment compensation, workmen's compensation, hospitalization, Christmas dividends, profit sharing, and others). They are paid on the little merchant basis; they are charged a wholesale rate and collect the retail rate. The wholesale rate declines with each year of service to yield an annual raise of at least $10 per week.

The St. Petersburg newspapers face one of the strongest competitive markets in the nation because their city zone abuts the city zones of Tampa, Bradenton, and Clearwater dailies. Reliable circulation employees are but one strategic response to the competition. The part-time employees participate in sales efforts, which are supplemented by door crews and a special multiple-unit sales force. The circulation manager opposes telephone sales because he believes they unduly irritate subscribers and nonsubscribers.

The home delivery division is responsible for the entire circulation territory; there is no separation between city and state zones. Similarly, the single copy sales unit embraces both the metro area and the counties north of St. Petersburg. This system reflects the strong home delivery circulation in the entire area and functional focus on either delivery or single copy sales. The St. Petersburg growth area is north along the coast, so a satellite printing plant north of the city produces special sections, delivered to carriers who insert them, for those counties.

Newspapers are distributed in the metro zone through a substation system, which employs specially designed buildings suited to inserting newspapers in the Florida climate. The substations also contain district manager offices and double as sites for sales motivation meetings.

To reduce collection problems in a market of transients, the newspaper demands advance payment for all new subscriptions with a minimum subscription of three months. Over 60 percent of customers pay by mail, many through automatic billing to credit card accounts. The third-generation computer system in circulation makes it possible for more subscribers to pay the office directly.

TORONTO SUN

When the *Toronto Telegram* closed in 1971, many of its staff moved to the brand new *Toronto Sun*, which began its life as a tabloid without home delivery. The *Sun's* owners, having limited capital, bought the *Telegram's* single copy boxes, hired a small staff of journalists, and contracted

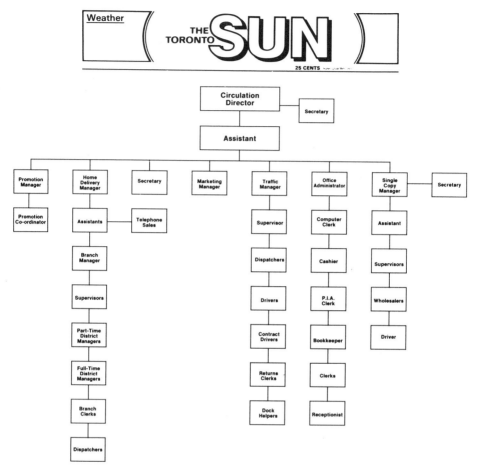

FIGURE 11.11

printing locally. The need for a low-cost, rapidly built circulation system produced a wholesale structure reminiscent of Ben Day's 1833 London Plan. More than a decade later, the *Sun* remains a single copy tabloid, sold to wholesalers off the dock, except on Sunday, when the *Sun* is home-delivered. A full-time district manager force (Figure 11.11) supervises only Sunday delivery!

The Toronto market hosts three dailies, which compete vigorously for a share of the rapidly growing population. An extensive and efficient subway and bus system supports single copy sales; in fact, the Toronto subway system is one of the wholesalers. The *Sun* sells to independent dealers, who sell through vending boxes, stores, and kiosks. Wholesalers rent boxes for the *Sun*, which retains a voice in their location. With 5500 boxes on the street, the *Sun* had a net paid circulation of 227,500 in 1982 and appeared to plateau at 250,000 after a major sales contest.

Circulation strategy for a single copy newspaper relies on employing point-of-sale timing, maintaining adequate supply, taking advantage of major news events, and creating interest through games and content. Point-of-sale timing for the *Sun* peaks between 6 a.m. and 6:30 a.m., but customers begin purchasing as early as 4 a.m. In order to assure maximum sales, the single copy newspaper must have 15 to 20 percent more copies at sales locations than needed in order to assure that everyone wanting a paper can purchase one. When a major event, such as the shooting of the Pope, occurs, the circulation manager must order an increased pressrun sufficient to cover sales. When major events don't occur, the newspaper must devise attention-getting methods to raise sales. Contests are one method; sensational content is another.

Despite such problems, the simplicity of a wholesale system leads some to argue against any home delivery. When *Sun* executives purchased the *Edmonton Journal* in western Canada, they discovered that deep snow and a windchill factor of −50 degrees drove off carriers and left routes undeliverable and undelivered. The shortage of carriers was compounded by problems with collections and service. At the *Sun*, it is up to wholesalers to adjust their daily draw in light of weather conditions, news stories, late press starts, and holidays; the dealer absorbs the problems of payment.

Why then did the *Sun* develop home delivery on Sunday? Because neither competitor mounted a Sunday edition in 1973. Canadian commercial laws require most stores to close on Sundays, so the newspapers developed large Sunday newspapers for the weekend. Rather than face Saturday competition, the *Sun* developed a home delivery force for 250,000 Sunday subscribers to augment 177,000 box sales. Delivery requires 68 full-time district managers, who mount sales efforts, recruit carriers, adjust route lists, and collect bad debts. Sunday home delivery sales are promoted through carrier sales contests and contract telephone sales. With the Sunday market all to itself, the *Sun* modified its basic system to take the fullest advantage of the opening. Otherwise, the *Sun* follows the format laid down 140 years earlier by Ben Day, except that metal boxes and subway kiosks have replaced shouting newsboys.

As these case studies amply demonstrate, the circulation of American newspapers is a complex and highly diverse system in which each newspaper makes hundreds of local adaptations. The result is a pattern that reflects the philosophy of the company, the human resources available for delivery and collections, the local environment, and the character of the audience. The fact that newspapers successfully accomplish what no other manufacturer even attempts—daily home delivery of a perishable product within a few hours after production—underlies the high sensitivity of circulation departments to subtle differences among the various parts of the system. This also explains why mastery of circulation in a particular community comes only with years of experience and the ability to organize a complex system without standardizing every phase. Newspapers will not only survive the next decade, they will thrive as they learn to fit the needs and desires of their audiences. Circulation, like every other part of the newspaper business, is well on the way to adapting to its changing audiences.

Index